An Economic Sociology of Law Reimagined

This book critically examines the concept of "embeddedness": the core concept of an economic sociology of law (ESL).

It suggests that our ways of doing, talking, and thinking about law, economy, and society, reproduce and re-entrench mainstream approaches, shaping our thoughts and actions such that we perform according to the model. Taking a deep dive into one example – the concept of embeddedness – this book combines insights from law, sociology, economics, and psychology to show that while we use metaphor to talk about law and economy, our metaphors in turn use us, moulding us into their fictionalized caricatures of *homo juridicus* and *homo economicus*. The result is a groundbreaking study into the prioritization throughout society of interests and voices that align with doctrinal understandings of law and neoclassical understandings of economics: approaches that led us into the dilemmas currently facing society. Zooming out from a detailed exploration of embeddedness in economic sociology and ESL literature, the book unpacks the fashionable post-2008 claim that the economy should be re-embedded in society and proposes two conceptual shifts in response. The book draws on personas and vignettes throughout, both to imagine and to realize shifting an ESL beyond embeddedness.

This timely engagement with the emerging field of economic sociology of law will appeal to socio-legal scholars and others with interests in the intersection of law, economics, and sociology.

Clare Williams is an ESRC–SeNSS funded Postdoctoral Research Fellow at Kent Law School, University of Kent, UK.

An Economic Sociology of Law Reimagined

Beyond Embeddedness

Clare Williams

Routledge
Taylor & Francis Group
a GlassHouse Book

Designed cover image: Orbon Alija

First published 2023
by Routledge
4 Park Square, Milton Park, Abingdon, Oxon OX14 4RN

and by Routledge
605 Third Avenue, New York, NY 10158

Routledge is an imprint of the Taylor & Francis Group, an informa business

A Glasshouse book

British Library Cataloguing-in-Publication Data
A catalogue record for this book is available from the British Library

ISBN: 978-0-367-76144-8 (hbk)
ISBN: 978-1-032-42022-6 (pbk)
ISBN: 978-1-003-35481-9 (ebk)

DOI: 10.4324/9781003354819

Typeset in Bembo
by Deanta Global Publishing Services, Chennai, India

For Oakley, who is crushed velvet and love.
And who is a constant reminder of what is important, and what is not.

Contents

Preface

The way we talk matters. Words, mere collections of sounds that synesthetically invoke concepts, ideas, and possibilities, give us windows into other worlds. The vocabularies and grammars we have available to us frame how we understand and respond to the world. Our ideas, our mental models, and our self-perception as social beings all rely on having adequate ways of talking. But the ideas we use to think of other ideas matter too: from small talk to the bigger concepts of doing, talking, and thinking about legal and economic phenomena. We are, as a society, currently searching for responses to financial crashes, social crises, and environmental catastrophes. If our current ways of doing, talking, and thinking are inadequate, how can we imagine new or better ideas?

Yet language is frequently inadequate. We are tripped up by pronouns, trapped within the mental straightjackets of old ideas, and misled by unhelpful metaphors. Usually, the inadequacy of our language passes by unnoticed, so entrenched are the linguistic tropes we rely on daily. But, as the most ubiquitous communicative tool we have, we should care that our language works, and works well. As a means through which our mental models and thoughtways are carved out, our language shapes our actions, defining how we perform and talk about legal and economic concepts. How can we respond to the crashes, crises, and catastrophes facing society if our language and mental models are those that led us into the problems in the first place?

The chapters that follow explore why we should care that our legal and economic metaphors are inadequate. They do this by taking a deep dive into one metaphor: embeddedness. Embeddedness-talk is everywhere, and the last decade has seen embeddedness become the "go-to" metaphor for describing relationships between the legal, the economic, and the social. Increasingly fashionable as a rebuttal to neoliberal ways of doing, talking, and thinking about the law and economy, embeddedness frequently pops up on the news, in the papers, in talks on the radio, as well as in books and journal articles. We are told that "the economy (or the law) has become disembedded" from society, and that the solution lies, quite simply, in "re-embedding markets and their regulation". At the same time, the opposite is also claimed, that "society has become embedded in the economy and its regulation" and that the solution lies in its disembedding. Start looking out for embeddedness-talk; I dare you. I also dare you to find an example that offers unambiguous definitions or context. What are we talking about? What is embedded? In what is it embedded? And what difference does it make?

As the core concept of an economic sociology of law (ESL), embeddedness has received a lot of attention in ESL literature that can shed light on current wider discourse. An ESL lens can show us how, where, and why some of the core assumptions of neoclassical economics and doctrinal legal scholarship are "baked in" to embeddedness-talk. By using ESL as our reference point, we can see how embeddedness reproduces problematic mental models that go largely unnoticed. Embeddedness, therefore, reproduces, re-entrenches, and re-affirms mainstream approaches to law and economics, and their relationships with society. But these are the mental models that led us into the financial crashes, social crises, and environmental catastrophes in the first place. Instead, this book suggests that we need innovative and imaginative responses to those crashes, crises, and catastrophes that are able to step beyond the confines of our current mental models. To do this, we need better ways of doing and thinking. And for this, we need better ways of talking.

This book suggests one option. It is written from a socio-legal perspective, but straddles, and occasionally wades into, sociology, economic history, psychology, linguistics, philosophy, neuroscience, and physics. In combining views from all these fields, it offers a unique perspective on how we currently do, talk, and think about the relationships between law, economy, and society. It explores the emerging academic field of economic sociology of law (ESL), and its core concept, embeddedness. It explores the multiple layers of metaphor in which our concepts and thoughtways are bound up, and identifies those fictions, those metaphorical leaps of faith, that we take every day when talking about the law or the economy. It shows the limitations of our current ways of doing, talking, and thinking when these fictions do not align.

An economic sociology of law (ESL) is set out as a useful and timely scholarly lens for conducting research at the interface of law, economy, and society. But, zooming out, ESL is a useful microcosm for exploring the life and times of its core concept, embeddedness, and how this metaphor operates in the real world. An ESL then gives us a helpful context for exploring how and why we might move beyond embeddedness, and what might happen as a result. The arguments have broader implications both for policy makers and for us all as we grapple with the roles of both law and economy in society; how we perform legal and economic phenomena, how we think about them, and how we talk about them. In short, if we aspire to respond effectively to those crashes, crises, and catastrophes, the way we talk matters.

Acknowledgements and return journeys

Summing up this book as a labour of love doesn't quite do justice to the years of stopping, starting, rewinding, and reviewing that have gone into the ideas here. It was a bumpy journey but, I hope, what follows has turned out the better for it.

Starting a PhD or research project can be like swimming out into the great, wide ocean. You've explored and mapped out your own island of knowledge, identified an interesting expedition that could lead to a new, unmapped area, and now begin wading out to discover your original contribution to the map. You splash out into the waves, eager at first to begin swimming and to feel the land drop away as the water lifts you, nudging you along this way and that. In your mind's eye, another small island lies just over the horizon, waiting for you to stumble upon it, map it, and then tell everyone else where it is and what's there.

Sometimes, though, things don't quite go to plan.

Throughout the (long) PhD and despite several interruptions, I had the opportunity and privilege to paddle, wade, and then swim a little bit more. By the time I stopped to look around, my original island had receded over the horizon and was out of sight. I may have discovered new territories, but I could no longer see my starting point, or how to get back there. Trying to explain to everyone else where I was, and what I was doing there, was often a frustratingly futile exercise.

As everyone else was still firmly on the mainland, or was off exploring their own islands far out of sight from mine, even trying to explain where my jumping-off point was could pose problems. But then, to explain that further out, much, much further over that horizon, there's a view worth swimming for … well, I became depressingly familiar with blank stares.

I needed a new plan. I needed not only to map out a new idea, but to explain clearly *how to get there* from the mainland of mainstream grammars, vocabularies, and mental models that are familiar (hopefully to you). I needed not only a return journey to the mainland, but I needed to map out the pathways, bridges, and links to be able to bring you back with me and show you the views. Safely. And without anyone getting lost *en route*.

This book is the result of many return journeys. It maps out the original island where my journey began, and then describes the glint on the horizon that I began swimming out to. It describes the journey, and what I found. It describes the view from that new bit of the map, as well as the view when we zoom out and look at the map as a whole. Only this time, as I've made some pathways, you don't need to swim. I hope I have made those paths as accessible as possible, and I hope the view is worth waiting for.

While the doctorate might have taken eight and a half particularly tortuous years, the book took a little over a year. This year was one of immense enjoyment and the thrill of new horizons and opportunities, albeit COVID-mandated virtual ones. These opportunities were made possible by my funders, ESRC–SeNSS, to whom I will owe an eternal debt of gratitude for opening the doors for me to spend time at Kent Law School. The intellectual stimulation, as well as the friendship, support, and guidance, have been an immeasurable boost after the drudgery of the PhD, and I can only hope that the resulting chapters do some small justice to the kindness I've received.

There are a few sets of shoulders that I have stood on to write this book, chief amongst those, Amanda Perry-Kessaris, whose work and no-nonsense approach to most things in life continues to be a huge source of inspiration. Similarly, Diamond Ashiagbor, who has also frequently gone above and beyond on my behalf and who, like Amanda, has fought for me when I was not able to do so myself. I'm indebted to both.

Despite their absence at the start of this journey, metaphors have turned out to play a central role in this story: both in its substance and in its narration. The power of metaphor to not only shift the narrative, but alter how we understand it, was demonstrated to me in real time by JL whose mentorship helped me climb the mountain of my PhD, but moreover helped me to enjoy the views along the way. These were developed into an online interactive game with the help, encouragement, and advice of Emily Allbon, to whom I owe a debt of gratitude for encouraging and facilitating a different type of visual project.

I'm indebted to Lara Bastajian, who has listened to various renditions and iterations of my thoughts over the years, and who has somehow remained interested. Her help in living up to our shared pedantry with grammar has been invaluable, and the mistakes that remain are mine alone. This applies equally to the substantive points made over the following chapters.

Thank you, Diana Burgess, for such careful and thoughtful feedback and comments, and Hamish Todd for encouragement and positive reviews along the way. I'm also immensely grateful to the Obligations Reading Group at Kent Law School for the opportunity to present and discuss the ideas in here, and for such thoughtful comments, and to generations of SLSA (Socio-Legal Studies Association) conference attendees for offering feedback on various aspects of the thesis as it developed over the past decade and sparking ongoing joy and interest in the core research. I also want to thank Colin Perrin and Naomi Round Cahalin at Routledge for their ongoing support (with no small hint of flexibility) and for letting me add so many creative elements to an academic monograph.

Finally, to dad, who never saw this completed, and to mum, for carrying me so far, and for whom thanks is so inadequate.

Visualizing socio-legal frames, concepts, and methods

This book uses visual techniques both to illustrate and interrogate the socio-legal frames, concepts, and methods explored in the chapters that follow. These include the use of personas and vignettes, and the three main characters who explore the propositions in the book are introduced at the end of Chapter 1. The text is also punctuated with diagrams that visualize the conceptual arguments.

Additionally, the first page of each chapter features a background image. These are more than merely decorative, and visualize key elements of the concepts described in the chapter that follows. The six small illustrations below can explain.

In the first illustration (top left), which also appears at the top of Chapter 1, we can note the straight lines of each of the interweaving strands. We might imagine these strands to be visual representations of hegemonic approaches in both law and economics and how these tend to elide the flexibilities, irregularities, and complexities of social phenomena. As Chapter 1 sets out, when our conceptual and linguistic tools fall out of alignment with our (inter-)actions in the real world, problems can arise.

In the second illustration (top right) which appears on the front page of Chapter 2, we see a regular pattern of the three interweaving strands of law, economy, and society. We can note that when we zoom out, a social "fabric" begins to emerge.

Then, in the third illustration (centre left, Chapter 3), we see a little more flexibility as curved lines are added to the initial illustration, and can note that sociological or socio-legal approaches demand empirical grounding. This illustration also imagines how we might visualize the flexibilities and dynamism of an embeddedness-based economic sociology of law (ESL) lens.

Then (centre right, Chapter 4), the fourth illustration visually imagines what might happen to our social fabric were one of the strands to be pulled or for the fabric to be somehow distorted.

The fifth illustration (bottom left, Chapter 5) imagines an interweaving of legal and economic strands that accommodates the flexibility and irregularities of everyday interactions, and which deviates from the straight lines and right

Chapter 1

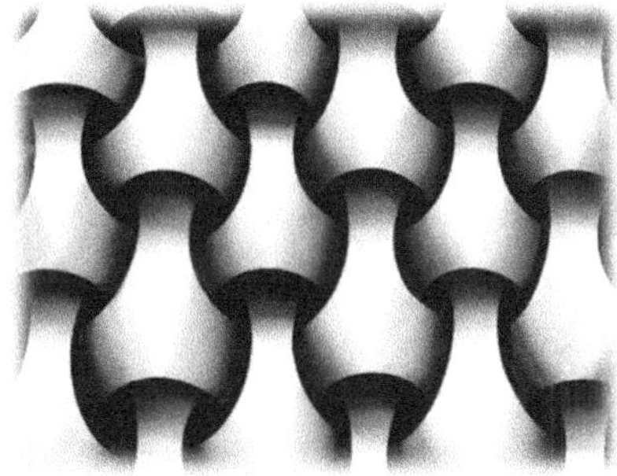

Chapter 2

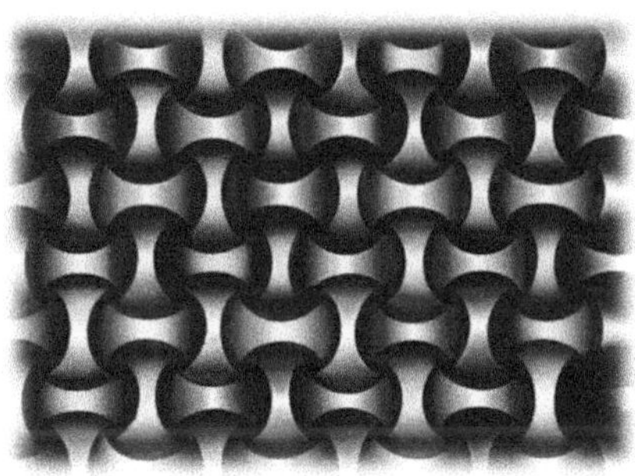

Chapter 3

Chapter 4

Chapter 5

Chapter 6

Visualizing socio-legal concepts. The background image on the first page of each chapter imagines how we might visualize the interweaving of legal, economic, and social phenomena. All artistic visualizations, including the illustrations on the first page of each chapter (pages 1, 33, 67, 93, 116, and 147) and the pages from Ann's sketchbook (pages 56 and 129) were hand-drawn by the author using the ProCreate app on an iPad Pro (2nd gen) and Apple Pencil (2nd gen). Other diagrams and figures were constructed in Microsoft PowerPoint.

angles of mainstream, hegemonic frames that the first image imagined. As such, we might appreciate this as a more accurate visualization of a constructivist economic sociology of law lens that has shifted beyond embeddedness, as the chapter suggests.

The final image (bottom right, Chapter 6) visualizes a composite that moves from the straight lines of mainstream frames, through the introduction of some curves and nuance to the full reflection of the irregularities of daily interactions with their myriad and diverse voices, values, and interests. This illustration therefore visualizes a progression, moving from left to right, from a hegemonic, mainstream lens through socio-legal and embeddedness-based ESL frames to a constructivist ESL lens that has shifted beyond embeddedness. The illustration therefore summarizes the core narrative set out in the book.

Chapter 1

Doing, talking, and thinking (and why we're not getting it right)

Crashes, crises, catastrophes

On a warm but overcast Friday, on 14 September 2007, people began to queue in highstreets up and down the UK. There was a rumour that Northern Rock, a familiar name in banking, had run into trouble and was about to collapse. Savers wanted their money back, but cash supplies quickly ran out. The first run on a bank in the UK in over 140 years heralded the start of what came to be known as the financial crash. Some 15 years later, in the throes of the Sars-COV-2 pandemic, the 2008 crash looks tame by comparison. Strategies to contain the virus that had been unthinkable prior to 2020 became normalized as entire economies were shut down in the name of public health (Tooze, 2021). Governments around the world struggled to manage the overwhelming consequences not just of the disease, but of the social crises and inequalities it highlighted (Dunford *et al.*, 2020). If health systems, social care systems, and supply chains collapsed, it was scant comfort to have protected the economy.

And yet, the crashes and crises of the century so far look set to be dwarfed by the looming environmental catastrophe wrought by climate change. The implications for humanity are unfathomably profound, necessitating that every aspect of human life on earth be reviewed (Matthews, 2021). These three "Cs", namely crashes, crises, and catastrophes, have a common thread. They comprise events that indicate that our ways of doing, talking, and thinking about law and economy might be inadequate. The financial crash forced a reconsideration of the boundaries between the freedom of self-regulating markets and the need for governments to regulate. The social crises of the pandemic in the UK so often boiled down to the pithy dualism of public health versus the economy, pit individual liberalism against government intervention, drawing on impoverished understandings of both health and wealth. And the environmental catastrophe of global warming, once again boiled down to the economy versus the environment, demonstrates the inadequacies of our mental models as we struggle to apportion value to nature, and assign legal rights to rivers, animals, and the wider environment.

DOI: 10.4324/9781003354819-1

In all of these contexts our mental models – those concepts and structures that we use to think about the world and our place within it – play a key role in how effectively we can understand and respond to problems. These mental models, and the "thoughtways" that link them, can be glimpsed through the way we talk: the vocabularies and grammars we use to describe and interact with the world (Cooper and Renz, 2021). But there is evidence that the way we talk plays a role in shaping the way we think. And if the way we talk shapes the way we think, then it also shapes the way we (inter-)act. To put it simply, then, the way we talk matters.

Doing, talking, and thinking

Imagine you are trekking through a jungle. Hacking out a new path is complex and time-consuming, but following an existing path is far easier. There is one problem though: the destinations that lie at the end of existing pathways are not where you want to go. You have been there before, and things did not end well. You want a different destination this time, and that means forging a new pathway through the jungle slowly and laboriously. Over time and with use though, paths solidify, the jungle relents, and you can carve out a discernible pathway to your new destination.

Human thought processes are similar. The mental models we use, and the thoughtways that lead us from one concept to another, are "channelled" gullies "carved out" for us by our language; gullies that "are formed by years of use" over our lifetime "and influenced by generations of linguistic evolution before that" (Shariatmadari, 2019, p. 152). Our mental models include shared expectations about the world too, including assumptions about how others will behave regarding rules and resources: will they stick to the rules about keeping off the grass or ignore them? Will they share that sandwich or not?

However, the more ubiquitous our mental models and thoughtways are, the less we pay attention to them, or to the concepts we are using, and how, and why. They become invisible, taken for granted, and unquestioned. But it matters "what ideas [...] we think with" (Norman, 2022, p. 5), just as "[i]t matters what ideas we use to think other ideas" (Harraway, 2016, p. 34).

We create the world when we interact with others. There might, objectively, be some form of mind and matter, but our reality can only be experienced through interaction and encouragingly, theories from fields as diverse as quantum mechanics, cognitive psychology, neuroscience, and linguistics all suggest the same (Lewton, 2021; Gefter, 2022). Similarly, as a "collective endeavour", language is a "[p]rocess of negotiation, a phenomenon whose structure only emerges when we interact with others" (Shariatmadari, 2019, p. 101). Our words then, soundscapes that synesthetically convey concepts, both describe and construct the reality that we experience; both the tangible and immediate (such as what you fancy for tea, for example) as well as the more conceptual, less tangible phenomena that are so central to the social structures we rely on (social institutions like the law and the economy).

Human thought processes are largely metaphorical, and our ways of talking about the law and the economy are no different (Lakoff and Johnson, 1980, p. 25; Geary, 2011). Our "ordinary conceptual system, in terms of which we both think and act, is fundamentally metaphorical in nature" from the "most mundane details" through to the concepts that "structure what we perceive, how we get around in the world, and how we relate to other people" (Lakoff and Johnson, 1980, p. 3). Metaphor is not merely an "optional, rhetorical flourish", but our "most pervasive means of ordering our experience into conceptual systems" (Bandes, 1996; Levit, 2009). The human brain is hard-wired to detect patterns, and images and symbols are retained to a far greater extent than words alone (Levit, 2009, p. 277). Metaphors, then, are those linguistic techniques that make language colourful, symbolic, and memorable. They are the ways in which we make sense of the world and our place within it.

So, we can think of "the law", "the economy", and "society" as metaphors; ways of talking about nonentities "as if they were things" (Lakoff and Johnson, 1980, p. 25). The problem is that these metaphors "are so natural and so pervasive in our thought that they are usually taken as self-evident, direct descriptions of mental phenomena" (Lakoff and Johnson, 1980, p. 28). We no longer pay attention to how we are talking about shared mental models like the law and the economy, because, well, that is just how we have always talked about them.

But, if our metaphors are inadequate or conceptually inconsistent, they can perpetuate injustice, mask problems, and obscure innovative responses to pressing social challenges. What's more, when these metaphors are overused to the point of invisibility, we lose sight of their implications, origins, and impact. By paying attention to how we talk about legal and economic phenomena, we can begin to see that preferences are "baked in" to our default ways of talking and thinking.[1] These baked in concepts, assumptions, and ideals that are intrinsic to certain words and phrases act as invisible yet powerful channels that direct what and how we are able to perceive and conceptualize, and how we respond.

But this story goes further. Metaphors not only describe reality, they create it, and in this sense, "metaphors can be self-fulfilling prophecies" (Lakoff and Johnson, 1980, p. 156; Schön, 2012; Slupska, 2021). Therefore, the metaphors we use to talk about the law, the economy, and society, deserve close scrutiny. The complexity of language with its tacit assumptions and preferences means

1 The phrase "baked in" is an analogy borrowed from computer modelling and animation and refers to part of a graphical process whereby 3D geometry textures are transposed into a 2D image texture, allowing the engine to render the texture and colour more readily. Baking consolidates a system of data into a simplified, more permanent form, and is usually non-reversible. Computer modelling originally borrowed the analogy from cookery.

that our metaphors not only construct our reality but construct us. They craft and shape our mental models and thoughtways, reflecting the "accumulation of a cultural experience", or a "fossil record of changing communicative strategies" (Shariatmadari, 2019, p. 240). To speak, then, is to "swim in an inherited stream of images and words" that we have neither chosen nor appreciate the impact of (Herder, cited in Shariatmadari, 2019, p. 240). More crucially, generations of use have attached to metaphors conceptual baggage that contextualizes and describes. For metaphors like "law" and "economy", this conceptual baggage tends to reflect the dominant approaches, or accepted ways of thinking, in each field that have seeped into the mainstream from their academic roots (Giddens, 1984). In turn, this has the unhappy effect of entrenching mainstream approaches, and reinforcing dominant narratives.

We are not faring well though. In the last 30 years or so, our legal and economic metaphors have led us into financial crashes, social crises, and environmental catastrophes. It is fair to ask, then, if they are serving us well. And if the answer is no, we might then ask how we could do, talk, and think differently about legal and economic phenomena, and what different concepts, perspectives, and preferences such a shift might enable. If our ways of talking repeat the assumptions and preferences of mainstream theories in law and economics, how can we imagine something different? How can we respond innovatively and imaginatively to these social dilemmas without first appreciating the role of our language in shaping how we understand the world, and how we respond to it?

The law and the economy don't really exist

Our reliance on metaphor might be more ubiquitous than you had realized. If, for example, I ask you to point to "the economy", you might point to a bank, some coins, shops, or even cryptocurrency. What you are pointing to is, respectively, a building, some pieces of metal, more buildings, and a computer. Similarly, if I ask you to point to "the law", you might show me a courtroom, a police officer, an Act of Parliament, and some case law. But, once again, you are pointing to a building, a person, and some pieces of paper. And yet we all understand that "the economy" and "the law" refer to certain collections of social behaviour that society deems acceptable, even useful. So then, "the law" and "the economy" are "ontological metaphors" for these collections of behaviours; useful and convenient linguistic short cuts for talking about nonentities as if they were real that save us time (Lakoff and Johnson, 1980, p. 25). These ontological metaphors then are the primary layer of meaning that we construct. They comprise a linguistic level at which we all take a collective leap of imagination, delving in to the fluidities of law's materialities, frequently without realizing (Cloatre and Cowan, 2019; Rose and Valverde, 1998).

Table 1.1 Three layers of ontological metaphors

Layer	*Example*
Tertiary metaphors (relational)	"The law and economy are embedded in society" "Society has become embedded in the law and the economy"
Secondary metaphors (personification)	"The law makes an ass of us all" "The markets have fallen" "The fabric of society is fraying"
Primary metaphors	Law Economy Society

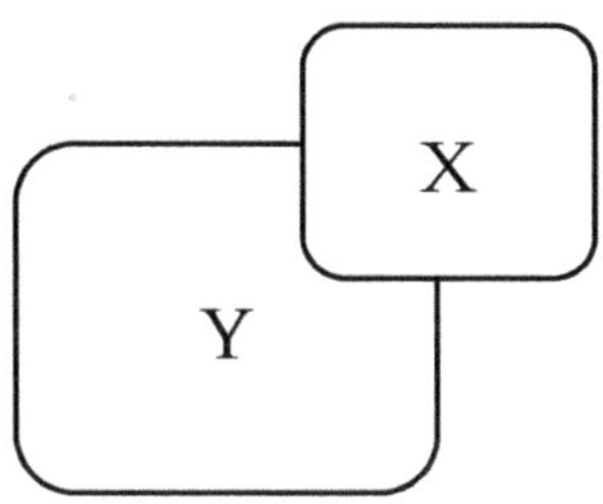

Figure 1.1 We say that X is embedded in Y.

The dilemmas appear at the second and third layers of metaphor that we construct on top of the first (see Table 1.1). We personify both the law ("the law makes an ass of us all") and the economy ("the markets have tumbled"), creating a secondary layer of metaphor that is equally ubiquitous, and equally invisible. It has become fashionable since the 2008 financial crash to identify a problem of distance between law, economy, and society through the embeddedness metaphor. We say that the economy (and its regulation) has become "disembedded" from society. Accordingly, the obvious solution to repair this relationship is the "re-embedding" of the economy and its regulation in society. We might think of this as a tertiary, relational, layer of metaphor that describes the relationship between two ontological metaphors, as Figure 1.1 sets out.

Yet, when we recognize that neither "the law" nor "the economy" exist, save for in our linguistic tropes, describing the relationship between these (non)entities as "disembedded" from society is clearly nonsense. How can we conceive of "a law" or "an economy" separate from society? Undeniably, a common understanding is communicated. But there are conceptual inconsistencies here; leaps of faith that we all take unquestioningly. What if those leaps meant that we were further entrenching concepts that brought us to these crashes, crises, and catastrophes in the first place?

PS: Nor does society

When Margaret Thatcher notoriously proclaimed in 1987 that there was "no such thing" as society, she was both right and wrong (Thatcher, 1987). Like "law" and "economy", we can understand "society" as an ontological metaphor; a linguistic short cut for a collection of concepts and behaviours that we lump together for convenience. We cannot point to society or touch it. We might claim to feel or sense it, but this depends on our subjective attribution of meaning. Durkheim's ultimate "social fact" of society here stands in opposition to Popper's assertion that all we can identify is a collection of concepts, constructs, and theoretical entities (McLachlan, 2020).

And yet, once again, it is undeniable that shared meanings are communicated. We may disagree on what exactly society is, or where it is to be found, but there is a common understanding of shared experiences and expectations. While a detailed social ontology is beyond the scope of this book (see inter alia Searle, 2006), questions of what makes "society" or "the social" special have troubled generations of anthropologists, sociologists, psychologists, and philosophers. For Latour, the "assembled" characteristic of the social was vital, alongside heterogeneity and composition (Latour, 2007). There is, though, a consensus that our metaphors, "conceptual models", and "overall vision" are lacking for understanding, predicting, influencing, or theorizing "society" (Delanda, 2006; Elias, 2010).

Look out for the secondary layers of metaphor that perch atop the primary, ontological metaphor of "society". Particularly fashionable over the last couple of decades has been the fabric metaphor, which has the potential, like a reel of cotton, to just keep giving. The fabric of society is said to be fraying, to have ripped, to be wearing thin, and to be in need of stitching back together or at least darning (see inter alia Tanner *et al.*, 2020).[2] These metaphorical threads symbolize and allow us to visualize relationships, institutions, and behaviours, as well as infrastructure and economic value. The metaphors frame the non-tangible as if it were tangible, allowing us to (metaphorically) grasp the concepts: to picture them, mentally, and envisage responses. Similarly, when referring to the strength and depth of bonds we might refer to the fashionable concept of "social capital", a curious metaphor that invokes economic thoughtways and values to describe social relationships (Putnam, 2001; Harriss, 2002). Each of these metaphors has baked in

2 My thanks here to Tobias Berkley and the Obligations reading group at Kent Law School for pointing out that the fabric metaphor, when applied to society, has further implications. Fabric cannot self-accrete or self-repair, but requires active intervention from someone, in a manner similar to the Intelligent Design approach. When we use the fabric metaphor, therefore, we imply that we need someone to come and repair the damage done. While the metaphor does not specify who, or how, it is inevitable that any repairer will have their own sets of preferences and assumptions which they will apply in the course of their repairs. The fabric metaphor, then, is an inherently and intrinsically political way of talking about society.

fictions that undeniably add colour and vivacity to the language, but which direct our thoughtways along specific paths, guiding our mental models to predetermined concepts, often without our realization. Both primary and secondary ontological metaphors are generally so ubiquitous as to pass unnoticed; invisible until we begin to pay attention to the ways that our language colours our thought processes. But what do these metaphors and their fictions do to the ways we are able to think and talk about legal, economic, and social phenomena? And if our ways of talking mould our ways of thinking and doing as legal and economic actors, how do our metaphors use us?

How metaphors use us

While we might like to assume that we craft and deploy our language independently, the following chapters and exploration of the impacts of embeddedness suggest that our language equally crafts and deploys us. We can understand embeddedness as a tertiary, generative, ontological metaphor that both gives us a word to describe the problematic relationship between law, economy, and society, but which also shapes our mental models and our interactions. Baked into the concept of embeddedness are mainstream or orthodox approaches: doctrinal legal and neoclassical economic assumptions and preferences. And our ongoing conceptual commitment to embeddedness entrenches these each and every time we describe the law or economy as "embedded in" society.

"Generative metaphors" shape our mental models, revealing some parts of the complex social puzzle while concealing others (Schön, 2012). We can understand embeddedness, then, as a generative metaphor that guides our thoughtways, tacitly and usually subconsciously. Metaphors like embeddedness tend to facilitate the reproduction of mainstream or orthodox approaches and ways of thinking about social phenomena. Crucially, though, metaphors like embeddedness tend to place intrinsic assumptions and preferences beyond the reach of ordinary, quotidian interrogation, leaving these concepts and thoughtways free to form the foundational building blocks of what we do intentionally talk about. In short, we reproduce mainstream concepts without realizing. And we perform the mainstream approaches central to law and economics – doctrinal and neoclassical respectively – equally subconsciously. Our language then, tacitly and invisibly, constructs a frame within which we are guided to perform the mainstream preferences assumed by the dominant models that frame our understanding of the world. We are, then, guided to act as those famed characters central to mainstream economic and legal theory: *homo economicus* and his lawyerly cousin *homo juridicus*.

While the function and career of the concept of embeddedness make for interesting reading, it is useful to step back and explore its origins. The academic field of economic sociology of law (ESL) here offers an unparalleled microcosm for this study, as embeddedness is the "core concept" of ESL and its sister field, economic sociology (ES) (Frerichs, 2009, p. 20; Cotterrell, 2013, p. 50). The "always embedded" market economy, and its regulation, have been the subject of much head-scratching and heated debate within ES and ESL literature for decades, and offer us unique insights into the implications of embeddedness-talk (Block, 2003, p. 276). Within this literature, the concept of embeddedness can be traced back to the 1944 work of political economist and economic historian Karl Polanyi.

By all accounts, Polanyi had been reading extensively about coal-mining practices in England prior to the 1944 publication of his most famous work, *The Great Transformation* (Polanyi, 1944; Block, 2001). Coal was said to be "embedded" in the walls of the mine, requiring smart tactics to secure its extraction. Nevertheless, Thurnwald, Tönnies, and Marx had all employed embeddedness in one context or another, and Polanyi's familiarity with their works indicates an element of borrowing and refashioning (Dale, 2011; Peck, 2013). More persuasively, though, recalling her life with her husband, Ilona Duczynska Polanyi noted that Karl's time in Britain in 1940, teaching economic history to the working classes in ex-mining towns in Kent and Sussex, brought him face to face with the horrors of the Industrial Revolution. In particular, she recalls that he was struck by what we might now term the intergenerational trauma that resulted from the dehumanizing effects of the free market. "Blake's 'dark satanic mills' lived on through the generations and the British working class – even after its economic rise and in spite of it – still bore the stigmata of the crippling events of its inception" (Duczynska Polanyi, 2006, p. 311). Ilona notes how Karl was surprised that the houses Engels had written about were still standing, and that there were people living in them. What's more, evidence of the social and environmental destruction wrought by the free market was everywhere: "black hills of slag stood in the green landscapes of Wales; from the depressed areas, young men and women who had never seen their parents employed, drifted away to London" (Duczynska Polanyi, 2006, p. 311). While *The Great Transformation,* with its embeddedness metaphor, was published in 1944, Ilona notes that it was conceived in 1940 during the couple's stay in Britain. One way or another then, coal – the fuel of the Industrial Revolution – seems to have birthed the embeddedness metaphor as we find it in economic sociology and economic sociology of law literature.

Nevertheless, Polanyi used embeddedness sparingly, and likely without a second thought; the term appears a handful of times in *The Great Transformation* before falling off the metaphorical page for the next 40 years.[3]

3 The term appears twice on page 60, and then on pages 64, 73, and 135 before making a reappearance in Polanyi's notes at the end of the book. It does make occasional appearances in Polanyi's later works and unpublished manuscripts. It would be little more than speculation to ask if the frequency of the term in unpublished works might indicate Polanyi's unease with the concept (Dale, 2011, p. 320). For further discussion, see Chapter 3, footnote 2, page 70.

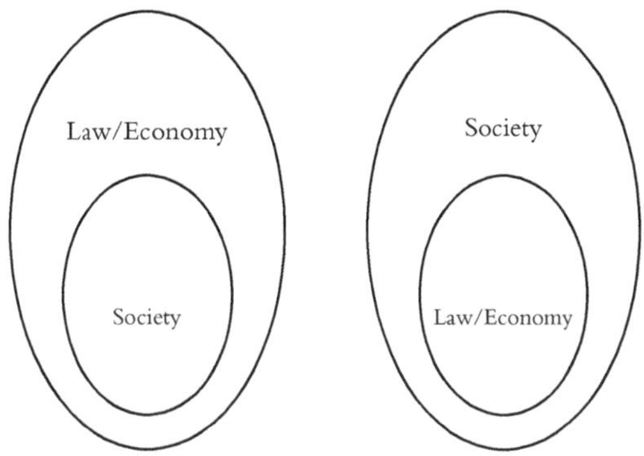

Figure 1.2 Are the law and the economy embedded in society, or is society embedded in the law and the economy?

As a relational descriptor, embeddedness implies the coexistence of two entities in space and/or in time: in this instance, the coal in the walls of a mine. As Figure 1.2 illustrates, it offers a useful visual metaphor when we are referring to ontologically separate objects. We can see that X is embedded in Y, and appreciate that they overlap to some extent, coexisting both spatially and temporally.

But when we are referring to phenomena that are distinguished only through a metaphorical fiction, the use of embeddedness to describe their relationship becomes problematic. If we accept that the law and the economy are collections of (social) behaviours, it is therefore anathema, disingenuous even, to speak of re-embedding the law or the economy *in society*. We are, then, describing the coexistence of (non)entities in space and time, by reference to phenomena that co-create each other. To revisit Figure 1.1, where X represents the economy or the law, and Y represents society, once we strip away the layers of metaphor we can appreciate that X does not, and cannot, exist unless and until it is performed or constructed by Y.

Nevertheless, our conceptual commitment to embeddedness continues to mask this point. Instead, repetition of embeddedness-talk in relation to law, economy, and society enforces their separation as distinct – albeit fictional – silos of inquiry and of action. And by re-entrenching the separation between the layers of metaphor and the silos of activity, our ongoing conceptual commitment to embeddedness enables the dominant, mainstream theories and frames within each of these silos to be reproduced and strengthened. Embeddedness-talk perpetuates dominant, doctrinal legal thoughtways and neoclassical economic thoughtways as well as the assumptions, values, and interests that are baked into these mainstream approaches.

Constructing reality[4]

As earlier paragraphs have hinted though, this goes further, with implications for how we think and act. In an accidental misstep by the Eurobarometer survey several years ago, preferences of respondents were seen to shift depending on how the respondents were identified. When they were referred to as "citizens" in the question, their preferences indicated more public-spirited behaviour, while respondents identified as "consumers" showed preferences for free markets and less civic obligations (Law, 2009).[5]

An essential step in understanding how we construct legal and economic phenomena goes back to the basics: how do we perceive the world? What is consciousness? What does it mean to be a human, social actor? While there are myriad theories of consciousness, these can be split into two broad camps: top-down, and bottom-up. Seth's theory of predictive processing sets out to combine both of these, proposing that perception involves two counterflowing streams of signals.

> There is an "inside-out" or "top down" stream that conveys predictions about the causes of sensory inputs. Then there are "outside-in" or "bottom up" prediction errors – the sensory signals – which report the differences between what the brain expects and what it gets.
>
> (Seth, 2021; but see also Thomson, 2016)

So, as Seth argues, by taking some data from the outside world and making predictions about this (and essentially hallucinating the rest), our brains constantly make "best guess" efforts to piece together sensory data about the world and this is what we consciously perceive. Thus, "we don't passively perceive our worlds – we actively generate them" (Seth, 2021).

There is a curious parallel here with some of the recent literature on consciousness and quantum theory which suggests that reality is constructed through interaction. While social constructivism might have become more fashionable in the social sciences as a way of understanding the reproduction of social institutions and behavioural patterns, enquiries into space–time suggest that "until two people interact, they don't share the same reality – because it is communication itself that creates it" (Lewton, 2021; Gefter, 2022). So, then, if we construct our (legal, economic, and social) reality through interactions, our thoughtways and how we communicate these take on enormous significance, as do initiatives to shift these or shape our actions.

4 Constructivist and constructionist approaches are explored further and differentiated in Chapter 2.

5 The survey did not set out to test this, but accidentally found a discrepancy in opinions correlated with respondent identification, so it is difficult to draw firm conclusions. The Eurobarometer analysis is discussed in more detail in Chapter 5, page 133.

The suggestion that we can shape behaviour through the frames and mental models we use builds on evidence from cognitive psychology, with the field of behavioural economics as the most obvious example of putting this theory into practice. Indeed, governments have set up their own "nudge" units to design choice architecture that encourages individuals to make decisions that are in their own, or society's, best interests, or at least their presumed best interests (Thaler and Sunstein, 2009). Cognitive psychology has begun to extend this proposition though, now also suggesting that even emotions are culturally and linguistically contingent, and that our entire mind-worlds might be shaped and coloured by language (Boroditsky, 2009; Dermendzhiyska, 2021).[6] If this is so, our legal and economic thoughtways derive their shape, colours, flavours, and textures from our available vocabularies and grammars.

This has implications for how we describe, define, and construct legal, economic, and social phenomena, and the extent to which our metaphors shape our behaviour, as well as our ability to perceive problems and conceive of solutions. For example, if our vocabularies and grammars are those that reproduce doctrinal legal assumptions and thoughtways, might we be (unwittingly) performing as the archetypal legal man with his built-in preferences? Similarly, if we talk and think with the language of neoclassical economics, might we be performing as the archetypal economic man with his built-in preferences? This has implications not only for our thoughts and actions, but the voices and values that we are able to perceive and accommodate. If we act as *homo juridicus*, the fictional man of law, how might we understand voices and interests that traditionally lie beyond mainstream doctrinal legal models, such as friendship obligations or altruism? And if we act as *homo economicus*, how might we understand and accommodate values and preferences that lie beyond the purview of neoclassical economics, such as the environment or social bonds?

Introducing homo juridicus and homo economicus

At this point, fictional caricatures that have been lurking in the shadows of the discussion demand introductions. These are the archetypal caricatures of mainstream legal and economic theories that align with assumptions about an average legal and economic person, respectively.

6 This rebuts, almost fully, Chomskian notions of a Universal Grammar, or the notion that language is somehow inbuilt or native to the human brain. Instead, the evidence is emerging that language, and the thoughtways and mind-worlds that it shapes, is socially constructed. While the Sapir–Whorf hypothesis has been largely disproven, there is still intense debate about the extent to which we can claim linguistic determinism, or the proposition that language shapes thought (Boroditsky, 2009; Shariatmadari, 2019).

Mainstream theories of, and approaches to, law – summarized as doctrinal – assume the figure of a *homo juridicus*, the "rational, autonomous, man of law" whose freedom is assumed to be pre-existing and who is imagined to exist before and apart from any concept of the social (Naffine, 1998, cited in Tata, 2020, p. 30; Teubner, 2021; Norman, 2022, pp. 4–5; although cf. Supiot, 2017). Liberated from the complex and messy social and affective ties that blight real humans, he – for "he" is invariably a "he" – acts "reasonably" and "effectively", contracting to realize his interests (Nedelsky, 2012). He enacts and applies the "black letter" of the law found in Acts of Parliament, statutes, legal opinions, and case law, performing subject to his pragmatic doctrinal reasoning that sits apart from any consideration of the social, the moral, or the political (Burrows, 2016). His language, with its precision and careful definitions, has tended to seep into wider social processes and institutions beyond Parliament or the courtroom, leading some commentators to call for a "complete reorientation in how we see the world and our place in it" (Nedelsky, 2012; see also, in particular, Fineman, 2019, 2022; Norman, 2022, pp. 5–6).[7,8]

Mainstream, or neoclassical, economics has an equivalent. *Homo economicus* is a devoted utility maximizer, asocial, with perfect information and generally fixed preferences. While this concept of the ideal economic agent is thought to have developed out of responses to the work of Adam Smith and John Stuart Mill, dissatisfactions with the model have not tempered its impact on how we think about economics, and how economics thinks about us. Fetishes for mathematizing and quantifying every aspect of social life in the latter half of the twenty-first century, along with the ability of neoclassical economics to offer scholarly foundations for neo-liberal political preferences, secured his place in history. *Homo economicus* acts "rationally" and "efficiently", once again eschewing matters of politics, morality, or ethics. Nevertheless, not all economists are happy with this caricature, and the groundbreaking work of Kahneman and Tversky bringing psychology into economics, developed by Thaler and Sunstein into the field of behavioural economics, is an example of a push-back, calling *homo economicus* out for the "social moron" and "rational fool" that he was … and still is (Kahneman and Tversky, 2000; Thaler, 2000, 2016; Thaler

7 The use of fictions in the law is not a new phenomenon and was a central feature in the justification of colonialism and slavery. John Locke's mental gymnastics enabled the claim that Indigenous communities had no ownership over the land, which, then being *terra nullius*, could be appropriated by settler-colonialists and used for extraction. Along the way, the assignment of rights to (some) humans only, placing animals and ecology in the category of property, continues to hamper efforts to rethink our relationship with the environment as well as with each other. The ongoing impact of these thoughtways is explored in Chapter 6.

8 The seepage of academic ideas and theories from the ivory tower or the courtroom echoes Giddens' "double hermeneutic". See (Giddens, 1984).

and Sunstein, 2009). For "he" still exerts a surprising influence on how we construct notions of economic behaviour.

As ontological metaphors, these two characters embody sets of assumptions and "unthought knowns" about the disciplines of law and economics (Lakoff and Johnson, 1980; Bernstein *et al.*, 2015). As generative metaphors, the caricatures both reveal and conceal thoughts, assumptions, and preferences (Schön, 2012). Embodied in the quotidian language and layers of the metaphors we use to talk about legal and economic phenomena, they represent "those fundamental assumptions" which people "unconsciously presuppose", being "so obvious" that people "do not know what they are assuming because no other way of putting things has ever occurred to them" (Whitehead, cited in Naffine, 2006).

In creating these fictional renders that simplify the average person, we create convenient mental and linguistic short cuts that communicate common understanding, similar to the ontological metaphors of "the law" and "the economy". And yet, as later chapters and the discussion on performativity explores, the problems arise when we lose sight of the fictions, the metaphors, and the conceptual heavy lifting we are asking them to do. The caricatures take on a life of their own, becoming normative markers of behaviour (Fleming, 2017). And, in the process, while we perform them, they perform us. Society is co-opted by the language and consequent thoughtways of mainstream approaches in law and in economics. The communicative potential of neoclassical economics, in offering us "clean" answers to "messy" social dilemmas, means that our preferences for quantification and mathematization have even co-opted the law (Hirsch, Michaels and Friedman, 1990; Teubner, 2021). "The image of the market became an increasingly captivating social metaphor" (Ruggie, 1982, p. 386), meaning that we are then forced "to confront, as Foucault put it, 'the problem of the inversion of the relationship of the social to the market'" (Foucault, 2008, p. 240; Rittich, 2014, p. 342).

Our preferences for the ways of doing, talking, and thinking of neoclassical economics, and to a lesser extent doctrinal legal reasoning, reproduce and re-entrench those same dominant approaches. By the same token, the voices and values that "fit" easily into these mainstream frames are those that are prioritized, highlighted, and that naturally form the focus of our attentions. These tend to be economic interests, economic voices, and notions of efficiency, productivity, and rationality. Through language, these dominant frames determine what and how we are able to perceive, conceive, and understand, and how we are able to respond. For if we only have the language of *homo economicus-juridicus* available to us, we can only think like *homo economicus-juridicus*, talk like *homo economicus-juridicus,* and act like *homo economicus-juridicus.*

Neither caricature engages in relational or particularly moral thought processes. Neither are deeply social, ethical, or political souls, and neither are particularly well networked within their communities. Instead, these caricatures assume an atomistic individual who is pre-socialized and lacking many of the traits that we might say make us human. As MacKenzie and Millo suggestively propose, what if we could imagine the fuller, richer, morally configured, socially situated figure of *homo sociologicus* (MacKenzie and Millo, 2003, p. 141)? And, if we had the conceptual and linguistic tools to act *as homo sociologicus,* what voices and values might we choose to then prioritize? But, this is jumping ahead. For now, let's zoom back in to explore embeddedness in more detail, starting with its role as the core concept of the fields of economic sociology and economic sociology of law (ESL).

An ongoing conceptual commitment to embeddedness

The contagion of the subprime crisis spread like wildfire through the markets, culminating in the 2008 financial crash. In its wake, a wave of literature appeared, desperately seeking answers to a crisis that had largely avoided prediction. Massive deregulation in the decades prior to the crash, coupled with an ideological belief in the ability of markets to self-regulate, had blinded regulators to the risk that some institutions had become too big to fail and could, therefore, imperil the structural organization of society. While the markets themselves – even subprime markets – continued to be socially constructed, our conceptual and linguistic tools had "floated free", increasingly portraying markets as naturally occurring phenomena that should be allowed to self-regulate (Perry-Kessaris, 2011b). In other words, the tools we had available to understand and make decisions about the markets no longer reflected their social origins or aligned with the social construction of markets.

In the search for answers, both as to the cause of the crash and to solutions, one of the problems identified in the response literature was the (metaphorical) distance between the economy, its regulation, and the society that both were supposed to serve. By deregulating, governments had stepped back from interfering in the markets, introducing more (metaphorical) space between regulators and markets. Following the post-2008 (re-) regulatory rush, embeddedness emerged as a convenient conceptual coat hook upon which many of the problems of the economy and its regulation could be hung. In identifying the relational distance between the spheres of law, economy, and society, the literature revealed the rise of a common phraseology based around the embeddedness metaphor. In "floating free", our ways of talking and thinking about the economy – the banks and subprime markets in particular – had come to understand markets as something separate from society; as "disembedded" (Perry-Kessaris, 2011b). The solution, seductive in its simplicity, was then to "re-embed" the economy in society. The problem, however, was the lack of context or definition. What was embedded, and in what was it – or should it be – embedded (Cotterrell, 2013)?

Two examples will suffice to illustrate the confusion. Kate Raworth's *Doughnut Economics: Seven Ways to Think Like a 21st-Century Economist* has become one of the lasting contributions to pluralistic economic thinking to emerge from the 2008 crash (Raworth, 2018). In her book, Raworth sets out a manifesto for living within our means on this planet, finding that "sweet spot" within the two concentric circles that comprise the title's doughnut where basic needs are met but where the planet's resources are maintained (Raworth, 2018, p. loc.19). Raworth's goal is to reorient economics towards valuing environmental resources for more than the sum of their narrow, economic values: "If the economy is so evidently embedded in the biosphere, how has economics ignored it?" (Raworth, 2018, p. loc.1069). We are urged to "[f]orget the free market, think embedded market" (Raworth, 2018, p. loc.1220). Her "Embedded Economy", (with capital letters), "ends the myth of the self-contained, self-sustaining market, replacing it with provisioning by the household, market, commons, and state – all embedded within and dependent upon society, which in turn is embedded within the living world" (Raworth, 2018, p. loc.1380). There are myriad possible answers here to our original questions, posed by Roger Cotterrell, of what is embedded, and in what (Cotterrell, 2013)? The most likely answer is that Raworth imagines that the economy is, and should be, embedded in society and in the regulations that society makes to define, control, and direct the economy. But there are myriad other potential interpretations we might draw.

By contrast, another widely read and influential book that emerged from the 2008 crash was *The Econocracy: On the Perils of Leaving Economics to the Experts*. Published in 2017 by three dissatisfied students of economics at the University of Manchester, the book responds to the monoculture within the discipline, and the lack of adequate responses to the financial crisis on the curriculum. They were, frankly, angry at being asked to learn the models and theories that had led to the crash, while ignoring other economic theories and concepts that might offer an alternative. The authors expressed their disappointment that "students are taught to study the economy without ever having to study or engage with real people" (Earle, Moran and Ward-Perkins, 2017, p. 49). Yet, early on in the book, the authors note that "[w]e are all embedded in the economy" (Earle, Moran and Ward-Perkins, 2017, p. 4). Who is the "we"? If the authors are referring to society here, this places the statement in direct contrast to Raworth's. This contradiction can be visualized in Figure 1.2 on page 9.

So then, is the market economy and its regulation embedded in society? Or is society embedded in the market economy? What about its regulation? And why does this matter? The following section introduces an economic sociology of law (ESL) – our microcosmic study for examining embeddedness-talk – as a direct challenge to the mainstream approaches in both law and economics. In so doing, it sets out the context in which we can begin to answer these questions.

Introducing an economic sociology of law (ESL): the home of embeddedness

If we define mainstream, or orthodox, approaches to legal and economic scholarship as doctrinal and neoclassical, respectively, we might define an economic sociology of law as a combined antithesis. An ESL-inspired lens asks "how and why" we might use sociologically inspired approaches (empirical, analytical, and normative) "to investigate the relationships between legal and economic phenomena" (Ashiagbor, Kotiswaran and Perry-Kessaris, 2013). An ESL lens, then, demands careful, empirical, sociological enquiry into legal and economic phenomena. Chapter 2 maps out what an ESL-inspired approach might look like and what it has done. But, for now, to understand what an ESL-inspired approach responds to and how its core concept of embeddedness can shed light on our current social needs, it might be helpful to explore what an ESL-inspired lens sets out to do, and how, and the following discussion is situated in the context of the field of law and economic development.[9]

An ESL-inspired lens challenges the assumptions we might characterize as mainstream and demands real-world observation and validation. It is useful here to recall characteristics of mainstream approaches that an ESL lens responds to. We were introduced to *homo juridicus* or the archetypal legal man above, along with the assumptions of doctrinal legal scholarship that "legal developments can be interpreted, critiqued and validated by reference to the internal logic of" the "sealed system" of law (Vick, 2004, 178–9, cited in Banakar and Travers, 2005, p. 2). The focus tends to be on statutes, legal opinions, and legal cases, analyzed within the assumption that law is a rational and coherent analytical construct based on logic and order (Banakar and Travers, 2005; Cotterrell, 1992, p. 2). There is little space for the informal, the normative, or the grey areas of ethics and affect.

Similarly, we were also introduced to assumptions that ground neoclassical economics, which deal "with an advanced capitalist world of perfect markets; consumer sovereignty; automatic price adjustments; decisions made on the basis of marginal, private-profit, and utility calculations; and equilibrium outcomes in all product and resource markets" (Todaro, 2012, p. 7). Mainstream economics assumes "economic 'rationality' and a purely materialistic, individualistic, self-interested orientation toward economic decision making" (Todaro, 2012, p. 7). It tends to quantify, mathematize, and compare phenomena, whether these phenomena lend themselves to being counted or not, and whether or not we recognize that "numbers are rhetoric" (McCloskey, 2006).

9 The discussion that follows introduces ESL in the context of law and economic development, and the timelines and orders in which fields, movements, and disciplines are presented may differ from other areas. Thanks to Ruth Dukes for pointing this out. I'm also indebted to Amanda Perry-Kessaris for phraseology and ways of speaking about "the economic life of the law" in various contexts, each with a subtle shift in focus and framing.

These empirical (counting), conceptual (adding, multiplying, dividing), and normative (comparing one with another) techniques have, over decades, been applied more widely to social phenomena, with the unhappy result that widespread social "indicators" have become technologies of surveillance and governance, especially in the field of "development" (Davis, Kingsbury and Merry, 2010; Perry-Kessaris, 2011a). Neo-liberalism, as the political realization of neoclassical economic concepts and techniques, has seen the triad of privatization, marketization, and deregulation place ever increasing faith in the self-regulation of free markets to govern society (Mudge, 2008).

So, we might say that mainstream approaches in both law and economics share the belief that social behaviour can be understood, analyzed, and modified without much recourse to the messy realities and grey areas of society. In response, socio-legal scholarship has challenged doctrinal legal analysis, while economic sociology has challenged neoclassical economics. This is, of course, an oversimplification, and we might point to myriad other approaches that have each taken issue with one or more of the core assumptions of orthodoxies.[10] Nevertheless, in combining the challenges to mainstream assumptions in both law and economics, an ESL lens might sit between socio-legal scholarship and economic sociology, borrowing from both, and responding to the limitations of doctrinal and neoclassical approaches.

To be clear though, an ESL lens asks us to approach legal and economic phenomena sociologically through empirical observation. It responds to scholarly movements like Law and Economics (the application of the empirical, analytical, and normative approaches of mainstream economics to the law) and Law and Development (the instrumental use of doctrinal law to effect economic development) and could therefore also be described as an anti-law and economics lens.

Inherited from the parent field of economic sociology, embeddedness is the "core concept" or "common denominator" of ESL, describing the variable relationship between the economy and the law with society (Krippner *et al.*, 2004; Block, 1990; Cotterrell, 2013). While there is a consensus on the central role of embeddedness within ESL, the concept itself has given rise to multiple interpretations over the decades, and there is still disagreement over exactly what is embedded, and in what it is embedded, as well as the overall accuracy and utility of the metaphor in general. Advantages and disadvantages of the concept and its many inconsistencies have been set out in the literature on economic sociology and ESL (Krippner *et al.*, 2004; Frerichs, 2011; Cotterrell, 2013). This makes ESL an invaluable starting point for exploring why we

10 In particular, law and political economy (LPE) scholarship in the US has sought to revive the insights of legal realists and critical legal scholars, interrogating the assumed separation and independence of the law from the economy. See inter alia (Blalock, 2015; Grewal, Kapczynski and Britton-Purdy, 2017).

might keep, reform, or abandon the concept of embeddedness in wider discourse, and the implications of any such decision.

To explain, empirically and analytically, why an ESL lens offers us such a useful starting point, a real-world context is helpful. Chapter 2 offers more detail, but for now it is useful to outline the World Bank's *Doing Business* reports and use of indicators to illustrate the problem. The *Doing Business* saga started in 2002 as the love-child of a Law and Economics approach that believed that there was an "ideal investment climate" that could attract foreign investors, thereby catalyzing economic development.[11] The World Bank, captivated by this notion and the new techniques of counting and measuring the uncountable and the unmeasurable, introduced indicators for phenomena like the rule of law and access to justice. These intangibles necessitated proxy indicators, and a global industry of counting the law sprang up. Unsurprisingly, "once you start keeping score, everyone wants to win", and the *Doing Business* indicators swiftly became a competitive undertaking by governments seeking to attract inward investment (Taylor, 2005; World Bank, no date).

This "rule of law Olympics" came to a screeching halt in 2021 with the publication of a scathing report by the law firm WilmerHale LLP into practices by the World Bank (Machen *et al.*, 2021).[12] The *Doing Business* initiative was closed in 2021 but is to be replaced by the *Business Enabling Environment*, meaning that the principles and concepts that underpinned it will continue to inform development policy and interventions. Based on mainstream approaches to law and economics, such policies reflect changes that have characterized the social sciences over the past 50 years. This has included a differentiation and departmentalization of disciplines that has seen schools within the academe separate out and become silos of endeavour, rarely engaging with each other. Within each silo, languages and themes – ways of apprehending the world – have developed. The continental drift of these fields of inquiry, and the silos of research that grew into Towers of Babel, characterizes not only the way we think about social life (is a problem a legal one, an economic one, a psychological one, and so on), but defines how scholars approach the world they study. "If you've got a hammer everything's a nail", and for those who research in the social sciences this reflects a tendency never to look beyond the confines of one's own discipline, however unrealistic this might be when contrasted with "the real world" (Ewick and Silbey, 1998, p. 226).

Nevertheless, as the natural sciences gained respect for their impartiality and objectivism across the twentieth century, the social sciences took note. Economics was the first to ape the methods of the natural sciences in a bid to buy the respectability and deference conferred by scientific methods. The

11 I'm borrowing the phrase "ideal investment climate" from Amanda Perry-Kessaris.

12 The Doing Business project is to be replaced with the World Bank's *Business Enabling Environment* indicators following the discovery of "data irregularities", political interference, bullying, management by Djankov of his team "by terror and intimidation", along with endemic conflicts of interest throughout the process (Machen *et al.*, 2021).

"physics envy" of economics in quantifying, mathematizing, and comparing social phenomena was then copied in some law schools, with the apogee of the law and economics movement realized in the World Bank's *Doing Business* rankings (Mirowski, 1992). And yet, much of the literature on which the *Doing Business* regime rested did not, and could not, establish causation between regulatory structures and economic activity in the same way that a double-blind, peer-reviewed, controlled trial in the biomedical sciences might. In the social sciences, we can work with correlation, and some causative inferences, but we must be careful not to overstate our hand. As Chapters 4 and 5 explore, a shift towards randomized controlled trials (RCTs) in development economics marks an important methodological shift that raises different sets of questions, but, in general, the language of natural science borrowed by economics (and then by law) has tended to act as a fig leaf of rigour and accountability, masking the lack of proven causation. At the same time, the voices and interests of those who do not "fit" neatly into the neoclassical boxes of development economics have been largely silenced by the mainstream discourse, leaving communities underserved.

An ESL lens responds to these limitations. By urging a sociological approach, an ESL lens seeks bridges between the silos that characterize modern social science departments. It seeks to shift the disciplines closer together, forging an understanding of the links between the economy and its regulation, and the sociological underpinnings of both. Discussed further in Chapter 2, an ESL is therefore an integrationist lens that lends itself to constructivism, or the assumption that we might start with observing those quotidian, micro-level, social interactions. And, in the process, an ESL lens challenges the normative silence of mainstream approaches. It not only seeks to reconceptualize the legal and the economic as two sides of the same, social, coin, but emphasizes the political and moral dimensions of all social enquiry.

Nevertheless, while timely and valuable in responding to the limitations of the mainstream, an ESL-inspired lens is not perfect. Its "core concept" (Krippner *et al.*, 2004), embeddedness, is problematic on two grounds: its internal conceptual inconsistency, and its external conceptual incompatibility with the wider goals of ESL. Some economic sociologists and ESL scholars have offered interpretations that seek to remedy the embeddedness problem and this debate can shed light on our wider and more recent ongoing conceptual commitment to embeddedness and how we might innovatively respond to the crashes, crises, and catastrophes facing society (Block, 1991, 2001; Krippner *et al.*, 2004; Ashiagbor, 2011; Frerichs, 2011; Perry-Kessaris, 2011b; Cotterrell, 2013).

The career of embeddedness in ESL and two conceptual conundrums

Literature from economic sociologists and ESL scholars has plenty to say about our ongoing conceptual commitment to embeddedness, highlighting two principal limitations. The first, echoing some of the more academic debates in ESL and our reference points above, is about "what is embedded, and in what is it embedded?" (Cotterrell, 2013). Through the following chapters, this first dilemma is referred to as the "*what* are we talking about?" problem, which relates to the internal inconsistency of the concept. As a metaphor, embeddedness has been applied so broadly, even within the niche area of ESL enquiry, that it now means all things to all people and is consequently largely meaningless (Krippner *et al.*, 2004).

Yet there is a second, more pressing concern which we can sum up as the "*how* are we talking about it?" problem. This refers to the concept's external incompatibility with the integrationist goals of an ESL lens in seeking to shift the disciplinary silos of law, economy, and society back into dialogue with each other. The concept of embeddedness entrenches the separation of law, economy, and society. If we think back to Figure 1.1 on page 5, by describing X as embedded in Y, we understand that these are two ontologically distinct entities. In other words, *embeddedness maintains the metaphorical fiction of the ontologically separate law and economy*. And, in doing so, it allows the dominant orthodox approaches in each of these silos to be maintained, preventing innovative and imaginative sociological approaches that might (re)unite the disciplines. It denies, then, the possibility of any social constructivist understanding that we might attribute to an ESL lens, contrary to the aim of ESL in reintegrating the silos of law, economy, and society.

In reinforcing disciplinary separation, an ongoing conceptual commitment to embeddedness shapes the words and thoughtways we have available to us to describe and make sense of our world and to construct our reality. In re-entrenching the ontological separation of metaphorical phenomena like law, economy, and society, embeddedness-talk moulds our thoughtways and speech as those of *homo economicus-juridicus*. The mental models that led us into the current crashes, crises, and catastrophes are repeated, while simultaneously blinding us to alternative, distinctly sociological possibilities for acting, talking, and thinking otherwise.

Embeddedness in academic literature: drawing parallels and drawing conclusions

While Karl Polanyi is generally credited with the first description of the economy as "embedded", there has been a good deal of ink spilt over what he might have meant.[13] But what can an historical appraisal of embeddedness do

13 We can be fairly certain that Polanyi used embeddedness as a throwaway term, likely giving the implications of the concept little thought. He uses the term sparingly in *The Great Transformation*, although the term does creep back into some of his later notes and papers. There is evidence that Thurnwald, in fact, used the metaphor before Polanyi, although in a slightly different context. For reasons of historical anomaly though, Thurnwald appears to have dodged the bullet for coining such

for our responses to current crises? It is worth returning to the two popular literary responses to the financial crash that were introduced earlier, Raworth's *Doughnut Economics* and Earle *et al.*'s *The Econocracy*.

Raworth's and Earle's contrasting claims about the relationship between the economy and society, respectively that the economy is embedded in society and that society is embedded in the economy, mirror two similarly opposing interpretations of Polanyi by two notable scholars of his life and work: Fred Block and Gareth Dale. While – to oversimplify – Block reads Polanyi as stating that the economy (and its regulation) is embedded in society, Dale argues that Polanyi shows us that society has become embedded in the economy (and its regulation) (Krippner *et al.*, 2004; Dale, 2010b). These claims can be visualized, with Block's reading of Polanyi aligning with Raworth's claims on the left, and Dale's claim, aligning with Earle *et al.*, on the right (see Figure 1.3).

Which is correct? Is the economy (and its regulation) embedded in society, or is society embedded in the economy (and its regulation)? Or is, as Mariana Mazzucato has recently suggested, the economy embedded in norms and regulations (Mazzucato, 2021)? And then, given our observations that the way we talk matters, what difference does it make in practice?

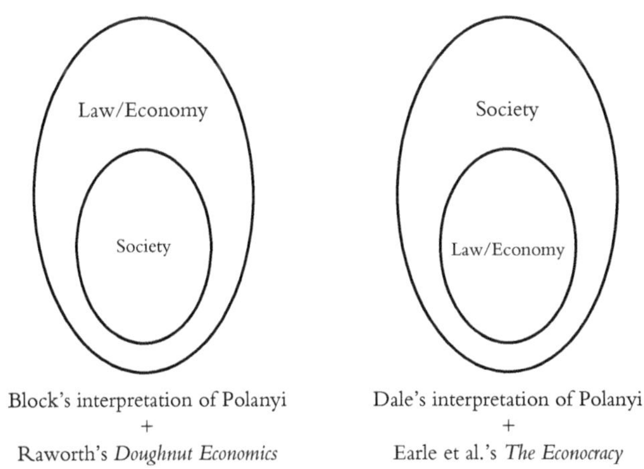

Figure 1.3 Are the law and economy embedded in society, or is society embedded in the law and economy? Raworth's claims, echoing Block's interpretation of Polanyi, are set out on the left. Earle *et al.*'s claims, echoing Dale's interpretation of Polanyi, are set out on the right.

an ambiguous and problematic term, and it is to Polanyi's works that scholars consistently return for enlightenment (Dale, 2010a, 2016).

In turning to the first limitation of embeddedness talk, namely its internal inconsistencies, or the "what are we talking about?" question, we can see that Polanyi's macro-level embeddedness, and the later, confusingly micro-level revival of the concept by Mark Granovetter in 1985 in the field of economic sociology, leaves little consensus as to "what is embedded, and in what" (Polanyi, 1944; Granovetter, 1985; Cotterrell, 2013). Sabine Frerichs, Diamond Ashiagbor, and Amanda Perry-Kessaris have all offered possible readings of embeddedness that add consistency, seeking to reinforce the concept (Frerichs, 2011, 2012; Ashiagbor, 2014; Perry-Kessaris, 2015), and these are discussed in more detail in Chapter 3 as it traces the career of the concept of embeddedness.

If we gaze beyond the confines of economic sociology and ESL literature, the concept of embeddedness has had a fruitful career in other fields, and two notable applications stand out as instructive. John Ruggie's theory of "embedded liberalism" and Peter Evans' theory of "embedded autonomy" offer us two examples of embeddedness-talk that have generally been regarded as successful (Ruggie, 1982; Evans, 1995). Both combine the concept carefully with an equal-and-opposite force to construct an oxymoron that reintroduces some of the flexibility and dynamism that Polanyi might have originally intended but which has been lost in the formation of disciplinary silos and the continental drift that has separated them. Both also apply their conceptual oxymorons to narrow, carefully defined contexts, and avoid sweeping statements of principle. Both theories offer us clues as to how the concept of embeddedness might be strengthened in response to the first charge of its internal inconsistency, and these conditions for a conceptually consistent use of embeddedness are explored in Chapter 4. Readers interested in how we might use embeddedness more consistently and coherently might skip ahead to this chapter.

But even if we rebut the first charge, the second remains: the "how are we talking about it?" question. If we understand ESL as a lens that seeks to challenge entrenched legal and economic disciplinarity, embeddedness-talk becomes conceptually problematic. While an ESL lens seeks to reintegrate the disciplinary fields, embeddedness-talk entrenches their separation. In reproducing the metaphorical fiction of ontologically separate law, economy, and society, the concept of embeddedness is irreconcilable with a constructivist understanding of legal and economic phenomena, understood as two sides of the same social coin. It reproduces this separation linguistically and metaphorically, but, as the above discussion has shown, by shaping how we talk, the concept shapes how we think, and how we (inter)act.

Given the disciplinary drift, departmentalization and differentiation between the academic fields, and their production of discipline-bound, static frames that channel doctrinal and neoclassical approaches, how can we reconcile a commitment to the concept of embeddedness with the limitations of the metaphors it seeks to describe? Even revisiting Ruggie's "embedded liberalism" and Evans' "embedded autonomy" here does not fully resolve this question. Either we must scale back the ambitions of ESL to reintegrate the disciplines, maintaining the metaphorical distinctions between spheres of behaviour, or we must reappraise the linguistic tools we use to describe how we construct and perform legal and economic phenomena. This latter is not such a daunting task, and Chapter 5 proposes one way of going about this. While our current focus lies with actors and their micro-level (dis)embeddedness, we might scale up to the macro- and meta-level (dis)embeddedness of institutions across space and time. Chapter 5 asks, speculatively, what if we were to shift our focus from actors to their interactions, and from embeddedness to the feedback loops that operate throughout these interactions? Readers interested in moving beyond embeddedness might jump straight to this chapter.

To be clear, what follows is not a treatise against embeddedness as a concept, word, metaphor, or even a term of art. As the following chapters show, when certain conditions are met, embeddedness can be helpful, illuminating, and entirely appropriate as a relational descriptor. The argument is more subtle, as danger lies where we lose sight of the metaphorical fictions we invoke, the concepts baked into these, and the theoretical heavy lifting that we are (tacitly) asking these concepts to do. But there are certain instances where optimal conditions of use cannot be met, and in these our ongoing conceptual commitment to embeddedness becomes unhelpful and circular. As such, Chapter 6 looks ahead, asking what the insights gained in these chapters mean for our ongoing responses to crashes, crises, and catastrophes, and what we risk by preserving our current frames in digital aspic as we are doing when we train AI systems of the future. Those interested in real-world applications of the insights of the following chapters and how we could be framing the future, might like to skip ahead to the final chapter.

Introducing our "guide" personas: Ann, Polly, and Lillian[14]

In keeping with ESL's insistence on the study and understanding of legal and economic phenomena empirically, the theoretical discussion that follows will be guided and applied by three personas: Academic Ann, Policy Polly, and Lay Lillian. Each will explore an embeddedness-based ESL frame in their life and work, before shifting to the proposed alternative to assess the differences that result.

14 The three characters, introduced here as personas and developed in vignettes throughout the book, are waiting to meet you online (Williams, 2020, 2022).

Apart from bringing the discussion back to its quotidian, real-world applications and implications, the personas and their development through vignettes reflect another of the core arguments made here. This is the inadequacy of language, both to accurately reflect what we are wishing to communicate, and to lodge permanently in the brain. The former of these is a theme explored in detail through the study of embeddedness over the following chapters. The latter derives from insights from neuroscience and narrative research.

"When people tell stories or listen to them, they form mental images that are stored in memory as symbols" (Berman, cited in Levit, 2009, p. 277). While people retain only about 20 percent of what they read, they recall up to 80 percent of symbols (Berman, cited in Levit, 2009, p. 277). Narratives "light up" areas of the brain that "produce an affective response", triggering "a release of neurotransmitters (catecholamines, such as epinephrine and dopamine) that affect both hemispheres of the brain", leading to holistic learning (Batt, cited in Levit, 2009, p. 276). The use of empathetic narratives in the form of personas and vignettes throughout the book challenges the way that scholarship is usually disinfected of the personal, the affective, and the emotional through the process of writing (Campbell, 2016). Each of the characters has their own back story, and each comes to the concepts and theories discussed here with different requirements. Some vignettes offer illustrations. Others raise questions or pose dilemmas from a different perspective. In introducing Ann, Polly, and Lillian, the hope is to maintain the "forceful link" with reality demanded of (econo-)socio-legal inquiry (Frerichs, 2012, p. 9; Williams, 2023).

In empirically grounding the conceptual, personas and vignettes can be described as "designerly" approaches (Cross, 1982; Perry-Kessaris, 2021). There is no clear dividing line beyond which persona becomes a vignette, however there is a consensus that personas are fictional renditions of characters that embody relevant characteristics, while vignettes tend to capture short snippets of context that explore the "perceptions, beliefs, and attitudes" of the characters (Hughes, 1998). In some cases straddling the two then, Ann, Polly, and Lillian explore three contexts relevant to the arguments set out here, offering a critical, practical, and imaginative space in which we can explore the problems and solutions arising from our ongoing commitment to the concept of embeddedness (Perry-Kessaris, 2021). They offer a way of making the discussion both visible and tangible, and in later chapters allow us to ask "what if" we had alternative ways of doing, talking, and thinking. As such, they operate both speculatively (asking "what if") and prefiguratively (acting "as if"), enabling an exploration of alternative possibilities and their implications for the three contexts chosen here: namely academic research, policy design and implementation, and then wider lay discourse across society (Perry-Kessaris, 2021). They will be our guides through the following five chapters, exploring alternative ESL lenses, and the implications and the impact of these.

Let's meet them.

ACADEMIC ANN

Ann works in the law department at a university in the UK. Her particular area of interest is the interface between law and the economy, especially in the field of economic development. She wants to find out how a legal system can be structured to maximize inward foreign (direct) investment (FDI) flows. She has funding for fieldwork and is planning a series of interviews with foreign investors in the country she is heading to. She's booked her flights, had all the necessary jabs, and has stacked the freezer with home-cooked dinners for her partner and two teenage sons.

Ann's links with the target country go back years. She had been backpacking there on her gap year as a teenager and had fallen in love with the country, revisiting as often as she could and taking her children as soon as they were old enough. She has friends there, and over time has made contacts in the civil service and government too.

Recently, things have changed though. Vast quantities of foreign investment have poured in and infrastructure projects that had initially mushroomed have since stalled. Some years ago, development banks were the go-to for infrastructure finance for development, and they imposed conditions on borrowers. These conditions principally sought to improve conditions for foreign investors by streamlining bureaucratic processes and strengthening the rule of law, and reforms were typically based on hunches rather than evidence. But then other sources of funding appeared, and the development banks no longer had the monopoly on lending. What did this mean for the role of the law in facilitating FDI?

POLICY POLLY

Polly was only a baby when her family emigrated to the Global North. Growing up, she was aware that she had opportunities that her cousins did not. A scholarship to study at the LSE brought her to London, followed by a masters at Sciences Po in Paris and then internships in think tanks and at the World Bank back in Washington. Frustrated by global inequalities and the development industry in general, Polly had always wanted to make a difference, and had hoped that working either in the third sector or at a development bank would give her the opportunity to do this.

After a few years at the bank, working in research and policy development, Polly enjoys her work, but isn't sure she is making the impact she wanted to. The implementation gap bugs her: the bank has policies and indicators, and on paper things should be getting steadily better for people around the world. But they aren't. Then, there was the "data irregularities" debacle, which was just the latest example of data not matching up with reports on the ground. At other times, the policies she helps to shape just don't produce the desired results.

She is still in touch with a couple of friends from her university days in London, and catching up virtually she tells Ann about some of the problems with her work: that sometimes the numbers are simply wrong, and that sometimes the theories and concepts she is using don't seem to align all that well with the realities on the ground.

LAY LILLIAN

Lillian is retired, although you wouldn't think so. She's kept busy with her grandkids and volunteering, but still does a bit of cleaning for cash. Before 2008, she was optimistic about her sons' futures, but they both lost jobs after the financial crash, and her local community has seen cuts and closures to virtually every service. These have been compounded by the pandemic, and Lillian's pension now barely covers the essentials. The decade of austerity has hit her family hard and she gives her sons whatever money she has, but they still need the local food bank from time to time.

Lillian has always been interested in politics though and reads the papers every day. While her family has struggled, she notices that not everyone has suffered the same. Some people have got much richer, and the unfairness makes Lillian angry. She brought up her family to play by the rules, but she feels the rules have let her down.

Bumping into her neighbour on the way home, Lillian begins to explain her day. Ann listens, patiently, agreeing with Lillian on every point. She knows it all to be true and starts to explain to Lillian that maybe we are all talking about this using unhelpful terms and metaphors. Lillian doesn't quite understand Ann's point, but she gets the gist that maybe better mental models would help decision-makers to make fairer decisions.

Ann, Polly, and Lillian will drop in and out of the following chapters, applying the discussion to their own lives and work in the contexts of academic research, policy design, and wider discourse respectively. They each find that an ESL-inspired approach is a useful tool for challenging the shortcomings of our current mental models. Then, unpacking the proposed alternative lens in Chapters 4 and 5 that moves us "beyond embeddedness", each finds that there are potential advantages revealed by shifting our focus to interactions and feedback loops. Ann explores the differences in her fieldwork resulting from different interpretations of embeddedness, finding that different actors and research questions are highlighted. Then, moving beyond embeddedness, she suspects that the proposed frame in Chapter 5 will offer a fuller and more accurate understanding of the complex interactions that she is hoping to investigate at the interface of the legal and the economic.

Polly finds that the proposed shift "beyond embeddedness" – focusing on interactions and feedback loops – allows her to more easily include a plurality of voices and interests in her work. She is optimistic that combined with more experimental approaches at the development bank this might reduce the implementation gap, where the results of interventions turn out to be underwhelming or have unexpected consequences. Finally, Lillian finds that focusing on interactions and their myriad ideal types allows her to describe the needs of her community in ways that are denied to her by mainstream discourse. She is hopeful that this offers her a way of challenging the mainstream narratives that have not served her, her family, or her community well. Zooming out further in Chapter 6, Lillian guides us through the real-world implications of the conceptual shifts proposed, as we explore what an alternative way of doing, talking, and thinking about legal and economic phenomena might mean for our responses to crashes, crises, and catastrophes. If we can *talk* better, this book argues that we might *think* and *do* better. The potential gains for society, were we to imagine alternative ways of talking and of thinking, could be immeasurable. An ESL-inspired lens shows us why this is important, what we might achieve, and how we might get there. So, to begin, let us turn to an economic sociology of law in Chapter 2.

Bibliography

Ashiagbor, D. (2011) 'Embedding Trade Liberalization in Social Policy: Lessons from the European Union?', *Comparative Labour Law and Policy Journal*, 32(2), pp. 373–404.

Ashiagbor, D. (2014) 'Embedding Trade Liberalisation in Social Policy: A Research Agenda on Social Regionalism and the Global South', *Northern Ireland Legal Quarterly*, 65(3), pp. 265–281.

Ashiagbor, D., Kotiswaran, P. and Perry-Kessaris, A. (2013) 'Introduction: Moving towards an Economic Sociology of Law', *Journal of Law and Society*, 40, pp. 1–6.

Banakar, R. and Travers, M. (2005) *Theory and Method in Socio-Legal Research*. Oxford: Hart.

Bandes, S. (1996) 'Empathy, Narrative, and Victim Impact Statements', *University of Chicago Law Review*, 63(2), p. 361.

Bernstein, R. et al. (2015) 'There is No Local Here, Love', in D. O'Brien and P. Matthews (eds) *After Urban Regeneration: Communities, Policy and Place*. Bristol: Policy Press at the University of Bristol, pp. 95–110.

Blalock, C. (2015) 'Neoliberalism and the Crisis of Legal Theory', *Law & Contemporary Problems*, 77, pp. 71–103.

Block, F. (1990) *Postindustrial Possibilities: A Critique of Economic Discourse*. Berkeley: University of California Press.

Block, F. (1991) 'Contradictions of Self-Regulating Markets', in Marguerite Mendell and Daniel Salée (eds) *The Legacy of Karl Polanyi: Market, State and Society at the End of the Twentieth Century*. Macmillan.

Block, F. (2001) 'Introduction', in *The Great Transformation, Karl Polanyi*. Boston: Beacon Press, pp. xviii–xxxviii. https://inctpped.ie.ufrj.br/spiderweb/pdf_4/Great_Transformation.pdf.

Block, F. (2003) 'Karl Polanyi and the Writing of the Great Transformation', *Theory and Society*, 32(3), pp. 275–306.

Boroditsky, L. (2009) 'How Does Our Language Shape the Way We Think?', *Edge*, 6 November. Available at: https://www.edge.org/conversation/lera_boroditsky-how-does-our-language-shape-the-way-we-think.

Burrows, A. (2016) 'Challenges for Private Law in the 21st Century', *Oxford Legal Studies Research Paper* 3/2016 [Preprint]. https://doi.org/10.2139/ssrn.2710270.

Campbell, E. (2016) 'Exploring Autoethnography as a Method and Methodology in Legal Education Research', *Asian Journal of Legal Education*, 3(1), pp. 95–105. https://doi.org/10.1177/2322005815607141.

Cloatre, E. and Cowan, D. (2019) Legalities and Materialities, in Andreas Philippopoulos-Mihalopoulos (ed) *Routledge Handbook of Law and Theory*. London: Routledge, pp. 433–452

Cooper, D. and Renz, F. (2021) 'Reimagining Gender through Equality Law: What Legal Thoughtways Do Religion and Disability Offer?', *Feminist Legal Studies*. https://doi.org/10.1007/s10691-021-09481-3.

Cotterrell, R. (1992) *The Sociology of Law: An Introduction*. 2nd ed. London, Dublin, Edinburgh: Butterworths.

Cotterrell, R. (2013) 'Rethinking Embeddedness; Law, Economy, Community', *Journal of Law and Society*, 40(1), pp. 49–67.

Cross, N. (1982) 'Designerly Ways of Knowing', *Design Studies*, 3(4), pp. 221–227.

Dale, G. (2010a) *Karl Polanyi: The Limits of the Market*. 1st ed. Cambridge and Malden: Polity.

Dale, G. (2010b) 'Social Democracy, Embeddedness and Decommodification: On the Conceptual Innovations and Intellectual Affiliations of Karl Polanyi', *New Political Economy*, 15(3), pp. 369–393. https://doi.org/10.1080/13563460903290920.

Dale, G. (2011) 'Lineages of Embeddedness: On the Antecedents and Successors of a Polanyian Concept', *The American Journal of Economics and Sociology*, 70(2), pp. 306–339.

Dale, G. (2016) *Karl Polanyi: A Life on the Left*. 1st ed. New York: Columbia University Press.

Davis, K.E., Kingsbury, B. and Merry, S.E. (2010) 'Indicators as a Technology of Global Governance'. Available at: https://ssrn.com/abstract=1583431 or https://doi.org/10.2139/ssrn.1583431.

Delanda, M. (2006) *A New Philosophy of Society: Assemblage Theory and Social Complexity*. Continuum.

Dermendzhiyska, E. (2021) 'Feeling, In Situ', *aeon.co*, 8 October. Available at: https://aeon.co/essays/what-if-emotions-arent-universal-but-specific-to-each-culture?utm_source=pocket-newtab-global-en-GB.

Duczynska Polanyi, I. (2006) 'I First Met Karl Polanyi in 1920', in McRobbie, K. and Levitt, K.P. (eds) *Karl Polanyi in Vienna: The Contemporary Significance of The Great Transformation*. Montreal: Black Rose Books, pp. 302–316.

Dunford, D. et al. (2020) 'Coronavirus: The World in Lockdown in Maps and Charts', *BBC News*, 7 April. Available at: https://www.bbc.co.uk/news/world-52103747 (Accessed: 15 January 2022).

Earle, J., Moran, C. and Ward-Perkins, Z. (2017) *The Econocracy: On the Perils of Leaving Economics to the Experts*. Kindle Edition. Penguin Books. https://www.penguin.co.uk/books/307289/the-econocracy-by-joe-earle-cahal-moran-and-zach-ward-perkins/9780141986869.

Elias, N. (2010) *The Society of Individuals: v. 10 (Collected Works of Norbert Elias)*. Edited by M. Schroter and R. van Krieken. Translated by E. Jephcott. Dublin: University College Dublin Press.

Evans, P. (1995) *Embedded Autonomy: States and Industrial Transformation*. Princeton: Princeton University Press.

Ewick, P. and Silbey, S. (1998) *The Common Place of Law*. University of Chicago Press. Available at: https://www.press.uchicago.edu/ucp/books/book/chicago/C/bo3615912.html.

Fineman, M.A. (2019) 'Vulnerability and Social Justice', *Valparaiso University Law Review*, 53. Available at: https://papers.ssrn.com/sol3/papers.cfm?abstract_id=3352825.

Fineman, M.A. (2022) 'What Vulnerability Theory Is and Is Not', *Vulnerability and the Human Condition*, 1 February. Available at: https://scholarblogs.emory.edu/vulnerability/2021/02/01/is-and-is-not/.

Fleming, P. (2017) *The Death of Homo Economicus: Work, Debt and the Myth of Endless Accumulation*. London: Pluto Press.

Foucault, M. (2008) *The Birth of Biopolitics; Lectures at the College de France 1978–79*. Edited by M. Senellart. Translated by G. Burchell. Palgrave Macmillan. Available at: https://1000littlehammers.files.wordpress.com/2010/02/birth_of_biopolitics.pdf.

Frerichs, S. (2009) 'The Legal Constitution of Market Society: Probing the Economic Sociology of Law', *Economic Sociology, The European Electronic Newsletter*, 10.

Frerichs, S. (2011) 'Re-Embedding Neoliberal Constitutionalism: A Polanyian Case for the Economic Sociology of Law', in C. Joerges and J. Falke (eds) *Karl Polanyi, Globalisation, and the Potential of Law in Transnational Markets*. Oxford: Hart Publishing (International Studies in the Theory of Private Law, Vol. 8), pp. 65–84.

Frerichs, S. (2012) 'Studying Law, Economy, and Society: A Short History of Socio-Legal Thinking', *SSRN eLibrary* [Preprint]. Available at: http://papers.ssrn.com/sol3/papers.cfm?abstract_id=2022891.

Geary, J. (2011) *I is an Other: The Secret Life of Metaphor and How it Shapes the Way We See the World*. New York: Harper Collins.

Gefter, A. (2022) 'Do We Create Space-Time? A New Perspective on the Fabric of Reality', *New Scientist*, 2 February. Available at: https://www.newscientist.com/article/mg25333720-800-do-we-create-space-time-a-new-perspective-on-the-fabric-of-reality/?utm_source=pocket-newtab-global-en-GB.

Giddens, A. (1984) *The Constitution of Society: Outline of the Theory of Structuration*. Oxford: Polity.

Granovetter, M. (1985) 'Economic Action and Social Structure: The Problem of Embeddedness', *American Journal of Sociology*, 91(3), pp. 481–510.

Grewal, D.S., Kapczynski, A. and Britton-Purdy, J. (2017) 'Toward a Manifesto', *The LPE Project*, 6 November. Available at: https://lpeproject.org/lpe-manifesto/.

Harraway, D. (2016) *Staying with the Trouble: Making Kin in the Chthulucene*. Duke University Press. Available at: https://www.dukeupress.edu/staying-with-the-trouble.

Harriss, J. (2002) *Depoliticizing Development: The World Bank and Social Capital*. London: Anthem Press.

Hirsch, P., Michaels, S. and Friedman, R. (1990) 'Clean Models vs. Dirty Hands: Why Economics is Different from Sociology', in Sharon Zukin and Paul DiMaggio (eds) *Structures of Capital: The Social Organization of the Economy*. Cambridge: Cambridge University Press, pp. 39–57.

Hughes, R. (1998) 'Considering the Vignette Technique and its Application to a Study of Drug Injecting and HIV Risk and Safer Behaviour', *Sociology of Health and Illness*, 20(3), pp. 381–400.

Kahneman, D. and Tversky, A. (eds) (2000) *Choices, Values, and Frames*. Cambridge University Press. Available at: https://www-cambridge-org.chain.kent.ac.uk/gb/academic/subjects/psychology/cognition/choices-values-and-frames?format=PB&isbn=9780521627498.

Krippner, G. et al. (2004) 'Polanyi Symposium: A Conversation on Embeddedness', *Socio-Economic Review*, 2, pp. 109–135.

Lakoff, G. and Johnson, M. (1980) *Metaphors We Live By*. Chicago: University of Chicago Press.

Latour, B. (2007) *Reassembling the Social: An Introduction to Actor-Network-Theory*. New York: Oxford University Press.

Law, J. (2009) 'Seeing Like a Survey', *Cultural Sociology*, 3(2), pp. 239–256.

Levit, N. (2009) 'Legal Storytelling: The Theory and the Practice - Reflective Writing across the Curriculum', *The Journal of the Legal Writing Institute*, 15, pp. 259–283.

Lewton, T. (2021) 'The Quantum Experiment that Could Prove Reality Doesn't Exist', *New Scientist*, 3 November. Available at: https://www.newscientist.com/article/mg25233590-800-the-quantum-experiment-that-could-prove-reality-doesnt-exist/.

Machen, R.C. et al. (2021) *Investigation of Data Irregularities in Doing Business 2018 and Doing Business 2020 Investigation Findings and Report to the Board of Executive Directors*. WilmerHale: Wilmer Cutler Pickering Hale and Dorr LLP. Available at: https://thedocs.worldbank.org/en/doc/84a922cc9273b7b120d49ad3b9e9d3f9-0090012021/original/DB-Investigation-Findings-and-Report-to-the-Board-of-Executive-Directors-September-15-2021.pdf.

MacKenzie, D. and Millo, Y. (2003) 'Constructing a Market, Performing Theory: The Historical Sociology of a Financial Derivatives Exchange', *American Journal of Sociology*, 109(1), pp. 107–145.

Matthews, D. (2021) *Earthbound: The Aesthetics of Sovereignty in the Anthropocene*. Edinburgh: Edinburgh University Press.

Mazzucato, M. (2021) *Mission Economy: A Moonshot Guide to Changing Capitalism*. Penguin. https://www.penguin.co.uk/books/315191/mission-economy-by-mazzucato-mariana/9780141991689.

McCloskey, D.N. (2006) 'Why Economics is on the Wrong Track', *Prudentia*. Available at: http://www.deirdremccloskey.com/articles/stats/why.php.

McLachlan, H. (2020) 'Why "There's No Such Thing as Society" Should Not Be Regarded with Moral Revulsion', *The Conversation*, 24 April. Available at: https://theconversation.com/why-theres-no-such-thing-as-society-should-not-be-regarded-with-moral-revulsion-136008.

Mirowski, P. (1992) 'Do Economists Suffer from Physics Envy?', *Finnish Economic Papers*, 5(1), pp. 61–68.

Mudge, S.L. (2008) 'What is Neo-Liberalism?', *Socio-Economic Review*, 6(4), pp. 703–731. https://doi.org/10.1093/ser/mwn016.

Naffine, N. (2006) 'Our Legal Lives as Men, Women and Persons', *Legal Studies* [Preprint]. https://doi.org/10.1111/j.1748-121X.2004.tb00265.x.

Nedelsky, J. (2012) *Law's Relations: A Relational Theory of Self, Autonomy and Law*. Oxford University Press. Available at: https://global.oup.com/academic/product/laws-relations-9780195147964?cc=gb&lang=en&#.

Norman, J. (2022) *Posthuman Legal Subjectivity: Reimagining the Human in the Anthropocene*. Oxford: Routledge (Law, Justice and Ecology).

Peck, J. (2013) 'Disembedding Polanyi: Exploring Polanyian Economic Geographies', *Environment and Planning A*, 45, pp. 1536–1544. https://doi.org/10.1068/a46253.

Perry-Kessaris, A. (2021) *Doing Sociolegal Research in Design Mode*. New York: Routledge.

Perry-Kessaris, A.J. (2011a) 'Prepare Your Indicators: Economics Imperialism on the Shores of Law and Development', *International Journal of Law in Context*, 7(4), pp. 401–421.

Perry-Kessaris, A.J. (2011b) 'Reading the Story of Law and Embeddedness Through a Community Lens: A Polanyi-Meets-Cotterrell Economic Sociology of Law?', *Northern Ireland Legal Quarterly* (Special Issue on *Socialising Economic Relationships*), 62(4), pp. 401–13.

Perry-Kessaris, A.J. (2015) 'Approaching the Econo-Socio-Legal', *Annual Review of Law and Social Science* [Preprint]. https://doi.org/10.1146/annurev-lawsocsci-120814-121542.

Polanyi, K. (1944) *The Great Transformation: The Political and Economic Origins of Our Time*. 2nd ed. Princeton: Beacon Press.

Putnam, R. (2001) *Bowling Alone: The Collapse and Revival of American Community*. New York: Simon & Schuster Ltd.

Raworth, K. (2018) *Doughnut Economics: Seven Ways to Think Like a 21st-Century Economist*. ebook (Kindle). Random House Business. https://www.penguin.co.uk/books/429710/doughnut-economics-by-kate-raworth/9781847941398.

Rittich, K. (2014) 'Making Natural Markets: Flexibility as Labour Market Truth', *Northern Ireland Legal Quarterly*, 65(3), pp. 323–345.

Rose, N. and Valverde, M. (1998) 'Governed by Law?', *Social and Legal Studies*, 4, pp. 541–551.

Ruggie, J.G. (1982) 'International Regimes, Transactions and Change: Embedded Liberalism in the Postwar Economic Order', *International Organization*, 36(2), pp. 379–415.

Schön, D.A. (2012) 'Generative Metaphor: A Perspective on Problem-Setting in Social Policy', in Ortony, A. (ed.) *Metaphor and Thought*. 2nd ed. Cambridge: Cambridge University Press, pp. 137–163.

Searle, J.R. (2006) 'Social Ontology: Some Basic Principles', *Anthropological Theory*, 6(1), pp. 12–29.

Seth, A. (2021) 'Consciousness: How Your Brain Creates the Feeling of Being', *NewScientist*. Available at: https://www.newscientist.com/definition/consciousness/ (Accessed: 4 March 2022).

Shariatmadari, D. (2019) *Don't Believe a Word: The Surprising Truth about Language*. Kindle. Weidenfeld & Nicolson.

Slupska, J. (2021) 'War, Health, and Ecosystem: Generative Metaphors in Cybersecurity Governance', *Philosophy and Technology*, 34, pp. 463–482.

Supiot, A. (2017) *Homo Juridicus: On the Anthropological Function of the Law*. Translated by S. Brown. London: Verso.

Tanner, W. et al. (2020) *The State of our Social Fabric*. Onward. Available at: https://www.ukonward.com/wp-content/uploads/2021/09/The-State-of-our-Social-Fabric.pdf.

Tata, C. (2020) *Sentencing: A Social Process-Rethinking Research and Policy*. Palgrave Macmillan (Palgrave Socio-Legal Studies). Available at: https://doi.org/10.1007/978-3-030-01060-7.

Taylor, V.L. (2005) *The Law Reform Olympics: Measuring the Effects of Law Reform in Transition Economies*. SSRN Scholarly Paper ID 893682. Rochester: Social Science Research Network. Available at: https://papers.ssrn.com/abstract=893682.

Teubner, G. (2021) 'The Constitution of Non-Monetary Surplus Values', *Social and Legal Studies*, 30(4), pp. 501–521.

Thaler, R.H. (2000) 'From Homo Economicus to Homo Sapiens', *Journal of Economic Perspectives*, 14(1), pp. 133–141.

Thaler, R.H. (2016) *Misbehaving: The Making of Behavioural Economics*. Penguin. Available at: https://www.penguin.co.uk/books/179/179906/misbehaving/9780241951224.html.

Thaler, R.H. and Sunstein, C.R. (2009) *Nudge: Improving Decisions about Health, Wealth and Happiness*. Penguin.

Thatcher, M. (1987) 'Women's Own Interview with Margaret Thatcher', *Women's Own Magazine*. Available at: https://www.theguardian.com/politics/2013/apr/08/margaret-thatcher-quotes.

Thomson, H. (2016) 'You Are Hallucinating Right Now to Make Sense of the World', *NewScientist*, 2 November. Available at: https://www.newscientist.com/article/mg23230980-400-you-are-hallucinating-right-now-to-make-sense-of-the-world/.

Todaro, M.P. (2012) *Economic Development*. 11th ed. Boston: Addison-Wesley (The Pearson series in economics).

Tooze, A. (2021) *Shutdown*. Allen Lane, Penguin.

Wheeler, S. (2020) 'Socio-Legal Studies in 2020', *Journal of Law and Society*, 47(S2), pp. S209–S226.

Williams, C. (2020) 'Making Research Relevant: Meet Ann, Pol, and Lil', *Clare's Research Blog*, 26 January. Available at: https://claresresearchblog.com/2020/01/26/making-research-relevant-meet-ann-pol-and-lil/.

Williams, C. (2023) 'Using Personas, Vignettes, and Diagrams in Legal Education', in Allbon, E. and Perry-Kessaris, A. (eds) *Design and Visualisation in Legal Education: Access to the Law*. New York: Routledge.

World Bank (n.d.) *Doing Business, Why Aggregate, and How to Do it*. World Bank Doing Business. Available at: http://www.doingbusiness.org/~/media/WBG/DoingBusiness/Documents/Methodology/Other/why-aggregate-doing-business-2006.pdf (Accessed: 17 November 2018).

Chapter 2

Introducing an economic sociology of law

What is an economic sociology of law (ESL)?

> **ACADEMIC ANN**
>
> *Previously, Ann had looked at correlations between legal reforms and investment rates in her target country. She had examined the figures, spoken with a few contacts, and had made some suggestions to the government and to other policy stakeholders based on her regression analyses of the data: it had all gone down very well and Ann was hoping to repeat the success this time.*
>
> *There was one memory of that research trip that played on her mind though. Chatting to the director of a foreign-owned company, Ann had asked about pre-investment legal inquiry and whether this research was borne out in their experiences. Instead of the carefully considered answers he had given to her other questions, he had laughed!*
>
> *He had then told her that, sure, the company had done some research into the laws before investing, but they didn't really care. If there were bribes to be paid, he said, all he wanted to know was how much and when. If there were delays to the systems, he continued, all he wanted to know was who to contact to speed things up. Wondering if he was being flippant, Ann had realized there and then that she was missing a piece of the puzzle.*

While there is a general consensus about what an economic sociology of law (ESL) *is* and *does*, and *why*, there are multiple suggestions of *how* we can go about this. Let's begin with the aspects about which there is broad agreement.

An ESL represents "shared understandings of how and why one might use sociologically-inspired approaches (analytical, empirical and normative) to investigate relationships between legal and economic phenomena" (Ashiagbor, Kotiswaran and Perry-Kessaris, 2013, p. 2). A focus on the role that "law and regulations play in the economic sphere" as well as the "economic constitutions

DOI: 10.4324/9781003354819-2

that make up market society" have both been offered as foci for an ESL lens (Swedberg, 2003, p. 2; Frerichs, 2009, p. 24). It therefore sits between legal sociology and economic sociology, facing both aspects of its heritage (Frerichs, 2012, p. 5), although the centrality of a sociological starting point, or lens, cannot be understated.

There is also general agreement that the "'legal' and the 'economic' [... are] social phenomena occurring on all, interconnected, levels of social life", hinting at a readiness to consider ESL a constructivist lens, and later sections in this chapter explore what this means (Perry-Kessaris, 2013, p. 69). In the context of economic development, we might imagine ESL and its heritage as set out in the diagram in Figure 2.1; in dialogue with its immediate "parent" fields represented by double-ended arrows, while responding to the more mainstream approaches represented by the single directional arrows.[1] Thus, an ESL unites insights from socio-legal scholarship and economic sociology. In the context of research on economic development, these in turn respond to other movements. So, we might note that socio-legal scholarship responds to the Law and Development and then the Law and Economics movements. Similarly, economic sociology might be seen as a response to neoclassical economics and the New Institutional Economics. Figure 2.1 visualizes what we might term the family tree of an economic sociology of law (ESL).

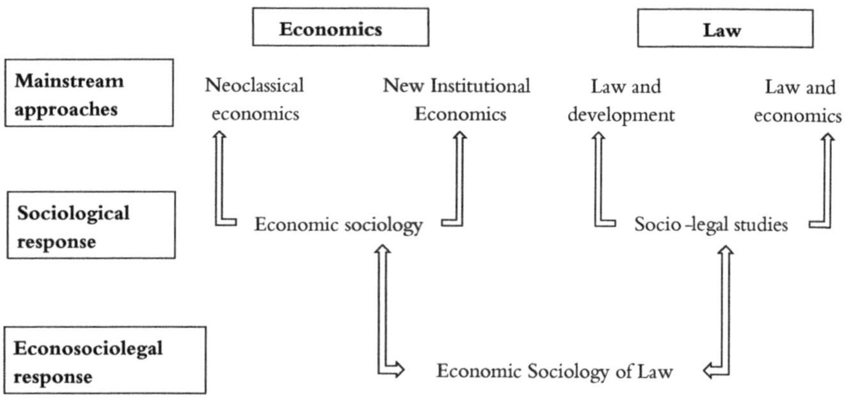

Figure 2.1 ESL's family tree, set in the context of the literature relating to law and economic development. Double-ended arrows indicate heritage and dialogue, while single direction arrows indicate a response.

1 Note that ESL's family tree might look different in different contexts or fields or inquiry (with thanks to Ruth Dukes for pointing this out). The core arguments made over the following chapters apply equally regardless of context.

Nevertheless, there is still some debate about where exactly within this landscape an ESL lens sits, and which way it faces (Ashiagbor, Kotiswaran and Perry-Kessaris, 2013, 2014). Some writers see an economic sociology of law as a socio-legal project, sitting neatly within socio-legal approaches, doctrines, and boundaries and borrowing the methodological categories that have already been established therein (Perry-Kessaris, 2012). Others have set economic sociology of law on a separate footing, spanning (both borrowing from and adding to) economic sociology and socio-legal literature (Frerichs, 2012). As a tool for examining the social interface of legal and economic aspects of interactions, ESL offers a way of accommodating diversity and appreciating flexibility. It also offers insights into the conflicting and overlapping requirements of multiple groups across time and space. It can be extended as a project demands, functioning magpie-like to "borrow" useful aspects from different theoretical lenses, traditions, or disciplines, encouraging the researcher to look beyond the boundaries of their field.

An economic sociology of law, moreover, "accommodates a wide range of methodologies and substantive fields" and is therefore available as an approach to "legal historians, sociologists and lawyers trained in more than one discipline" (Ashiagbor, Kotiswaran and Perry-Kessaris, 2014, p. 263). There is also, finally, a general agreement that as a "social phenomenon", law (and economics) "must be understood empirically (through detailed examination of variation and continuity in actual historical patterns of social co-existence, rather than in relation to idealised or abstractly imagined social conditions)" (Cotterrell, 1998, p. 183). Thus, an ESL should produce "careful empirical studies of the role that law and regulations play in the economic sphere" through an analysis that highlights both "social relations [and...] interests" (Swedberg, 2003, p. 2).

Consequently then, we have an extensive array of sociological lenses or tools to choose from. Some of those that have been developed range from the socio-legal communal networks lens (Cotterrell, 2013; Perry-Kessaris, 2013), to relational work (Zelizer, 2011; Block, 2013), via sociological levels of analysis based on embeddedness (Frerichs, 2009, 2012; Perry-Kessaris, 2013), to the more constructivist theories of the "third generation" of sociologists (Giddens, 1984; Bourdieu and Wacquant, 1992; Luhmann, 2004; Wallerstein, 2004). Each of these offers a different point of departure and focus. Some deal directly with the dualisms that have developed in modern sociology (agency/structure, ontology/epistemology, realism/constructivism, macro/micro, embeddedness/relatedness, and so on), while others instead have a more particular locus of interest.

ESL tends to look back to the work of economist and sociologist Max Weber, not only in the multidisciplinary sense of providing a sociological account of legal and economic phenomena, but also in offering a series of categories for understanding society and the economic and legal phenomena found therein (Perry-Kessaris, 2015). Weber was writing at a time before the disciplines had drifted apart, differentiating themselves in the process. Building on the work of the father of sociology, Comte, Weber had more time for the theoretical, non-empirical models that both Comte and Durkheim argued against, reflecting his belief in the dual value of theoretical economics and empirical studies that were reliant on a sociological understanding and frames of reference for accuracy. This pre-disciplinarity, a characteristic of the scholarly landscape in which Polanyi later wrote *The Great Transformation*, understood the dynamism and flexibility of social relations and the interconnectedness of social phenomena that is so anathema to the mainstream approaches we work with today.

The role of economic sociology of law: responding to disciplinarity

ACADEMIC ANN

Ann's previous work on law and economic development had asked what shape a legal system should take to maximize inward investment flows. In other words, what were foreign investors looking for in a legal system? She had, along with the World Bank and Law and Development literature, assumed that a rational legal system with strong respect for the rule of law would make the best "investment climate", and there was a sense that this "received wisdom" was beyond doubt. The World Bank even measured and compared the rule of law around the world annually, posting country rankings on their website.

Sure, there had been some years when the figures had changed – apparently a computer glitch that a Bank employee had apologized about when Ann had enquired why her spreadsheets no longer matched the Bank's. And then there were the frequent alterations to methodology that meant you couldn't make comparisons over time. And then there had also been the "data irregularities" debacle and the closing of the Doing Business *programme.*

But, replaying in her head the investor's laughter when she had asked him about the legal system bothered Ann more than she cared to admit. What if law wasn't all that important after all? What if the tools she was using didn't reflect what was really happening?

But this pre-disciplinary vista of inquiry in the social sciences in which Weber and Polanyi, amongst others, were writing, did not survive the twentieth century. The continents of the disciplines drifted apart, becoming islands and then states that built walls rather than bridges. In the context of economic development and its associated research, this continental drift resulted in two appropriations. Economics, and then law, borrowed approaches from the natural sciences, aping their objective impartiality and sating some of their "physics envy" by copying their supposed "neutrality" (Mirowski, 1992). Then, the more insidious "economics imperialism" marks a second appropriation, whereby economists "dipped their toes, waded, and then swam ever further from the jetties of trade, finance and investment, eventually 'discovering', à la Columbus, the shores of law and development" (Fine and Milonakis, 2009, p. 1; Perry-Kessaris, 2011a, p. 405). Indeed, a recurring theme of this book is the co-option by neoclassical economics of other regimes such as the law, and the application of the conceptual and linguistic tools of neoclassical economics to fields of enquiry for which they were never designed.

The differentiation, departmentalization, and disciplinarity that occurred during the second half of the twentieth century in social science departments across the Global North enabled these two appropriations. At the same time, the methods and supposed neutrality of the natural sciences had seemingly elevated these fields beyond the messy realms of opinion and preference. These methods claimed irrefutable knowledge about the world, free from bias and supposedly free from the rhetoric in which the persuasive and the political were cloaked. With this elevation came prestige and privilege, and respect bordering on deference.

While prestige is not necessarily a zero-sum game, no one likes to "lose" standing. The social sciences, and in particular economics, were compelled to respond to the elevation of the natural sciences, and did so by borrowing, adapting, and developing objective methods; the empirical (counting, or quantification), analytical (marketization and comparison) and normative (privatization and competition) tools of what we might now describe as neoclassical economics. The resulting rational choice theory grew to become mainstream and set out a series of assumptions about human behaviour centred on an atomized individual with perfect information, fixed preferences, and infinite capacity for rational decision-making (you may recognize the description of *homo economicus* who was introduced in Chapter 1). Accordingly, a methodological preference for aggregated data and deductive modelling accompanied claims of objectivity that elided the subjective, the political, and the human. The refinement and reductionism of models meant that the core assumptions became universal: in being able to do less and less, they were applied to more and more.

These steps mirrored the politics of the day, with neoliberalism's preferences for privatization, competition, and deregulation expressed in the newly scientized discourse of rationality. There was a veneer of objectivity, cloaked in the irrefutable logic of mathematics, supposedly removing any space for moral, ethical, or personal biases. Of course, all that had really happened was that these had been pushed beyond reach. The models still made choices about what to count – about what was deemed important and what was not – and herein lay the political. But in addition to placing the subjective in an internal black box, "mathemetization reinvent[ed] a verbal wheel", adding mystique to everyday phenomena but little insight, and excluding most of society in the process who had not been indoctrinated through formal training in economics (McCloskey, 1998, 2006; Bronk, 2009; Perry-Kessaris, 2011a, p. 411; Schön, 2012).

The second appropriation has been referred to as "economics imperialism", whereby the tools of neoclassical economics came to be applied to non-economic phenomena (Fine and Milonakis, 2009; Perry-Kessaris, 2011a). While economics has suffered the most accusations of "physics envy", law, too, developed methods that could be presented as objective, scientific, and subject to its own internal logics (Mirowski, 1992; Burrows, 2016; but cf. Samuel, 2016). But "economics imperialism" or the Law and Economy movement saw swathes of the law come under the spell of quantification. Becker's treatment of children as "durable goods" offers an example of an apogee (Perry-Kessaris, 2011a, pp. 411–12). Yet these approaches also relied on metaphor, and economic metaphors and categorizations seeped into our ways of doing, talking, and thinking about the law subconsciously. Some of these metaphors introduced through economic analysis remain "live" and visible if we pay attention, while others have become so well worn and familiar as to pass into our daily vocabularies unchecked. They are, nevertheless, still there, and still shaping our thoughtways along economic lines.

In 2016, Lord Justice Burrows delivered a speech in which he passionately advocated for a revival of doctrinal legal reasoning and interpretation (Burrows, 2016). In setting out plans for a renaissance of research into "black letter" law, Burrows cited the brilliance of Supreme Court legal reasoning in two conjoined judgments that had been delivered the same year.[2] This brilliance was, for Burrows, "practical doctrinal reasoning" at its very best, without any "hint of economic or philosophical reasoning" (Burrows, 2016, p. 7). Yet, returning to the cases in question, at paragraphs 98, 107, and again at 109 of *Parking Eye [UKSC 67]*, the Court repeatedly refers to the "efficient" use of the resource in question: a car park. The Court could have focused instead on the most effective use of the resource, but deliberately chose to frame the discussion in terms of efficiency, immediately invoking the language and framing of neoclassical economics. Whether the Supreme Court wants to admit it or not, its Justices were engaging in economic analysis. Economics imperialism might have peaked, but its effects live on and live long in our vocabularies, grammars, and mental models, not only when we talk about the economy, but in myriad other social spheres and contexts.

We can similarly discern a more subtle, metalevel shift in wider discourse that mirrors the two appropriations set out here, namely the appropriation of natural

2 The cases in question, where the "reasoning is practical doctrinal reasoning at its very best, (note without a hint of economic or philosophical reasoning)" are "the conjoined appeals of *Cavendish Square Holding BV v Talal El Makdessi* and *ParkingEye Ltd v Beavis* [2015] UKSC 67 (on penalty clauses) and *Menelaou v Bank of Cyprus* [2015] UKSC 66 (on subrogation and unjust enrichment)" (Burrows, 2016, p. 7). See paras 98, 107, and 109 of the judgement in *Parking Eye* for analysis of the most "efficient" use of the resource, in this context a car park. I am grateful to the Obligations group at Kent Law School for drawing these cases to my attention and for letting me test out theories regarding reasoning used in the cases.

science methodologies by economics, and then of economics' methodologies by other social sciences. Through myriad micro-shifts in framing, we can discern a gradual shift in our wider social narratives. Over decades, the political right has funded research into economics and law that explicitly sets out to reframe the narrative and, over time, this has seeped into everyday discourse. We might think of the examples of "tax relief", a phrase devised by the White House under George Bush that immediately paints tax as an affliction from which the public can be saved (Lakoff, 2014). Similarly, we can see the emergence in the UK of the phrase "taxpayers' money" to refer to what had, previously, been "public" or "the government's money".[3] The effects of these multiple, micro-shifts have been to bring wider discourse more closely into alignment with the conceptual and linguistic tools of the private sphere of interactions, where protection of property rights and freedom to contract are prized. The individual and their agency take centre stage, while the state, government, and notions of collective, social, or public regulation and responsibilities are sidelined. Problematically, though, as Lakoff's work shows us, inadequate or misleading frames can only be successfully challenged by reframing; simply repeating "tax relief is bad" or that "taxpayers' money is government money" entrenches and reinforces existing frames (Lakoff, 2014). Instead, we might talk about "tax cuts" or "cuts to investment", depending on how one sees tax.[4]

Thus, "[t]he" economics approach came to be "a way of thinking" that covered the totality of human, social life (Heyne, cited in Hirsch, Michaels and Friedman, 1990, p. 46). The "clean models" of neoclassical economics, with their clear, binary answers, came to be increasingly valued by time-poor policy makers. As Hirsch *et al.* note, "having a clear argument" is often more important than "being right", and "consistency, purity, and elegance" are themselves highly valued (Hirsch, Michaels and Friedman, 1990, p. 54). In contrast, the discipline of sociology resembled a Tower of Babel, with its research carried out by the "dirty hands" of sociologists who grubbed around with the messy complexity of social life (Hirsch, Michaels and Friedman, 1990). There are frequently no clear or precise answers offered by sociological accounts. The attraction of the clarity of orthodox, neoclassical economics was obvious, and it is, perhaps, unfair to term economic incursions into law and sociology as invasions, as the term "economic imperialism" implies. To some extent, neoclassical economics was invited in. And yet, the analysis of social spheres as if they were markets, and the widespread application of rational choice theory, leaves an invisible linguistic legacy. As the following sections pick up, and as an ESL lens continues to grapple with, where are the limits of the law and of the markets, or, more precisely, where *should* we find them?

3 I'm grateful to John Wightman and the Obligations reading group at Kent Law School for this example.

4 Chapter 6 returns to these examples in the context of how and why we might reframe wider narratives.

The intellectual heritage of ESL: economic sociology and socio-legal scholarship

> **ACADEMIC ANN**
>
> *A few years ago, at a conference, Ann had listened to a presentation that set out how an economic sociology of law lens could be used to accommodate diverse interests and voices. She hadn't really been paying attention; it had been a long day and her son's school had been in touch again. She couldn't see what use an ESL lens had for her.*
>
> *Her subconscious must have been paying attention, she thought, because this ESL lens played on her mind for a while before she found the time to delve into some of the literature. She wanted to be sure that she wasn't missing something and, scanning the literature, she quickly realized that an ESL might be helpful. In planning her imminent fieldwork trip to interview foreign investors about their experiences with the host state legal system, she realized that in mapping out sites of similarity and difference, of conflict and agreement, and of legal and economic interests as well as the non-economic and non-legal, she might be prompted to look at wider sets of relations. The more she read, the more different interview questions presented themselves along with different sets of interviewees, and she was curious to see where this lead her. Might this be a way of investigating why the investor had laughed at her question all those years ago?*

Socio-legal heritage

We noted in Figure 2.1 on page 34 that ESL derives much of its intellectual heritage from economic sociology and from socio-legal scholarship. Socio-legal studies can be interdisciplinary in nature, drawing (analytically) on the concepts and relationships, and (empirically) on the facts and methods of the social sciences and (occasionally) the humanities (Perry-Kessaris, 2012, p. 10). In contrast to some of the so-called "Grand Theories" of sociology, socio-legal approaches are more accurately portrayed as a "mid-level" theoretical approach, straddling the larger theories and the empirical detail. All legal approaches have their own empirical, conceptual, and normative tendencies, and doubt has been cast on efforts to identify *the* "overarching independent variable that would operate in all social processes" (Perry-Kessaris, 2012).

Nevertheless, socio-legal enquiries tend to focus on the descriptive and the explanatory, leaving questions of the normative for legal philosophers to grapple with (Banakar and Travers, 2005, p. 7). A detailed differentiation of socio-legal scholarship from sociology of law, legal sociology, or Law and Society scholarship in the US is beyond the scope of the discussion here (Banakar and

Travers, 2005, p. 2; Banakar, 2014). For present purposes, socio-legal scholarship is understood as a broad response to doctrinal or "black letter" studies of law that explores "the 'legal' in the everyday": the "cultural practices and adoptions of authority that are considered to be legal by those who exercise them and by those who are subject to them" (Wheeler, 2020, p. 216).[5] It combines "ambitious theory" with "empirical researches" into the complexity and diversity of "local contexts of legal life" (Cotterrell, 2005, p. v). There is a consensus though that while overarching theories may be useful in relating hypotheses or sets of theories, grand narratives are less helpful, and socio-legal approaches can sit between the micro and meta, linking or challenging both (Hirsch, Michaels and Friedman, 1990).

Historically, though, the socio-legal can tend to be frustratingly imprecise, "woolly", and lacking clear definitions and strict methodologies and while socio-legal lenses will have empirical, analytical, and normative aspects, each socio-legal lens prioritizes aspects of these differently (Perry-Kessaris, 2012, p. 4). We can generalize that while positivist approaches tend to focus on the text itself, naturalist approaches tend to privilege the moral reasoning between the lines of the text, and a historical approach "favours a holistic understanding of law as a social phenomenon" (Frerichs, 2012, p. 10). Indeed, for Weber or Polanyi, writing in a time before the disciplinarity that occurred in the later twentieth century, the need to state that the law was a social phenomenon would have seemed laughably axiomatic. Additionally, there have been many movements within legal scholarship that have sought to bring law more closely back to its roots as a social science and as a study of human interaction. Amongst these we can count legal realism, the law and society movement, critical legal studies, feminist jurisprudence, critical race theory, and economic theories of law among many others.[6] These have sought to include, more or less directly, other aspects of interactions that the authors see as important in shaping the social interactions at the heart of the study.

5 Wheeler has argued that "Socio-legal" scholars see themselves as operating in the "hyphen" space, and that the hyphenation of socio-legal, in the creation of a compound noun or adjective, is of particular significance. It delineates the space in which legal phenomena are placed, and then studied (Wheeler, 2020, pp. 216–17).

6 For legal realism, which is generally cited as a response to legal formalism, see the works of Oliver Wendell Holmes and Karl Llewellyn. The law and society movement sees law and legal institutions as socially constructed phenomena and cites the works of inter alia Friedman. Critical legal studies, with its focus on power and how this is exercised, can be found in the works of inter alia Duncan Kennedy and Martti Koskenniemi. Feminist jurisprudence and legal theory speaks to broader matters of equality as well as the exercise of power and is exemplified by the works of Catharine MacKinnon, Andrea Dworkin, and Nicola Lacey. Critical race theory, which critiques the exercise of hegemonic power, can be found in the works of Derrick Bell, Angela Harris, Patricia Williams, and Kimberlé Crenshaw. Economic theories of law apply the rationalities of neoclassical economics to the law and build on the work of Ronald Coase whose study of institutions showed their importance in shaping the regulatory landscape in which choices are made.

There have been similar movements in social theory which can complement movements in legal sociology and economic sociology. Drawing on three categories identified by Gephart, we can appreciate firstly "the unity of legal and social theory" as seen in the works of Karl Marx, Émile Durkheim, and Max Weber (Gephart, 1993, cited in Frerichs, 2012, p. 11). Secondly, the "loss of the law in social theory" in the works of George Herbert Mead, Alfred Schütz, and Thomas P. Wilson was, then, followed by the third movement which saw "the rediscovery of the law in social theory" and can be seen in the works of Talcott Parsons, Niklas Luhmann, and Jürgen Habermas. However, while each brings the law back within a social sphere, they assume that "modern society is differentiated into a number of functional spheres [... each] with distinctive ways of communication and forms of power" (Frerichs, 2012, p. 12).

Economic sociology heritage

Economic sociology is differentiated from "social economics" here and detached from both economic theory and economic history. It has also been referred to as a "sociology of economics", and although slow in "acquiring its own identity", the field has strong traditions (Swedberg, Himmelstrand and Brulin, 1987, p. 169). Economic sociologists are united in the belief that economics is too important to be left to economists alone, and that the economy constitutes an important area of society that should be approached sociologically, historically, and empirically. In addition to Weber, Schumpeter, Durkheim, and Marx, economic sociologists look to Simmel, Parsons, and Smelser as the founding fathers of the discipline. While it is important to note that economic sociology was a recognized approach prior to 1985, Mark Granovetter's revival of embeddedness and networks in that year marked a renaissance and the birth of the "New Economic Sociology" (Granovetter, 1985; Krippner, 2001; Frerichs, 2012, pp. 6–7). This has been referred to as the third generation in economic sociology, distinguishing it from the holistic and historical approaches that had characterized the first generation and the scientific approaches within the sociological tradition of the second (Frerichs, 2012).

In keeping with its belief about the social foundations of economics, the field makes three assumptions about the actors it analyses which differentiate the approach from classical economic theory. These are that "the actor is always connected to other actors and the social environment", that "a broad spectrum of actors and actions must be taken into account", and that "contradictions in the behaviour of actors is to be expected" (Swedberg, Himmelstrand and Brulin, 1987, p. 175). Economic history is also used to great effect to contextualize the economic, broadening enquiry. Finally, the centrality of empirical observation and scientific method, as well as sociological interpretations of the economy and economic aspects of interactions, is emphasized as a defining feature.

Sitting between socio-legal scholarship and economic sociology, then, ESL-inspired frames have a plurality of methods and mindsets to respond to, and to respond with. What differentiates an ESL lens is its goal to bring the spheres of law, economy, and society into closer dialogue, and to analyze both law and economy sociologically. Nevertheless, as a lens, ESL offers a series of taxonomies – categories of criteria that nudge the researcher to look out for certain aspects of those social interactions she is investigating. The hope is that, in having checklists of phenomena, the resulting research will be empirically grounded, theoretically informed, and methodologically rigorous. To this end, some key taxonomies are set out below.

"Black boxes" and taxonomies

ACADEMIC ANN

Ann pauses. She still remembers the disbelief and ringing laughter of the foreign business owner when she had asked him about his expectations and experiences of the legal system in that country. Determined to get a fuller picture this time, she asks herself how she would approach the research through an ESL lens. She begins to sketch out the different individuals and groups who might be affected by the legal reforms made by the government at the behest of the development bank. She is surprised that there are so many people who might potentially be impacted by legal reform. She had never considered the wider social implications of legal change and is surprised at the ripples that a small alteration could make.

Pausing, she reviews what she has written, and scribbles "economic" and "non-economic" next to actors and groups according to the impact of the reform they experience. Feeling that a deeper understanding of the complexity of the community in which regulations were applied could not be a bad thing, she decides to continue.

You have probably heard of a "black box". Usually, these appear in the context of a flight recorder on a plane, or in science and engineering where we are referring to a system with opaque internal workings. In science, a black box can only be viewed and analyzed in terms of its inputs and outputs and the causal relations that can be imputed to these. In essence, because we cannot see into it, a black box is something that we have to understand through the effects it produces. Something similar occurs in economic sociology and ESL, although this time it is the product of linguistic fictions, metaphors, and inconsistent mental models. Chapter 5 explores the implications of the black box produced by embeddedness-talk but for the present discussion, the black box of ESL deserves acknowledgement before further taxonomies are set out.

While vulnerable to its own black box problems, an ESL lens reminds the researcher of the interconnectedness "that characterizes the intersections between economic and legal aspects of social life" and the way that we think about those intersections (Perry-Kessaris, 2015, p. 16.2). Thus, we might understand an ESL as an aspect of a wider approach to reintegrate the social sciences, but in particular to reconnect law, economy, and society "both as spheres of reality and as fields of scholarly interest" (Frerichs, 2012, p. 5). But while drawing primarily on sociological, socio-legal, and economic sociology-based approaches, the movement also takes inspiration from political economy, development studies, feminist and critical approaches; in short, "whatever it takes to improve analytical, empirical, and normative clarity in the field" (Perry-Kessaris, 2015, p. 16.2).

This stands slightly apart from interdisciplinary, multi-, or transdisciplinary research in the sense that, as this book argues, a constructivist ESL lens understands economic and legal phenomena as two sides of the same (social) coin. While interdisciplinary research seeks to transcend the boundaries of the discipline and gain insights from alternative perspectives, adopting different methodologies or challenging norms, concepts, or analyses, it can by its very nature repeat existing disciplinary boundaries. By contrast, a constructivist ESL lens understands the construction of legal and economic institutions and the performance of legal and economic behaviours as aspects of the social, acknowledging that one cannot exist without the other. Similarly, there are no social interactions that do not have legal and economic aspects to them, be this in the use, abuse, or avoidance of law and economy, and where both are understood as social phenomena (Perry, 2004).[7]

Keen-eyed readers will, of course, have already spotted ESL's very own "black box" problem concerning the name of the lens. This is, in short, the assumption and acceptance that these three aspects of social interaction are (empirically and conceptually) – and *should be* (normatively) – studied and observed separately, with different approaches, literature, methods, and terminology. Nevertheless, having flagged this, this book does not set out to change the name of an economic sociology of law. For those coming to ESL for the first time, the name is helpfully descriptive, setting out the fields of interest and indicating that these are – and *should be* – related. By asserting that ESL is a constructivist lens, the logical conclusion is that if we name a constructivist lens "an economic sociology of law", we implicitly separate out and entrench the division between the three spheres of enquiry. Is it not the case, you therefore argue, that advocating for the social construction or performance of legal and economic phenomena is contradictory to the name of the lens? Well, perhaps. While ESL scholars have acknowledged that the name of the lens is somewhat "clunky", in looking back to the pre-disciplinarity days of Weber and Polanyi,

7 As noted in Chapter 1, "social" in this context simply means the presence of two or more persons.

this book recognizes that an ESL responds to and proposes an approach to a post-disciplinary world in which economic, legal, and social scholars rarely spend much time together, if they encounter each other at all. There is a contradiction inherent in the name, but this book asks the reader to suspend disapproval for the time being, accepting that the current name conveys the purpose, aspiration, and goal of the lens, while sitting uncomfortably like grit in an oyster.

A further word on terminology is necessary here too. ESL is presented as a (metaphorical) *lens* rather than a theory, method, methodology, or frame. This is a deliberate way of indicating the purpose of ESL, and the use to which it is put; namely a conceptual device through which we can see the relationships between legal and economic phenomena differently.[8] As a lens, we look *through* ESL-inspired taxonomies to explore how law, economy, and society interface, noting that we can appreciate and accommodate a wider range of voices, interests, and values through the re-sociologizing of economic and legal phenomena – usually those silenced by mainstream approaches. So, in a manner similar to a microscope that brings different voices in and out of focus, an ESL lens nudges us to appreciate the complex, dynamic, shifting networks of community that might form the basis of any empirical study of law and economy.

Some proposed definitions, typologies, and taxonomies and their relations to each other are set out in the discussions that follow. These draw together and illustrate conceptual and analytical categories developed throughout the works of Amanda Perry-Kessaris and Sabine Frerichs, amongst others. Taxonomies include *what* is approached (text, context, and subtext), *how* it is approached (the empirical, conceptual or analytical, and normative), the *scale* of what is approached (micro, meso, macro, and meta rankings of social interaction), and finally the *relationship* between these (the econo-socio-legal relationship). While this chapter does not aspire to offer a "how to" of "doing" ESL, it does suggest prompts that might remind a researcher, policy maker, or interested social activist to consider various aspects of any complex, social dynamic. These taxonomies of substance (what), method (how), scale (where), and relationship (where and why) offer a means of using an ESL lens to structure empirically grounded, theoretically informed, and methodologically rigorous research at the interface of socially constructed legal and economic phenomena.

The categories are neither cumulative nor exhaustive. The checklists set out below are illustrated by Ann as she explores foreign investment and the role of the legal system in her own research. Ann builds an example of an ESL lens by combining Roger Cotterrell's community lens that uses Weberian interaction ideal types (instrumental, traditional, belief-based, and affective). Then, Ann adds

8 The "lens" analogy is borrowed from Roger Cotterrell's definition of his own work on communal networks.

Sabine Frerichs' embeddedness-based rankings of social interaction that give us the language of regimes (what we do, on a society-wide scale) and rationalities (how we think about what we do, including our conceptual and linguistic tools). As the beginning of this chapter emphasized, this is simply one of many possibilities for sociologically examining the economic life of the law and is presented as an example to show what an ESL can offer. Thus, the headings are offered as guides that may be more or less present or more or less useful depending on context, to be incorporated or disregarded according to the demands of the task at hand. As is generally the case, reflexiveness about research, one's own positionality, and one's own ways of approaching both are always useful.

Text; subtext; context

ACADEMIC ANN

Ann starts with the text. For her research, this includes the directives and recommendations issued by the World Bank as well as the investment laws drafted and implemented by the government of the host state. This is a similar starting point to a typically doctrinal approach familiar to most academic lawyers. She then turns to the subtext or the normative frames that informed the drafting and enactment of these laws. She asks herself what the development bank and the (central and local) government were trying to achieve and why, and whether their goals and interests aligned.

Turning to the context, Ann looks at the enacted laws and regulations as social phenomena. Are they performed, or ignored, entirely? Did they change anything in real life or, as the laughter of the businessman at her previous question might indicate, were these laws ignored completely? With a sinking feeling, Ann suspects that the new regulatory requirements made less impact than the development bank might have intended. But thinking of those groups of actors and their interaction ideal types, Ann begins to wonder if other actors might have been inconvenienced or priced out by laws that look good on paper but made little difference to the foreign investors they were designed to help.

As a starting taxonomy, this is most helpful in reminding the researcher to look beyond the written rules, the immediately obvious, and the easily accessible, while at the same time asking whether the reality matches up to the stated aims. The rules might appear clear, but as both Ann and Polly have found in relation to the World Bank's data sets and development policies, theory and practice can be two very different things.

By "text", we can refer to "the legal text, that is, the written rules and doctrines, or what can be considered black-letter law" (Frerichs, 2012, p. 9).

This can then include the text of the law itself and what this sets out in terms of rights, responsibilities, and mediation or restitution, the text of interviews, questionnaires, and other empirical data, as well as the quantified comparison of figures, theories, and rationales informing the collection, processing, and interpretation of that data. Subtext is defined as "the moral subtext of a legal text, that is, its implied or deeper meaning", which "includes notions of justice underlying a legal argument, which also make it necessary to read between the lines" (Frerichs, 2012, p. 9). In terms of the subtext, "socio-legal approaches allow a normative advance" in the literature, in particular "the location of sites of domination and [...] of resistance [of] the moral subtext of international economic law" (Perry-Kessaris, 2012, p. 10). Finally, we can understand context as "the social context of a legal text, that is, its forceful link with reality", by which perspective "law is not a self-contained discourse but an entrenched social institution" (Frerichs, 2012, p. 9). Here, then, we are looking at the actions and interactions of actors "(producers, distributors, exchangers, consumers, regulators, debtors, etc), [who] are always embedded in wider social life" (Perry-Kessaris, 2012, p. 7).[9]

ESL's focus on all three of these categories stands in contrast to the prioritization of one over the others by preceding approaches; positivist traditions' tendency to focus on the text, naturalist traditions' tendency to focus on moral subtext, and historicist schools' tendency to focus on social practices and context (Frerichs, 2012, p. 9). Given this, an economic sociology of law is not to be seen as "an overspecialized approach which dissects legal, economic and social aspects and focuses on the smallest possible subset only" (Frerichs, 2012, p. 5). By contrast, an ESL lens aspires to reintegrate and reconnect law, economy, and society, both as they are constructed and performed in day-to-day interactions and as they are studied. An ESL-inspired lens, therefore, "mediates between the perspectives of legal sociology, on the one hand, and economic sociology, on the other", and this is partially achieved by a balanced focus on the text, the subtext, and the context of the interactions (Frerichs, 2012, p. 5).

Empirical; conceptual; normative

ACADEMIC ANN

Ann turns over to a new page in her notebook and jots down the three headings. She begins with the empirical, which is her fieldwork interviews, emails, and other conversations that she has consent to cite. It also includes her literature reviews and observations of the role of law in investment flows; in short, this is the sum of the evidence she can gather relating to interactions at the interface of law, economy,

9 Use of "embedded" here is uncontroversial given that it refers to conceptually distinct entities.

and society as they are performed in real life. Then, turning to the concepts and relationships, she scribbles down "ESL: community lens" as a title and underneath it "relationships between groups and their differing regulatory needs". Having identified groups of actors, she draws lines between each and thinks that some of these interactions might be more interesting from a regulatory perspective than others. Thirdly, under the normative heading she considers the values and interests of the groups she is investigating: what shared expectations do they have? What do they regard as important? What regulations are in place already and what values do these enact?

These categories essentially ask *what, how,* and *why*. As the discussion above showed, all socio-legal approaches have empirical, conceptual, and normative elements, although some approaches place more emphasis on one of these at the expense of the others. By "empirical", we are talking about the "facts and methods" informing the substantive inquiry. The "analytical" or the "conceptual" are the "concepts and relationships" that also inform the substantive, while the "normative" includes the "values and interests" that sit behind, or underpin, the research (Perry-Kessaris, 2012, pp. 4–5). This triad of categories responds to the narrower purview of doctrinal, positivistic, or autopoietic approaches that tend to focus strictly on the legal and calls for a willingness to consider the relevance of wider social realities. The constructivist ESL lens set out in the following chapters assumes that legal and economic aspects are intrinsic to each social interaction, denying the possibility that the legal can be separated out or differentiated as its own sphere of influence or observation. It is worth noting that while there may be some overlap and intersection, the empirical, conceptual, and normative do not map directly on to the text, subtext, and context, but rather complement these, asking slightly different questions.

Econo-socio-legal

ACADEMIC ANN

On another new page, Ann scribbles down this latest triad, and then puts her notebook down and frowns. Why was this a separate taxonomy when it was already the name of the lens? Suspending judgement, she draws two thick lines down the page, demarcating three columns, and begins to scribble out first the economic aspects, then the legal, and then the social. She wasn't sure she was doing this right, but decided to give it a go and see what materialized.

> *The economic aspects of the research were easy: the government of that country wanted to increase flows of foreign investment because this would act as an economic catalyst, generating jobs, growth, technological progress, training, and education (or so the textbooks said). But there were also the knock-on economic effects of increased trade for local businesses (hotels and restaurants, for example) and job opportunities for local communities. On the flip side though, if a multinational opened a franchise it could mean the demise of local businesses.*
>
> *The legal aspects seemed relatively easy too. The development bank had advised the government that to attract foreign investors they needed to reform the legal system to cut red tape, reduce investment costs and time, and to strengthen the rule of law and access to justice (or so the textbooks said). This was called the "investment climate", and the development bank had a series of indicators that they would measure annually to quantify and compare the legal system with others around the world. But there were other legal implications, Ann realized. Local lawyers would be consulted about business and tax regulations (either to use, abuse, or avoid them), while property laws would regulate where and how a business could start operations. Labour laws would regulate employment … and before long, Ann had filled another page in her notebook.*

At first glance, this taxonomy might seem both axiomatic (isn't this what we're already doing?) and problematic (the "black box" issue of separating out concepts by naming them, addressed above). The taxonomy is included as a reminder that the economic and legal are intrinsic to the social, and that focusing on one aspect without regard to the others can result in myopic or partial insights. In other words, "[r]eal life is "an econo-socio-legal" and "mutually constitutive" tangle, and the entrenchment of disciplinary silos has the capacity to shape the way we approach an understanding of real-world interactions (Perry-Kessaris, 2013, 2015, p. 16.6). An ESL lens is not the only approach capable of drawing out these interconnections. Approaches like Giddens' structuration, Latour's actor–network theory (ANT), Foucault's *epistemes*, and Bourdieu's *habitus*, amongst others, can all offer approaches for understanding the relations between economic and legal phenomena, and might be added to offer colours to the lens, prompting closer focus on particular elements of relations as desired.

These categories may seem at odds with a pseudo-constructivist lens, but as one of ESL's goals is the identification of existing ways of doing, talking, and thinking, and how they operate generatively, it can be helpful to start out with a mainstream (neoclassical and doctrinal) list of the economic and legal phenomena that might be involved. We can then appreciate how these are products of our vocabularies and grammars, and how existing mental models can be shaped accordingly. Then, using insights from a pseudo-constructivist ESL lens, we can begin to appreciate the economic and the legal as two sides of the same (social) coin. When we look for legal phenomena, we are prompted to flip over the coin and consider the accompanying, co-constructed economic phenomena, and vice versa. We can then begin to appreciate how these – usually separate – areas overlap, coalesce, merge, collide, or inflame the other and this, in turn, can help to produce a fuller, richer, more realistic account.

Sociologically informed approaches can emphasize the importance of the ties between actors, whether this is in the language of social capital (Bourdieu and Wacquant, 1992; Putnam, 2001), networks (Granovetter, 1985; Uzzi, 1997), or the importance of mutual interpersonal trust between actors (Granovetter, 1985; Fukuyama, 1995; Uzzi, 1997; Cotterrell, 1998; Harriss, 2002). This challenges the individualism and atomization of actors commonly assumed in mainstream legal and economics approaches, while broadening an appreciation of the drivers of economic aspects of interactions in a way that is denied by orthodox or mainstream frames. In the pooling of "facts, concepts and values" (the empirical, analytical, and normative) that currently characterize economic, legal, or social matters, we can recognize that we are not, usually, dealing with a "legal" or an "economic" problem (Perry-Kessaris, 2013). Instead, we are dealing with one that is social in nature with legal and economic aspects, facets, or "flavours" (Ewick and Silbey, 1998, p. 217). So, while the legal system can "further economic growth", a sociological approach to law and economy can begin to recognize where "the spirit of a commercial society can come to pervade parts of the law other than those that directly have to do with the economy" (Swedberg, 2003, p. 2).

Thus, market rationalities and law are "socially constructed or given meaning through social interaction" (Edelman and Stryker, 2005, p. 531), and recognizing the "constitutive" role of law in most economic phenomena entails the realization that law, economy, and society cannot be separated out (Swedberg, 2003, p. 4). While listing out the economic, again we have choices to make as to what we classify as important or not, acknowledging that any categorization is an inherently normative process. Are we defining "economic" as instrumental, and looking for shared objectives or values? Are we looking for types of decision-making in which we determine that economic decision-making approximates to "rational" decision-making? This can shift the focus from rationality as understood by neoclassical economics to the "non-rational" or "differently rational" that acknowledges other interests and values (Cotterrell, 2006, p. 2). It also simultaneously challenges the tacit assumption that the "non-rational" is incapable of providing us with the truth, or, more precisely, that there might be multiple truths. Similar epistemological questions apply to the identification of legal phenomena, and the necessity of recognizing the subjective and the normative as intrinsic to any processes of categorization.

Instrumental; affective; belief-based; traditional

ACADEMIC ANN

Ann flicks back to the page in her notebook where she jotted down the actors and groups who might – even vaguely – be impacted by law reforms. She had scribbled down the obvious candidates here: foreign investors, multinational enterprises, local business. But, in thinking about one legal reform where the government had tried to cut waiting times in the processes necessary to set up a business, she realized that local entrepreneurs had also been affected. Local government officials had been caught unawares and were no longer able to advise business communities which forms they needed, or who to speak to. Community leaders had become involved, although – Ann recalls – this was around the time of the riots against the opening of a new industrial zone and the widespread clearing of land for foreign investors to build on.

Looking at her list of actors, Ann decides to colour-code their interactions according to the dominant ideal type in each case. She draws red lines for instrumental relations, green for affective, blue for belief-based, and black for traditional. Soon, there are colourful lines criss-crossing her page and she realizes that some of these lines run in parallel. She notices, in particular, that instrumental and affective relations tend to mirror each other frequently in the local business community where business deals are done with friends and family. Traditional relations, where locale or language are shared, also tend to run alongside instrumental relations. Despite her familiarity with her research participants and her knowledge of the communities, Ann had never considered whether familial ties or shared social bonds that economic actors relied on, consciously or subconsciously, might be relevant to the econo-socio-legal tangle that she was trying to understand.

The impact of Weber's work in shaping assumptions about the role of law in economic development has been noted, specifically, his assertions about rational legal systems that have justified and underpinned the investment climate industry. Weber also set out a fourfold typology of social relations that has been developed by Roger Cotterrell through his community lens. While Dworkin treats the law as webs of understanding about social relations sustained by a community of legal interpreters, Cotterrell places this in a sociological frame with his communal networks lens (Cotterrell, 1997, p. 79–80. There are, then, many types of legal consciousness, myriad sites and contexts of legal interpretation, and many and varied forms of law coexisting in the same time and place. Unpicking the different relations by reference to Weber's relational ideal types, then, is one way of understanding the complex web of interrelations across society.

Instrumental relations are those where actors have shared goals or where their interests converge. This can, then, incorporate both legal and economic phenomena, indicating that a purposive approach might be necessary. Traditional relations are those in which space, culture, environment, or language is shared, offering an immediate point of connection between the actors. Affective relations are those based on family or friendship ties, while belief-based relations are those where beliefs converge. This may or may not imply religion, or religious belief as popularly understood, but may include a devotion to conspiracy theories or the fight against them. It may include a trenchant and ardent belief in the power of free markets to solve society's ills, or of politics to do away with rampant capitalism altogether.

For Cotterrell, relations of community must have some degree of stability; involvement must be continuing and reliable, and there must be a sense of attachment and belonging (Cotterrell, 1997, p. 82). This need not necessarily entail rejoicing at having found one's tribe, but might include membership of a community that one might not even want to be part of but cannot escape. Similarly, community itself does not imply warm, fuzzy relations of goodwill, but can also describe the exercise of power, domination, and coercion. The key characteristic, though, is that relations of community are generally "imbued with a high degree of trust" which can only be built over time (Cotterrell, 1997, p. 86). In fact, "mutual interpersonal trust is the basic element of the idea of community as a web of understandings about social relations" (Cotterrell, 1997, p. 86).

Of note at this point is the role of law in supporting these relations of trust. While each type of collective involvement has its own ideal regulatory requirements or types of law that can best support the kind of trusting relationships that are necessary for that particular community to thrive, Cotterrell places the law as something external to these relations. Nevertheless, "actual social relations of interpersonal trust are, by the nature of their intimacy and individuality, removed from external control and depend entirely on subjective understandings between those involved" (Cotterrell, 1997, p. 88). This means that "law's main support and encouragement of trusting relationships is indirect" (Cotterrell, 1997, p. 88). This understanding of law, of its boundaries and borders, and its sites of shared expectations is contrasted with the two shifts proposed in Chapter 5 which move ESL beyond embeddedness and which suggest a way of realizing a fully constructivist lens.

Micro; meso; macro; meta

ACADEMIC ANN

Finally, on yet another fresh page in her notebook, Ann jots down the four headings, first across the top of the page and then, realizing that she might have more to say than space to say it in, down the side. These headings, she realizes, ask her to consider how all the other headings and scribbles so far scale up across space and time. Flicking back to the first page on which she listed the actors and groups in society that might be impacted by the investment climate and the legal reforms, she begins sketching out the micro-level interactions between actors (investors, Board of Investment representatives, fixers, contractors, employees, and so on), circling each actor and then drawing lines symbolizing interactions that reach between them. Investors, she thinks, would definitely interact with other investors and maybe local businesses and contractors. They would have dealings with civil servants when applying for permits, as well as with gatekeepers, the inevitable "fixers", and local communities who they might employ, contract with, or evict. She realized that it was important to check these assumptions in her fieldwork though.

Zooming out, she expects patterns to emerge at the meso level, as accepted "ways of doing things" within, and between, these (groups of) actors appear. Zooming out even further, Ann draws a larger circle around these interactions that remind her to look for "regimes" at the macro level – institutions or structures. She notes law and the legal system here, and the economy, but then also notes the more context-specific regimes indicated by the Board of Investment; their procedures and processes for foreign investors. Finally, drawing another circle around the whole diagram, she sketches out the meta level "rationalities", or the mental models that make sense of the world. She realizes that macro level regimes and meta level rationalities must interact and develop closely together, and she makes a note in her sketchbook to consider how she will look for this in her fieldwork. Discussed more fully in Chapter 3, Ann adds in arrows to indicate cognitive and normative embeddedness. Ann's notebook is reproduced, with her permission, in Figure 2.3 on page 56.

The concept of embeddedness has enjoyed a varied and colourful career but, as the following chapter reveals, suffers from internal inconsistencies and external incompatibilities. The main cleavage causing internal inconsistencies – the "what are we talking about?" argument – is Polanyi's use of embeddedness at the *macro* level and Granovetter's use of embeddedness at the *micro* level. Are we talking about the embeddedness of concepts and metaphors, or the embeddedness of actors? In proposing a schemata to put both of these interpretations on the same page, and potentially rescue the disciplines of economic sociology and ESL in the process, Sabine Frerichs has proposed four rankings of social interaction. These start at the micro, individual, level of interactions and gradually zoom out, encompassing an increasingly broad overview of the totality of social interaction as it extends across time and space.

While the "Grand Theories" of sociology that seek to set out a general understanding of social behaviour and interaction are, on occasion, met with derision, Frerichs' taxonomies are lightweight, scalar, and modular in the sense that some can be used without others (Hirsch, Michaels and Friedman, 1990). There is no overbearing epistemology needed to underpin the terms, with plain-language understandings preferred that avoid the paywall of impenetrable terminology, although Frerichs does offer careful definitions. The rankings of interaction can complement the categories and taxonomies already discussed. Figure 2.2 visualizes the four layers, along with the levels at which we can identify regimes (how our interactions coalesce into structures or institutions) and rationalities (how we think about how we interact).

The language of regimes and rationalities adds a way of understanding the actor's mental models as well as her perception and understanding of her surroundings played out in the feedback loops, both within interactions and within the actor's own self-monitoring. This gives us a way of talking about the institutions and practices metaphorically called "the economy" and "the law" as *regimes*. It also gives us linguistic tools for speaking about the way we mentally conceptualize, rationalize, and justify these regimes through the mental models of economics and law *rationalities*. It reminds us that, consistent both with constructivist approaches and with Giddens' structuration theory aims, regimes, and rationalities are continually re-co-constituted through and within each and every social interaction, mirroring the so-called cognitive turn in some sociological theories without getting too caught up in epistemology.[10]

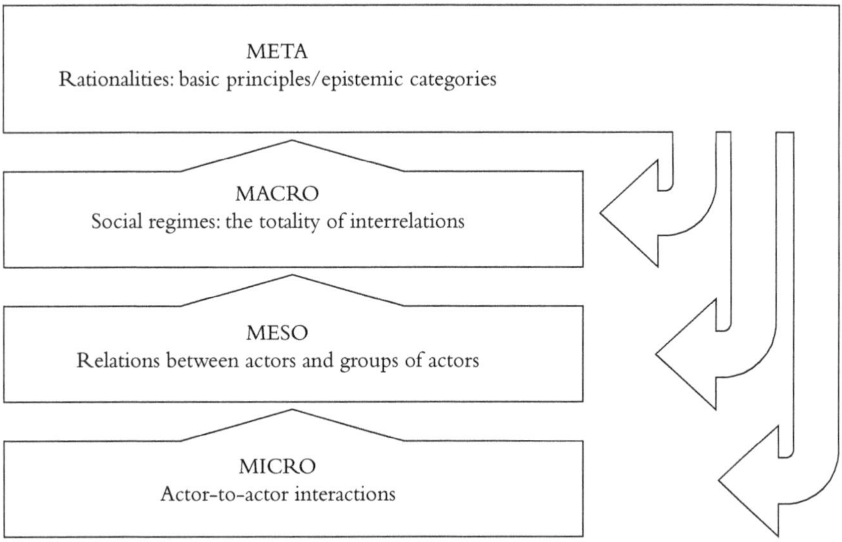

Figure 2.2 Visualizing the four rankings of social interaction, showing macro-level regimes and metalevel rationalities, and the re-co-constitutive feedback loops between all levels.

10 This was also Giddens' aim in setting out his theory of structuration in *Constitution of Society* (Giddens, 1984). While structuration theory can be unwieldy in the round, it offers some useful terms and phrases to complement Ann's (and our) emergent ESL lens.

A focus on interactions at the individual, group, society-wide, and meta levels gives us an alternative to atomistic understandings of the actor found in both neoclassical economic theory and Parsonian sociology. The focus on patterned relations ties in with Granovetterian networks at the meso level, while the macro and meta levels echo Polanyian analysis, recognizing the contingency of regimes and rationalities across space and time. Polanyi, then, "can be said to have focused on how our meta-level thinking and our macro-level policies in respect of economy were first disembedded from wider social life in the course of the Industrial Revolution and then re-embedded in wider social life through regulatory counter-movements" (Perry-Kessaris, 2011b, p. 402).

However, we are left wondering how regimes and rationalities are mutually re-co-constituted, as it is clear that ongoing dialogue between our regimes and rationalities – our (inter)actions and our conceptual and linguistic tools – are in a constant state of bidirectional dialogue.[11] There is a little room in this approach for language, and given its central role in shaping (and being shaped by) our mental models and interactions, along with the maintenance of a conceptual commitment to embeddedness, the frame is prevented from realizing its full constructivist ambitions. Nevertheless, we can appreciate, as Ann sketches out for us in Figure 2.3, that our regimes and rationalities might be normatively and cognitively embedded, respectively. We can then see that these are performed through interactions, offering a quasi-feedback loop that is developed further in Chapter 5.

Nevertheless, these four rankings of social interaction, along with the vocabulary of regimes and rationalities, give us ways of referring to "doing, talking, and thinking" about the relationships between law, economy, and society. Although not a hard and fast rule, we can assume that "doing", or the performance or construction of legal and economic aspects of interactions, manifests at the micro and meso levels through social interactions. Then, when we talk about law and economy, we use ontological metaphors at the macro level to refer to the *regimes*, or the social institutions and structures that we re-co-constitute through (micro-level) interactions. Similarly, thinking manifests at the meta level in the form of the *rationalities* or mental models that we use to apprehend and understand the world, and that shape our actions and interactions as we re-co-constitute those institutions and structures spoken about at the macro level. The interrelation between these levels, along with their combination with different socio-legal and ESL lenses, is explored in greater detail in the following chapters. With her kind permission, Ann's initial sketch of her fieldwork, understood through the lens constructed here, is reproduced in Figure 2.3.

11 I'm grateful to Iain Frame for highlighting the existence of feedback mechanisms regardless of how we understand our social interactions. This notion is developed further in the form of feedback loops in Chapter 5.

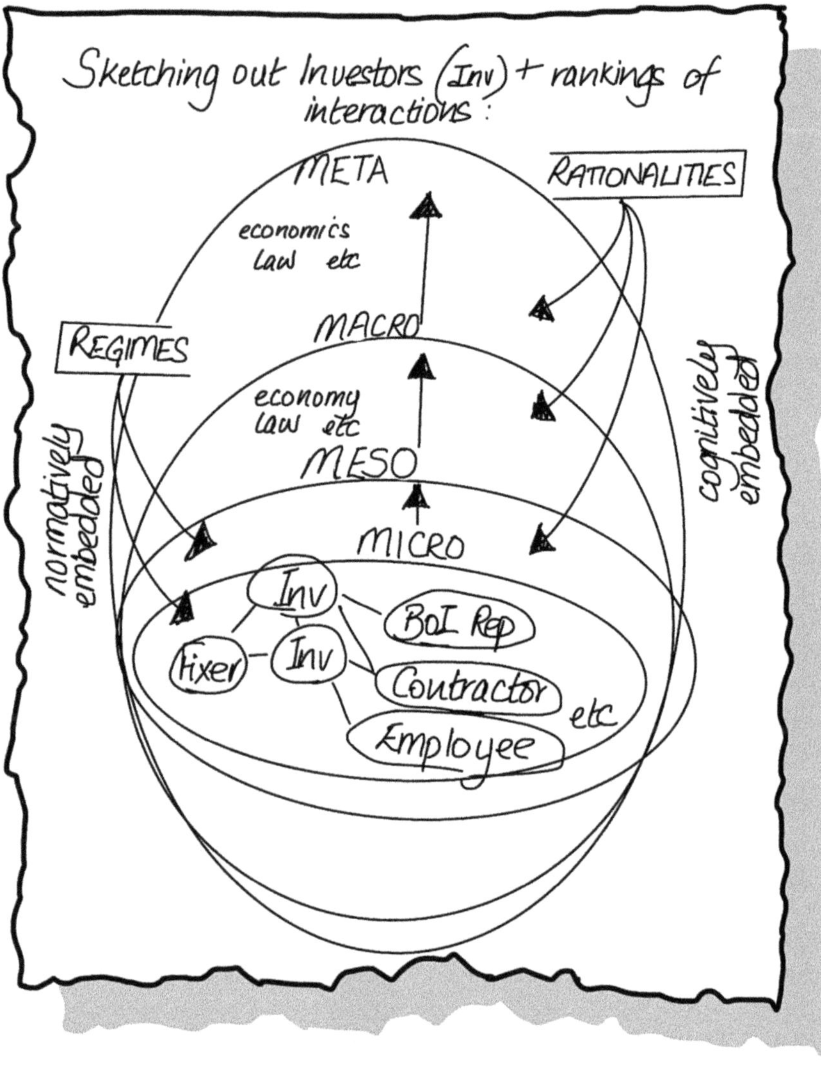

Figure 2.3 A page from Ann's sketchbook, exploring how it might look through an embeddedness-based ESL lens combining Cotterrell's communal networks with Frerichs' four rankings of social interaction. Page reproduced with the kind permission of Academic Ann.

Writing the rules of the game: indicators as technologies of governance

The discussion above has touched on the disciplinary developments that ESL responds to. It noted that the law and economics movements (exemplified by Posner) and the law and society movement (exemplified by Freidman) both derived from realist responses to the "specialization, professionalization, departmentalization, and fragmentation" of the surface structures of academic institutions (Frerichs, 2012, p. 12; Perry-Kessaris, 2012, p. 10). In turn, reacting to these movements, the most recent "generations" of both legal and sociological scholarship see legal, economic, and social phenomena as socially constructed. While there is no monolithic approach, there is a consensus that each of the "functional spheres" into which society is differentiated have "distinctive ways of communication and forms of power" that demand understanding through "careful empirical studies" (Frerichs, 2012, p. 12; Cotterrell, 2008, p. 65). Others have called for a "responsive" or "reflective" law, and see law as either "excessively coloni[zing]" the life world (Habermas), or describing a self-referential aspect of the social (Teubner, Luhmann, 2004) (De Souza Santos, 1987, pp. 279–80).

But this approach, while valuable, raises the problematic spectre of boundaries, a territorial borderland fraught with disagreements that is also familiar to the concept of embeddedness that the following chapter will explore. When our ways of talking and thinking are about "spheres" of social phenomena, each must necessarily have a border; a boundary where one phenomenon yields to, or merges with, another. Where does the economic become the legal? Where does the social become the economic? How do we define borders in a constructivist world-view? And how can we avoid reproducing unsatisfactory borders through existing thoughtways and mental models? How does one rationality become another? Which rationalities feedback to which regimes?

To begin to answer some of these questions, we can return to the World Bank's *Doing Business* indicators as an example of the apogee of disciplinarity, economics imperialism, and one rationality gaining dominance over others (without much evidence to back up the assumptions).[12] Questions of the natural limits of the law reflect similar, perhaps even more trenchant, discussions about the limits of the markets and of the discipline of economics to explain the totality of social life. These questions have become ever more urgent in recent decades as they respond to the economics imperialism discussed earlier. Indeed, the gradual creep of the empirical, analytical, and normative tools of neoclassical economics – quantification, mathematization, and competition

12 Complex links between legal systems and foreign direct investment, the dominance of economics and resulting impacts on national legal systems, had been laid bare in work from as early as 2008, and I'm grateful to Amanda Perry-Kessaris for bringing this to my attention. See inter alia (Perry, 2001, 2008; Perry-Kessaris, 2008).

respectively – into domains that might be considered anathema to economics has not gone unnoticed. In the context of economic development, an industry has grown up over decades measuring and comparing social phenomena. Usually, this is accomplished through the use of proxy indicators; how else could you *measure* social indicators like access to justice or the rule of law?

As the discussion in Chapter 1 has alluded to, the World Bank found a way. While counting might give the impression of progress and clarity, some things lend themselves to quantification and comparison more readily than others, and a range of ingenious proxy indicators appeared. The famed "LLSV" literature, an acronym deriving from the first letter of the name of each of the four main contributors to the development of this approach, Lopez, La Porta, Schleifer, and Vishny, revolutionized how the Bank was able to understand social institutions such as the law (La Porta *et al.*, 1999; Djankov *et al.*, 2002; La Porta, Lopez-de-Silanes and Shleifer, 2008). Remember, at this juncture, that "the law" is an ontological metaphor for a collection of social behaviours with common characteristics. Like time, or the economy, we can argue that it does not exist, tangibly, in the real world. Thus, proxies were needed to measure it. To take an extreme – and probably the most egregious – example, mortality rates faced by European colonialists were used as proxies "to estimate the effect of institutions on economic performance" (Acemoglu, Robinson and Johnson, 2001). Counting can be a double-edged sword, especially when the "net is cast widely, and whatever is caught is classified as fish" (Yusuf *et al.*, 2009, p. 41).

Indicators though have a curious effect, acting in a similar way to targets and inciting the contestants (countries, in this instance) to competition. The "law reform Olympics" were no different, and the monolithic set of *Doing Business* indicators make an interesting case in point (Taylor, 2005; World Bank, n.d.). Each country's legal systems were measured and compared annually, giving each country an overall ranking of how attractive their legal system was to businesses. The assumption here is that countries are net beneficiaries from foreign investment, owing to technology transfer, training, and infrastructure investments, as well as inflows of capital. There are complex sets of requirements to ensure that countries benefit from foreign investment though – this is not a "plug-and-play" method of legal reform where beneficial investment and economic growth will automatically result, and there are also multiple assumptions informing both the key messages and key methodologies.

But in creating and shaping incentives, indicators – in particular those like the *Doing Business* project – operate as "technologies of governance", creating competition between states for investors, and ultimately markets among legal systems (Davis, Kingsbury and Merry, 2010; Machen *et al.*, 2021). So, we might say that the indicators shape incentives and shape rationalities, which in turn shape regimes. The pressure exerted on Bank officials to reach politically acceptable rankings and conclusions demonstrates the moral authority and capital held by these indicators. And yet, empirical research establishing causation between rule of law-style legal reform with increased inward investment flows is thin on the ground. The *Doing Business* project assumed that Western-style legal systems saw higher levels of investment and causation was imputed from correlation, with a nod along the way to Max Weber's theory that rational legal systems better supported economic needs. Yet, as we have seen in the context of a pandemic, correlation can work in both ways, neither, or be completely irrelevant.

The use of counting, and of econometrics, as a supposedly neutral, scientific method often obscures what are significant conceptual and normative biases underpinning research methodologies (McCloskey, 1998, 2006). All thinking is political, and this applies equally to statistics. What we choose to count and how, are important questions with normative dimensions. When these preferences are masked by the scientific veneer of impartiality and neutrality that economics, and to some extent law, has aped from the natural sciences, we lose sight of their sites of contestation.

Add to this the complexity of language that has evolved in each of the disciplinary spheres, and we can appreciate that telling stories about social (non) entities is inherently political, and – when couched in jargon – exclusionary. Those who have not been indoctrinated into the ways of talking and thinking, the methodologies and analyses of mainstream economics or, to a lesser extent, law through the form of a degree are generally excluded from the bulk of mainstream discourse. Certainly, some terms have "leaked" into our shared social reality – we collectively worry about growth, productivity, and efficiency and, as later chapters show, we perform as *homo economicus-juridicus* – but the detail of the stories told in economics and in law is masked.

The apogee of this movement can be summarized with reference to the work of both Gary Becker and James Buchanan, both Nobel Prize winners. Both are renowned for "extending economic methodology to what are usually regarded as non-economic phenomena like politics, bureaucracy, racism, the family, and fertility" (Fukuyama, 1995, p. 17). This "rational choice theory" approach has "colonized" virtually every other area of social inquiry, explaining the political purely in terms of numbers (Fukuyama, 1995, p. 17; Perry-Kessaris, 2011a). Along the way, in appreciating the certainties of "clean", binary answers to complex problems over the "dirty hands" of messy sociological inquiry, we have lost sight of the fact that "numbers are rhetoric, which is to say humanly persuasive" (Hirsch, Michaels and Friedman, 1990; McCloskey, 2006). As the dominant rationality, though, these are the approaches that we have available to think with, talk with, and reason with, and we are left impoverished when we lose sight of the normative dimensions of the rationalities and regimes that we use, and that use us. In the context of the social crises of the pandemic, and the environmental catastrophes wrought by global warming, there is a growing consensus that pitting one interest against "the economy" is a fool's errand, as Chapter 6 explores in greater depth. We are beginning to realize that our mental models – those ways of thinking crafted over generations of scholars, writers, and discursive interactions across society – are shaped strongly by neoclassical economics. And these mental models, with their accompanying vocabularies and grammars, tend to reproduce themselves, along with their inadequacies. It is in this context of realization that we need better ways of doing, talking, and thinking that an ESL has emerged, offering not *the*, but *a* glimpse of an alternative. To this end, an ESL offers us a different way of conceptualizing the relationships between economy, law, and society. It offers an alternative means of balancing voices and values that might not fit with mainstream models, but which events show are vitally important.

ESL is (currently) a pseudo-constructivist lens: boundaries and borderlands

While the chapter has described ESL as a constructivist lens, it might be better characterized as a pseudo-constructivist lens. It aspires to reunite the three core disciplines. It applies a sociological lens to understanding both the law and the economy. It acknowledges feedback loops between our regimes (what we do) and our rationalities (how we think about what we do). But, in clinging to embeddedness as the core concept, this ontological metaphor entrenches the distinction of the phenomena an ESL lens seeks to rejoin. As Chapter 1 noted, embeddedness maintains the metaphorical fiction of the ontologically separate law and economy. And, in so doing, it prevents current ESL lenses from fully realizing their constructivist potential.

By "constructivist", we can refer to the so-called "third generation" of sociological scholarship that might understand the legal and the economic as *aspects*, or *flavours*, of the social, re-co-constructed through and within each social interaction (Crotty, 1998; Schwartz, 2007; Frerichs, 2012).[13] The importance here is that a constructivist lens "highlights the social constructed nature of reality and rejects any independent qualities of it" (Nilsen, 2009, p. 84). Central to this is a "critical stance towards taken-for-granted knowledge", "historical and cultural specificity", acceptance that "knowledge is sustained by processes", and agreement that "knowledge and social action go together" (Burr, 2003). While an ESL does not offer any normative or any conceptual content, but merely offers categories and taxonomies, these can shape perceptions (of the researcher, and of her subjects), creating the categories through which she perceives, conceptualizes, and acts with the world. Similarly, it is worth noting that the archetypal ESL lens outlined here does not set out to challenge the legal or the economic as *knowledge claims*, but instead seeks to reconceptualize these as regimes (such as "the economy" or "the law") and rationalities ("economics" or "law"). It illuminates the analytical and normative assumptions that shape the approach. This does mean though that, inevitably, legal

13 As many authors carefully distinguish between constructivism and constructionism, and then go on to use the terms interchangeably, the following chapters refer to constructivism only. In brief, while constructionism focuses on the artefacts or "knowing" created through shared production, constructivism places the individual at the centre of each meaning-making process (Crotty, 1998, p. 58). Nevertheless, the distinction has become a "shibboleth" (Crotty, 1998, p. 58). See Chapter 5, footnote 3 (page 119), for further discussion.

and economic aspects of interactions, in being identified as such, necessarily become truth claims, although the veracity, or verisimilitude, is not the focus.

Law or legal inquiry tends to be "marginal" in economic sociology, while economic phenomena rarely take centre stage in socio-legal inquiry (Edelman and Stryker, 2005, p. 527). But we can propose that the legal and the economic are two sides of the same social coin. An ESL lens that sees legal and economic phenomena as re-co-constructed through and within social interactions offers us a way of analyzing and understanding the social reproduction of the relations between economic and legal phenomena. An ESL lens can be a useful vehicle for reframing research at the interface of law and economy because of the challenge it can mount to mainstream or orthodox approaches and their hidden normativity. Nevertheless, current tools available for building an ESL, such as the one set out in this chapter, tend to retain the embeddedness metaphor. They also tend to neglect the role of language in the re-co-construction of our regimes and rationalities. For this reason, an ESL might only be termed "pseudo"-constructivist currently. As Chapter 5 shows, there are ways of addressing these areas to realize a fully constructivist ESL lens that is both internally conceptually consistent and external conceptually compatible with the aims and goals of an ESL more generally.

POLICY POLLY

A few years ago, quite by chance, while working in-country on a financed project, Polly spotted a face in the crowd she hadn't seen since they were at university together.

Over coffee the following morning, Ann explained her research goals and told Polly that, as FDI (foreign direct investment) was so important for stimulating economic growth, she was trying to establish what foreign investors were really looking for in a host state legal system. They swapped ideas and frustrations, as well as some questions about whether the underlying assumptions were quite as objective as commonly assumed. Polly understood and was on a similar quest, but from a different perspective.

Ann mentioned a new "lens" that she was exploring, called an economic sociology of law. Polly was sceptical. Despite her frustrations with implementation gaps, Polly still believed in the work she was doing. She had seen it make a difference, and she doubted whether a new conceptual approach with a complicated name could really bring anything useful. Nevertheless, Ann promised to send her some papers, and when they arrive in her inbox, Polly finds that she has five minutes to flick through one or two of them. She picks out some common themes and the gist of how a sociological lens on legal and economic phenomena can enhance the discussion. She downloads the papers and begins to skim read…

Despite ESL's status as an emerging field, this chapter has identified points of consensus as well as a series of useful taxonomies to help approach a research question sociologically at the interface of law and economy. We can state that an ESL lens:

1. Encourages careful, empirical observation
2. Prompts consideration of both *is* and *ought*, encouraging empirical, conceptual (or analytical), and normative analysis of any problem and its proposed solution
3. Suggests an examination of the legal text, its context, and subtext for any exploration to be comprehensive
4. Proposes that both law and economy are understood as social phenomena, re-co-constructed or performed through social interactions
5. Avoids sweeping generalizations of what the law or economy is, does, ought to do, or ought not to do, unless these statements are based on widespread, detailed empirical studies
6. Encourages exploration of theories, methods, methodologies, frames, and points of reference from other areas of the sciences, social sciences, and humanities, believing that approaches can be strengthened through multiple layers of understanding and points of reference
7. Suggests a reflective approach to problems, including an awareness of researcher positionality, when seeking to understand how we do, talk, and think about legal and economic phenomena

Having introduced what an ESL is, its heritage, and some taxonomies, as well as the application of the lens to Ann's research project, we turn to the core concept of the lens, embeddedness. The concept of embeddedness has had a convoluted career, the history of which can shed light on its operation as a secondary, generative metaphor in wider discourse and how it might operate to limit our responses to financial crashes, social crises, and environmental catastrophes. Academic Ann and Policy Polly continue to explore how an ESL lens might be applied in their respective inquiries, and they are joined by Lay Lillian in later chapters as we zoom out again.

Bibliography

Acemoglu, D., Robinson, J. and Johnson, S. (2001) 'The Colonial Origins of Comparative Development: An Empirical Investigation', *American Economic Review*, 91(5), pp. 1369–1401.

Ashiagbor, D., Kotiswaran, P. and Perry-Kessaris, A. (2013) 'Introduction: Moving towards an Economic Sociology of Law', *Journal of Law and Society*, 40, pp. 1–6.

Ashiagbor, D., Kotiswaran, P. and Perry-Kessaris, A. (2014) 'Continuing towards an Economic Sociology of Law', *Northern Ireland Legal Quarterly*, 65(3), pp. 259–64.

Banakar, R. (2014) 'Social Scientific Studies of Law', in *Normativity in Legal Sociology*. Cham: Springer, pp. 41–58.

Banakar, R. and Travers, M. (2005) *Theory and Method in Socio-Legal Research*. Oxford: Hart. Available at: https://www.bloomsbury.com/au/theory-and-method-in-socio-legal-research-9781841136257/ (Accessed: 27 April 2018).

Block, F. (2013) 'Relational Work and the Law: Recapturing the Legal Realist Critique of Market Fundamentalism', *Journal of Law and Society*, 40(1), pp. 27–48.

Bourdieu, P. and Wacquant, L.J. (1992) *An Invitation to Reflexive Sociology*. University of Chicago Press.

Bronk, R. (2009) *The Romantic Economist: Imagination in Economics*. Cambridge: Cambridge University Press.

Burr, V. (2003) *Social Constructionism*. New York: Routledge.

Burrows, A. (2016) 'Challenges for Private Law in the 21st Century', *Oxford Legal Studies Research Paper* 3/2016 [Preprint]. https://doi.org/10.2139/ssrn.2710270.

Cotterrell, R. (1997) 'A Legal Concept of Community', *Canadian Journal of Law and Society*, 12.

Cotterrell, R. (1998) 'Why Must Legal Ideas Be Interpreted Sociologically?', *Journal of Law and Society*, 25(2), pp. 171–192.

Cotterrell, R. (2005) *The Sociology of Law: An Introduction*. 2nd ed. Oxford and New York: Oxford University Press.

Cotterrell, R. (2006) *Law, Culture and Society: Legal Ideas in the Mirror of Social Theory*. Aldershot: Ashgate Pub. Co (Law, justice, and power).

Cotterrell, R. (2008) *Living Law: Studies in Legal and Social Theory*. Aldershot: Ashgate (Collected essays in law).

Cotterrell, R. (2013) 'Rethinking Embeddedness; Law, Economy, Community', *Journal of Law and Society*, 40(1), pp. 49–67.

Crotty, M. (1998) *The Foundations of Social Research: Meaning and Perspective in the Research Process*. St Leonards: Allen & Unwin.

Davis, K.E., Kingsbury, B. and Merry, S.E. (2010) 'Indicators as a Technology of Global Governance'. Available at: https://ssrn.com/abstract=1583431 or http://dx.doi.org/10.2139/ssrn.1583431.

De Souza Santos, B. (1987) 'Law: A Map of Misreading. Towards a Postmodern Conception of Law', *Journal of Law and Society*, 14(3), pp. 279–302.

Djankov, S. et al. (2002) 'The Regulation of Entry', *The Quarterly Journal of Economics*, 117(1), pp. 1–37.

Edelman, L. and Stryker, R. (2005) 'A Sociological Approach to Law and the Economy', in N.J. Smelser and R. Swedberg (eds) *The Handbook of Economic Sociology*. Princeton: Princeton University Press, pp. 527–551.

Ewick, P. and Silbley, S., (1998) *The Common Place of Law*. Chicago: University of Chicago Press.

Ewick, P. and Silbey, S. (2003) 'Narrating Social Structure: Stories of Resistance to Legal Authority', *American Journal of Sociology*, 108(6), pp. 1328–1372.

Fine, B. and Milonakis, D. (2009) *From Economics Imperialism to Freakonomics*. Routledge Ltd. Available at: https://www.amazon.co.uk/Economics-Imperialism-Freakonomics-Social-Theory/dp/0415423236.

Frerichs, S. (2009) 'The Legal Constitution of Market Society: Probing the Economic Sociology of Law', *Economic Sociology, The European Electronic Newsletter*, 10.

Frerichs, S. (2012) 'Studying Law, Economy, and Society: A Short History of Socio-Legal Thinking', *SSRN eLibrary* [Preprint]. Available at: http://papers.ssrn.com/sol3/papers.cfm?abstract_id=2022891.

Fukuyama, F. (1995) *Trust: The Social Virtues and the Creation of Prosperity*. London: Hamish Hamilton.

Giddens, A. (1984) *The Constitution of Society: Outline of the Theory of Structuration*. Oxford: Polity.

Granovetter, M. (1985) 'Economic Action and Social Structure: The Problem of Embeddedness', *American Journal of Sociology*, 91(3), pp. 481–510.

Harriss, J. (2002) *Depoliticizing Development: The World Bank and Social Capital*. Wimbledon, London: Anthem Press.

Hirsch, P., Michaels, S. and Friedman, R. (1990) 'Clean Models vs. Dirty Hands: Why Economics is Different from Sociology', in Sharon Zukin and Paul DiMaggio (eds) *Structures of Capital: The Social Organization of the Economy*. Cambridge: Cambridge University Press, pp. 39–57.

Krippner, G. (2001) 'The Elusive Market: Embeddedness and the Paradigm of Economic Sociology', *Theory and Society*, 30(6), pp. 775–810.

La Porta, R. et al. (1999) 'The Quality of Government', *Journal of Law, Economics and Organization*, 15(1), pp. 222–279.

La Porta, R., Lopez-de-Silanes, F. and Shleifer, A. (2008) 'The Economic Consequences of Legal Origins', *Journal of Economic Literature*, 46(2), pp. 285–332.

Lakoff, G. (2014) *Don't Think of an Elephant: Know Your Values and Frame the Debate*. Kindle. White River Junction: Chelsea Green Publishing.

Luhmann, N. (2004) *Law as a Social System*. Edited by F. Kastner et al. Translated by K.A. Ziegert. Oxford: Oxford University Press (Oxford Socio-Legal Studies).

Machen, R.C. et al. (2021) *Investigation of Data Irregularities in Doing Business 2018 and Doing Business 2020 Investigation Findings and Report to the Board of Executive Directors*. WilmerHale: Wilmer Cutler Pickering Hale and Dorr LLP. Available at: https://thedocs.worldbank.org/en/doc/84a922cc9273b7b120d49ad3b9e9d3f9-0090012021/original/DB-Investigation-Findings-and-Report-to-the-Board-of-Executive-Directors-September-15-2021.pdf (Accessed: 3 February 2022).

McCloskey, D.N. (1998) *The Rhetoric of Economics*. 2nd ed. Madison: University of Wisconsin Press.

McCloskey, D.N. (2006) 'Why Economics is on the Wrong Track', *Prudentia*. Available at: http://www.deirdremccloskey.com/articles/stats/why.php.

Mirowski, P. (1992) 'Do Economists Suffer from Physics Envy?', *Finnish Economic Papers*, 5(1), pp. 61–68.

Nilsen, A. (2009) 'From Questions of Methods to Epistemological Issues: The Case of Biographical Research', in P. Alasuutari, L. Bickman and J. Brannen (eds) *The SAGE Handbook of Social Research Methods*. London: Sage Publications, pp. 81–95.

Perry, A.J. (2001) *Legal Systems as a Determinant of FDI, Lessons from Sri Lanka*. Kluwer Law International. Available at: https://lrus.wolterskluwer.com/store/product/legal-systems-as-a-determinant-of-fdi-lessons-from-sri-lanka/.

Perry, A.J. (2004) 'Use, Abuse and Avoidance: Foreign Investors and the Legal System in Bangalore', *Asia Pacific Law Review*, 12(2), pp. 161–189.

Perry, A.J. (2008) 'Effective Legal Systems and Foreign Direct Investment: In Search of the Evidence', *International & Comparative Law Quarterly*, 49(04), pp. 779–799. https://doi.org/10.1017/S0020589300064654.

Perry-Kessaris, A.J. (2008) *Global Business, Local Law: The Indian Legal System as a Communal Resource in Foreign Investment Relations*. Ashgate. Available at: http://eprints.soas.ac.uk/10473/.

Perry-Kessaris, A.J. (2011a) 'Prepare Your Indicators: Economics Imperialism on the Shores of Law and Development', *International Journal of Law in Context*, 7(4), pp. 401–421.

Perry-Kessaris, A.J. (2011b) 'Reading the Story of Law and Embeddedness through a Community Lens: A Polanyi-Meets-Cotterrell Economic Sociology of Law?', *Northern Ireland Legal Quarterly* (Special Issue on *Socialising Economic Relationships*), 62(4), pp. 401–13.

Perry-Kessaris, A.J. (2012) 'What Does it Mean to Take a Socio-Legal Approach to International Economic Law?', in *Socio-Legal Approaches to International Economic Law: Text, Context, Subtext*. Routledge. Available at: https://papers.ssrn.com/sol3/papers.cfm?abstract_id=2085007.

Perry-Kessaris, A.J. (2013) *Socio-Legal Approaches to International Economic Law: Amanda Perry-Kessaris*. Routledge. Available at: https://www.routledge.com/Socio-Legal-Approaches-to-International-Economic-Law-Text-Context-Subtext/Perry-Kessaris/p/book/9780415510165.

Perry-Kessaris, A.J. (2015) 'Approaching the Econo-Socio-Legal', *Annual Review of Law and Social Science* [Preprint]. https://doi.org/10.1146/annurev-lawsocsci-120814-121542.

Putnam, R. (2001) *Bowling Alone: The Collapse and Revival of American Community*. New York: Simon & Schuster Ltd.

Samuel, G. (2016) 'Have There Been Scientific Revolutions in Law?', *Journal of Comparative Law*, 11(2), pp. 186–213.

Schön, D.A. (2012) 'Generative Metaphor: A Perspective on Problem-Setting in Social Policy', in Ortony, A. (ed.) *Metaphor and Thought*. 2nd ed. Cambridge: Cambridge University Press, pp. 137–163.

Schwartz, T.A. (2007) *Dictionary of Qualitative Inquiry*. Thousand Oaks: Sage Publications. Available at: https://methods.sagepub.com/reference/the-sage-dictionary-of-qualitative-inquiry.

Swedberg, R. (2003) 'The Case for an Economic Sociology of Law', *Theory and Society*, 32, pp. 1–32.

Swedberg, R., Himmelstrand, U. and Brulin, G. (1987) 'The Paradigm of Economic Sociology: Premises and Promises', *Theory and Society*, 16(2), pp. 169–213.

Taylor, V.L. (2005) *The Law Reform Olympics: Measuring the Effects of Law Reform in Transition Economies*. SSRN Scholarly Paper ID 893682. Rochester: Social Science Research Network. Available at: https://papers.ssrn.com/abstract=893682.

Uzzi, B. (1997) 'Social Structure and Competition in Interfirm Networks: The Paradox of Embeddedness', *Administrative Science Quarterly*, 42(1), pp. 35–67.

Wallerstein, I. (2004) *World-Systems Analysis: An Introduction*. Durham and London: Duke University Press.

Wheeler, S. (2020) 'Socio-Legal Studies in 2020', *Journal of Law and Society*, 47(S2), pp. S209–S226.

World Bank (n.d.) *Doing Business, Why Aggregate, and How to Do it*. World Bank Doing Business. Available at: http://www.doingbusiness.org/~/media/WBG/DoingBusiness/Documents/Methodology/Other/why-aggregate-doing-business-2006.pdf (Accessed: 17 November 2018).

Yusuf, S. et al. (2009) *Development Economics through the Decades: A Critical Look at Thirty Years of the World Development Report*. 30th Anniversary Edition. Washington, DC: World Bank Publications.

Zelizer, V. (2011) 'How I Became a Relational Economic Sociologist and What Does This Mean?', in Princeton: Centre for the Study of Social Organization, *Working Paper No*.5. Available at: www.princeton.edu/csso/working-papers/WP5.pdf.

Chapter 3

Embeddedness

A biography of a concept

Embeddedness: the origins

> **ACADEMIC ANN**
>
> *Ann already had a mental list of questions she wanted to ask her investor-interviewees. Some questions were follow-ups from her last trip, but other questions were new, reflecting the fact that the country had changed significantly since she was last there. There was a new government for a start, and funding had poured in from other states rather than development banks. Infrastructure was being planned and built at a phenomenal rate, and Ann tried hard to shelve her deep personal worries that the country might not be able to afford the repayments. She didn't want to think what might happen if the country defaulted.*
>
> *Focusing, she wondered if her interview questions would alter or shift if she applied an ESL (economic sociology of law) lens. Previously, she had spoken to investors and regulators: those directly involved, economically and legally, in foreign investment. But, applying an ESL lens, she realized that the effects of the project extend well beyond the investors. Thinking about wider community impact, Ann considered the new export processing zone (EPZ) that sat on ancestral lands, and remembers the riots that had been quashed by the police as the park was being built. The local community had hoped for jobs and schools, but they were still waiting.*

"Embeddedness"-talk is everywhere. Start looking out for this useful little metaphor, and you might be surprised at its ubiquity and sheer versatility. Embeddedness has increasingly come to be used to describe the problematic relations between the spheres of law, economy, and society. As a metaphor, it succinctly identifies our dissatisfaction with the (metaphorical) distance between the spheres of law, economy, and society. But simply stating that "the law is embedded in society", or "the economy should be re-embedded in society" does little more than conceal the fact that we are talking about fictions and their metaphorical relationships. Used both explicitly and implicitly,

DOI: 10.4324/9781003354819-3

embeddedness – as an unthought rationality – both reveals and conceals information about the dynamic relationship between legal and economic phenomena. And yet, being so familiar, so ubiquitous, the concept flies largely under the radar, invisibly shaping our mental models or rationalities, and our conceptual and linguistic tools.

As embeddedness is the core concept of economic sociology, and given that ESL grew out of, and continues to draw on much of that literature, it was somewhat inevitable that ESL would inherit the "core concept" of embeddedness (Cotterrell, 2013). Additionally, a key commonality of most ESL lenses is an acknowledgement of the works of both Max Weber and Karl Polanyi. As Chapter 1 noted, Polanyi's use of embeddedness as a visual metaphor, referencing the coal being extracted from the walls of the mine, was undeniably useful in offering a representation of the relationship between economy, its regulation, and society. But the disciplinarity, departmentalization, and differentiation that have occurred in academia and knowledge spheres more generally since then make our ongoing use of embeddedness problematic. This chapter follows the career of the concept from Polanyi's initial coinage, through its turbulent role as the "common denominator" in economic sociology, through to post-2008 applications of the concept (Cotterrell, 2013). Along the way, the chapter will differentiate the works of John Ruggie and Peter Evans as examples of embeddedness-based discourse that might offer us clues as to how embeddedness might be employed consistently and coherently.

Talking about embeddedness

Before setting off though, another word on terminology is necessary: namely, is embeddedness a "concept", a "paradigm", a "term" (of art), a "metaphor", a "theory", or all of these? It has been referred to as a "concept" in some of the ESL literature, although there is much to commend its description as a paradigm (Uzzi, 1997, p. 35; Kuhn, 1970). The "receding utility" of the "*concept*" of embeddedness, with its "oxymoronic and ill-defined qualities", and the centrality of this for how we respond to pressing social crises, demands that we reappraise embeddedness (Ashiagbor, Kotiswaran and Perry-Kessaris, 2013, p. 4). Unlike a "theory", defined as a "system of concepts and statements, models, or principles, which, in concert, make the empirical world more intelligible", embeddedness demands more nuance (Krimsky and Golding, 1992, p. 6).

Embeddedness has also been described as "a metaphor denoting a state of dependence upon or subordination to, refer[ing] to the relationship between 'economy' and 'society'" as well as a theoretical puzzle, "methodological axiom", or a "theoretical proposition" (Dale, 2011, pp. 307–8, 323). As Chapter 1 set out, in a constructivist context where we accept that "the law" and "the economy" are ontological metaphors, or linguistic shortcuts for describing collections of social behaviours, we can understand embeddedness as a tertiary metaphor, resting on the primary metaphorical layers of law, economy, and society as set out in Figure 1.1 on page 5. This gives us three layers of metaphor. Primary metaphors are those ontological metaphors such as "the law", "the economy", and "society", which are collective leaps of imagination we take when we use linguistic shortcuts to describe collections of behaviours. Secondary metaphors then personify and describe ontological metaphors: "the law makes an ass of us all", or "the markets have tumbled". Tertiary metaphors can then be understood as describing the relationship between two primary, ontological metaphors: "the law is embedded in society".

Used precisely and carefully, embeddedness can describe the temporal and spatial relationship between two phenomena, and thus also functions both as a concept and as an ontological metaphor (Lakoff and Johnson, 1980). While the term was originally used as a dynamic visual metaphor, it has become so central to wider discourse and so ubiquitous that we can now speak of a general *conceptual commitment* to embeddedness.[1] By identifying embeddedness as a concept, we need not acknowledge the inherently normative nature of the "paradigm", or the prescriptive aspects of a "theory". Embeddedness can have both of these depending on its context, or neither. Identifying embeddedness as a concept also enables a discussion that centres on its historical and contextual contingency.

Karl Polanyi's always (or never) embedded market

ACADEMIC ANN

Ann's ESL lens uses the core concept of embeddedness and she wonders what impact this might have on her research. Some of the literature has suggested that this might be a rabbit hole to avoid, and Ann wants to keep her project empirically focused, but she is curious. Reading that there are many and varied interpretations of embeddedness, she decides to choose two and compare them in the context of her own research.

It is fair to say that the concept of embeddedness has had a long and colourful career. Its genealogy in the context of economic sociology is generally traced back to Karl Polanyi's 1948 magnum opus, *The Great Transformation*, in which embeddedness is used sparingly as a visual descriptor of relations between

1 I'm grateful to Amanda Perry-Kessaris for this phrasing, and also for the point that, while not a complete theory, embeddedness does have empirical and normative dimensions and implications, whether it is deployed as part of a wider theoretical framework or, as is more common, on an ad hoc, discrete, basis.

market and society, offering what was probably little more than a throwaway description of macro-level relations. We can be fairly certain, given his lack of attention to the concept in core publications or his private notes, that Polanyi never intended the term to take on a life of its own (Dale, 2010, 2016). Given the inherent integration enjoyed by law, economics, and sociology in the pre-disciplinary time that Polanyi was writing, the concept likely appeared unproblematic. At that time, spheres such as law and economy would have been understood as dynamic, flexible, and essentially sociological in nature without this needing to be spelled out (Frerichs, 2011).

This has, over time, led to conflicting interpretations of what Karl Polanyi might have originally meant through his concept of the "always (or never) embedded" economy (Block, 2001, 2003). Are we talking solely about markets? And can Polanyi be read, as Fred Block suggests, that the economy is embedded (to a greater or lesser extent) in society, or as Gareth Dale proposes, that society has become embedded in the economy (Block, 2001; Dale, 2011)? Between these two extremes lies a range of differing views, and over the years many proposals for marrying macro- and micro-level (Polanyian and Granovetterian) embeddedness, along with the constructivist goals of ESL, have appeared (Krippner *et al.*, 2004; Frerichs, 2011; Perry-Kessaris, 2012; Ashiagbor, 2013).

While Polanyi is traditionally cited as the first to coin the "always embedded market economy", the term itself makes surprisingly few appearances in *The Great Transformation* (Block, 2001).[2] In *The Great Transformation*, Polanyi states, somewhat ambiguously, that "man's economy, as a rule, is submerged in his social relationships", using the terms "embedded", "enmeshed", "submerged", and "absorbed" interchangeably to describe the position of all observable economies in both economic and non-economic institutions (Polanyi, 1944, p. 48). Moreover, Dale notes that Thurnwald employed the term before Polanyi, although in a slightly different context (Dale, 2011, p. 320).

Nevertheless, Polanyi was building on existing approaches in sociology and economic sociology. In the social sciences, Marx spoke of the "group consciousness based on connected individuals experiencing common environmental realities", which has been taken as the roots of the concept of social embeddedness (Mckeever, Anderson and Jack, 2014, p. 223). Park's theories

2 The term "embedded" in relation to the economy appears twice on page 60, then on pages 64, 73, and 135. Polanyi also describes economies as "enmeshed in non-economic institutions", although this term only appears once in his notes on sources, reprinted in 2001 along with the text of the main work. Dale notes that the term crops up repeatedly in Polanyi's published books and articles from the post-war period, and even more frequently in his unpublished notes and manuscripts, leaving us to wonder if Polanyi edited the term out of his publications, or whether he glimpsed the embedded economy but ran out of time to publish the full version of this. As Dale notes, Polanyi's tendency for "epistemological breaks" along with the changes in institutional context makes it difficult to "read back" into *The Great Transformation* what we would like to find. (Polanyi, 1944; Dale, 2010, 2011).

of communal subgroups and the "condition of affective belonging" complemented Weber's proposition that economic behaviour was deeply "grounded in the cultural realm of customs, language and the collective ethos", as well as Simmel's work on "group identities" and interactions that produce society (Park, 1924; Weber, 1946; Simmel, 1950).[3]

Polanyi wanted to convey "the fluid mixing of social objects in a way that defied disciplinary boundaries", referencing the work of Weber when he described the focus of *The Great Transformation* (Krippner, 2001, p. 778). Other influences, such as the works of Frazer, Malinowski, and Lévi-Strauss emphasized the social nature of exchange and the interface between social and economic spheres, and Polanyi is said to have been "thrilled" by Malinowski's descriptions of the Trobiand islanders which resulted in the "scotching of the legend of *homo economicus*" (Mckeever, Anderson and Jack, 2014).[4] In these primitive societies, "purely economic" institutions did not exist, nor did "the economy", but "economic systems of 'primitive' societies were [...] submerged in the totality of social relationships" (Dale, 2011, p. 319). They urged a rethinking of the assumptions on which the capitalist, self-regulating market sat in society, along with the relationship between society and economy (Dale, 2011, p. 319).

In later work, Polanyi distinguishes between the "substantive economic" and the "formal economic", stating in his later work that the "economy, then, is an instituted process" (Polanyi, 1957; Maucourant and Plociniczak, 2013). This is this work that brought Polanyi closer to fully exploring the ramifications of the "always embedded economy", even though he was never able to fully explain his position. In discussing processes and institutions, he concluded that the human economy "is embedded and enmeshed in institutions, economic and non-economic", the inclusion of the latter being "vital" (Polanyi, 1957). He therefore noted that "[t]he study of the shifting place occupied by the economy in society is therefore no other than the study of the manner in which the economic process is instituted at different times and places", which he concludes "requires a special tool box" (Polanyi, 1957). Polanyi thus came closer than any other commentator at the time to a nuanced understanding of the social nature of the economy.

While there is a consensus that Polanyi was writing against the clock and keen to get *Transformation* out and into the world before the Bretton Woods institutions solidified into accepted structural form, Polanyi was also writing

3 This was later developed by Giddens to include the influence of social relationships on the behaviour of the agent themselves. See (Simmel, 1950; Giddens, 1979).

4 (Simmel, 1950; Giddens, 1979; Dale, 2011, p. 319; J.G. Frazer, *Folklore in the Old Testament* (Vol. 2, London, Macmillan 1919); B. Malinowski, *Argonauts of the Western Pacific* (New York, Dutton 1922); C. Lévi-Strauss, *The Savage Mind* (Chicago, University of Chicago Press 1969), all cited in Mckeever, Anderson and Jack, 2014).

from a political standpoint. Having spent years researching the disastrous impact of the gold standard, Polanyi was worried that Bretton Woods would, in making the dollar the international reserve currency, repeat the mistakes of the gold standard. He was also politically opposed to the politics that went into the post-war settlement as well as geographically distanced from the site of the action, being in America while Keynes and Hayek nipped between London and Switzerland. These pressures have been blamed for Polanyi's "epistemological breaks". Block suggests that while Polanyi *meant* to say that the economy was always embedded, he never quite glimpsed the bigger picture (Block, 2001). We will, though, never be sure how charitable this reading is. What we can be sure of is that in finding limitations with the progeny of Bretton Woods, and in looking back to Polanyi's alternative reading and thesis, the embeddedness (or not) of the economy has come to command a great deal of attention.

In fact, even if we can (unproblematically) read *The Great Transformation* through the lens of Polanyi's later publications and infer what he might have meant, there remain ambiguities. He appears to treat the market as disembedded, as "[i]nstead of economy being embedded in social relations, social relations are embedded in the economic system" (Polanyi, cited in Krippner, 2001, p. 780). But this contrasts with his statements that the self-regulating market is a fiction. Dale sums up the dual readings of Polanyi's "embedded" economy, stating that for some, "he is held up as the originator of a line of sociological analysis that treats 'the economy' as a subsystem 'embedded in' a social system" (Dale, 2011, p. 306). This reading places emphasis "upon the moral underpinnings of market behaviour, in contrast to the naturalism of Ricardo, Malthus and their heirs" (Dale, 2011, p. 306). However, for others, "his 'disembedding' thesis contains a more radical tale of the market economy coming to dominate 'society', bringing forth a sorcerer's apprentice world of untrammelled market forces that, although human creations, lie beyond conscious human control" (Dale, 2011, p. 306).

An alternative reading of Polanyi's embeddedness thesis whereby the economy could become disembedded, but where the historical trajectory "does not yield a *general* 'theoretical proposition' about this" offers another possibility (Cotterrell, 2013, p. 53). In other words, "a politico-social reaction [...], exposing and cancelling the 'dangerous fantasy' of the self-regulating economy, is *not bound to occur* – at least not without disaster overtaking social and political life first" (Cotterrell, 2013, p. 53). This shifts Polanyi's work from general social theory to more interpretive history, but still does not solve the second problem of conceptual incompatibility that is discussed below. Nor does it provide any neat answers to what the economy, or market, is embedded *in*, as once again we are reminded to keep in mind Cotterrell's main questions of *what* is embedded, and *in what* is it embedded. "[P]olitical institutions, legal controls, state policy or social conditions" have been suggested as answers to the second question, as well as "institutional regulation", "social relations", and "ongoing networks of social relations", although there is little consensus here (Randles, 2003; Krippner *et al.*, 2004; Cotterrell, 2013; Ashiagbor, 2014). Indeed, this may be one of the attractions of a specifically Polanyian reading of embeddedness; that it can support flexible interpretation and application, and properly defined can convey the broad outline of a concept. Alternatively, if one were being uncharitable, the embeddedness thesis offers sufficient ambiguity to support a range of propositions. Accordingly, when there have been so many and varied definitions of the term, its use without clear reference has come to leave it virtually meaningless. This is increasingly problematic in the context of our responses to pressing social dilemmas, as it means that the embeddedness metaphor is malleable to the political and moral whims of anyone who deploys it.

The resulting imprecision and lack of consensus has generated "some light and not a little heat" (Dale, 2011, pp. 306–7). To take some of this heat out of the discussion, we might imagine a simplified version of the two main interpretations of Polanyi's embeddedness thesis set out in Figure 1.3 in Chapter 1 on page 21 as a starting point for the following discussion.

The "accidental" revival of embeddedness

POLICY POLLY

Polly was intrigued. She had become frustrated with the narrowness of the models, theories, and concepts that the development bank used. But in the last 20 years there had been a shift towards experimentalism, and a rise in the use of randomized controlled trials (RCTs) to investigate development initiatives. Nevertheless, her in-country experience had shown her that there were voices and interests that still never quite made it into the calculations and cost–benefit analyses that the bank required. These were generally the non-economic values and interests. How could she put a price on familial attachment to land, or ecological devastation, when people would get jobs and education in return?

Flicking through the papers Ann had sent over again, Polly wondered whether a lens like an ESL might offer one way of capturing a greater plurality of voices and values.

One word kept cropping up that bothered her though: embeddedness. What difference might this make for her policy design?

"I had, in fact, forgotten about Polanyi [...] when I wrote that paper" (Granovetter, in Krippner *et al.*, 2004, p. 114). Thus, in 1985, so began the second life of embeddedness. However, this risks being unfair to Mark Granovetter, whose unintentional revival of the concept of embeddedness (re)launched what had been a relatively modest career.[5] The concept of embeddedness had flown largely under the radar until Granovetter's 1985 micro-level network analysis that launched the "New Economic Sociology" (Granovetter, 1985). In it, Granovetter describes actors as "embedded in" networks at the micro level. This stood in opposition to Polanyi's embeddedness of markets at the macro level. The seeds of the first challenge to embeddedness – the "what are we talking about?" argument – were duly sown, and as the field of economic sociology developed, the "core concept" of embeddedness grew.

Mark Granovetter was "attempting to chart a course" between the under- and over-socialization of actors in economic sociology and focused on the "embeddedness" of economic actions in "ongoing structures of social relations" (Granovetter, 1985, p. 481). As such, his course between Parsonian and Smelserian sociology on the one hand, and neoclassical economics on the other, developed a network analysis of micro-social and microeconomic interactions (Krippner *et al.*, 2004, p. 111). His ultimate proposal stated that all economic behaviour was "embedded in networks and communities of interpersonal relationships" (Mckeever, Anderson and Jack, 2014, p. 225). Granovetter remarked that "economic action is affected by actor's dyadic relationships and by the structure of the overall network of relations", avoiding any sweeping claims about the relationship between market and society (Granovetter, cited in Mckeever, Anderson and Jack, 2014, p. 225).

Granovetter's use of the concept "envelope[d] and submerge[d] the asocial market construct in social relations, all the while preserving intact the notion that somewhere there was a hard core of market behaviour existing outside of social life (and hence that needed to be 'embedded')" (Krippner, 2001, p. 778).

This dichotomy, Krippner argues, has led to "a neglect of the concept of the market" with the results that "*the market has tended to elude researchers as a sociological object*" (Krippner, 2001, p. 778).[6] Moreover, Granovetter's approach, described by Dale as what "one may charitably assume to have been a slip of the pen" contains its own contradictions, describing both the Polanyian "extreme" and his own middle course as "*the* embeddedness approach" (Granovetter, 1985, 481, 487, cited in Dale, 2011, p. 326).[7] Krippner and Alvarez have suggested that Granovetter is not engaging with Polanyi but "advancing a wholly different concept" that leaves Polanyi's critique of the "analytically autonomous economy" intact (Dale, 2011, p. 327). This is echoed by Beckert, who notes the "cumulative interpretative misunderstandings" pitching embeddedness at the heart of economic sociology, and by Maucourant and Cangiani,

5 With reference to economic sociology and economic history. Ruggie's "embedded liberalism" thesis had appeared two years earlier in the field of international political economy (see below, on page 84).

6 Emphasis in original. Ironically, this echoes criticisms by Coase and other New Institutional Economists who realised that analysis of the market itself was lacking in their approaches too.

7 Emphasis in Dale.

who point out the difference in focus of both writers; Granovetter of economic agents, Polanyi of the institutional arrangements of the economic system as a whole (Beckert, 2009; Maucourant and Plociniczak, 2013). Lie, by contrast, has described Polanyi's concept of market exchange as "disembedded" (Lie, 1997). Instead, he accuses Polanyi of a "moral critique of the sociologically empty market concept of neoclassical economics without probing its weakness by way of investigating 'the concrete social relations of those who buy and sell'" (Dale, 2011, p. 328).

Nevertheless, Granovetter's work on the nature of social ties and the implications of embeddedness "created a paradigmatic shift and bridged the structural hole which previously existed between economic sociology and [other disciplines]" (Mckeever, Anderson and Jack, 2014, p. 224). Granovetter's focus on strong, weak, and non-existent ties was derived through what he called "a rough intuitive basis", and he later used his theory of embeddedness as a method for analysing the use of weak ties that allowed individuals to use and manipulate their position within networks to access distant ideas, influences and information (Mckeever, Anderson and Jack, 2014, p. 225). Using the language of rationality, Granovetter later noted that "[w]hat looks to the analyst like non-rational behaviour may be quite sensible when situational constraints, especially those of embeddedness, are fully appreciated" (Granovetter, 1985, p. 506).

Instead, through his use of the term, Granovetter endorses "the analysis of institutions in terms of a single aspect, the configuration of network ties" in a way that almost inverts Polanyi's initial meaning and echoes Parsons' strategy for establishing sociology some 50 years earlier (Krippner, 2001, p. 777). Frustratingly though at this point, Parsons' "introduction of an analytical schema marking off discrete economic and social domains of knowledge" tends to "shade into an ontological proposition" (Krippner, 2001, p. 777). This is regardless of the fact that Parsons himself never realized this in so many words, and this distinction still haunts and shapes economic sociology to this day.

Nevertheless, the career of embeddedness had been revived, and it came to be applied to more and more, ultimately meaning less and less and sharing a similar fate to the orthodox neoclassical economics models discussed in Chapter 1. Additionally, its original dynamism and flexibility were lost, as the concept solidified and congealed into a static descriptor of relations between what were quickly developing into silos of research and practice – the spheres of law, economics and sociology that differentiated throughout the twentieth century, led by the "scientization" of economics and thereby wider policy (Christensen, 2018). This was reflected in the fictional metaphors of law, economy, and society that reinforced their ontological separation as distinct phenomena, each with their own dominant mental models and theories; doctrinal in law, and neoclassical in economics. Using the four rankings of social interaction set out by Frerichs and introduced in Chapter 2, we might visualize the contributions to the career of embeddedness as Figure 3.1 sets out.

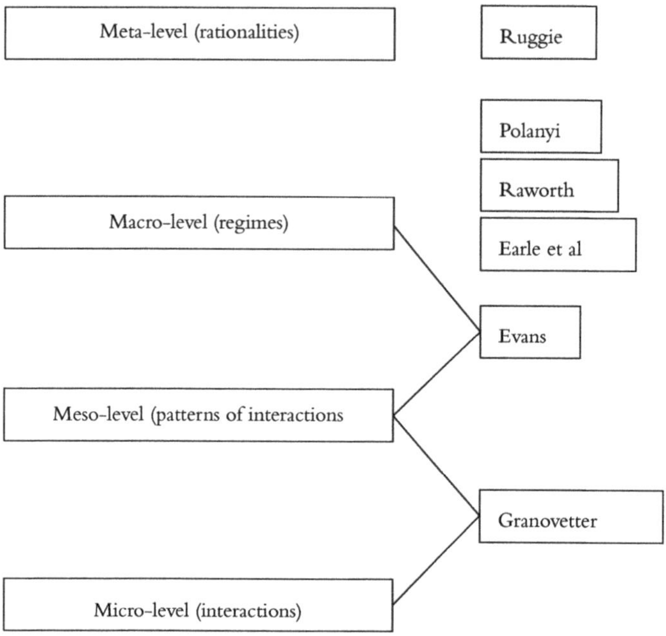

Figure 3.1 Rankings of embeddedness: applying Frerichs' four rankings of social interaction to the concept of embeddedness we might situate the key contributors according to the level at which they use the concept of embeddedness.

Critiques of embeddedness

LAY LILLIAN

Lillian's frustrations were growing. Her granddaughter had just graduated and Lillian was so proud, but worried about how she would find a job and buy a house, or even rent one.

Her granddaughter had told Lillian that sometimes her working hours would change from week to week, and she didn't know if her contract would be renewed. She was looking for a permanent job, but they were hard to come by. The world, it seemed, had changed a great deal since Lillian had joined the workforce.

She thought back to the conversations she had had with Ann recently and was still trying to make sense of what Ann had told her about framing. At the time, Lillian could only think of window frames, and hadn't understood Ann's description of her work as a "lens". But, realising that a window frame, when you look through it, can alter your perception of the view outside, she realized that Ann might be talking about the way we understand the world, and our place within it.

One thing about Ann's research that had lodged in Lillian's imagination was whether the economy should be more (or less) embedded in society. Was this the problem with society at the moment? Had the economy become too separated from society? Wasn't the economy supposed to function for society, rather than vice versa?

Critiques of macro-level embeddedness

While two prominent interpretations of Polanyian embeddedness are explored, contrasted, and compared in Chapters 4 and 5, critiques of Polanyi's embeddedness thesis – the always (or never) embedded economy – tend to fall into three main groups. The first picks away at the inherently contradictory and ambiguous nature of Polanyi's embeddedness thesis and the fact that while Polanyi might have "glimpsed the idea of the always embedded market economy, [...] he was not able to give that idea a name or develop it theoretically because it represented too great a divergence from his initial theoretical starting point" (Block, 2003, p. 276). Despite the "deep ambiguities in [Polanyi's] discussion of embeddedness", this approach remains "the most powerful and enduring way to make sense of Polanyi's core arguments" (Block, 2003, pp. 294, 276; Krippner *et al.*, 2004, p. 125). Polanyi "persuasively demonstrates" that the economy has to be – and historically has been – "embedded in law, politics, and morality" to avoid "social or economic disaster" (Block, 2003, p. 295). But this is through the maintenance of fictions: the three fictitious commodities, and the maintenance of institutional structures set up to manage the so-called self-regulating market.[8] Yet, as "there can never be a self-regulating market system" according to Polanyi, "so the idea of impairing its functioning is an absurdity" (Block, 2003, p. 297). This, then, "is the equivalent of complaining that one's perpetual motion machine was damaged when it was inspected by sceptical scientists" (Block, 2003, p. 297).

This has ramifications for the second critique which we can identify as the "black box" problem or the rationale that embeddedness leaves the market unavailable to sociological analysis, essentially denying one of the objectives of an economic sociology or ESL lens. As noted, the ontology of self-regulating markets that we can establish from *The Great Transformation* is then contradicted 13 years later when Polanyi contends that all markets are instituted in some way or another such that an unregulated market "never finds ontological reality" (Randles, 2003, p. 420). Regardless, recourse to embeddedness assumes and

8 "The commodity description of labour, land and money is entirely fictitious" (Polanyi, 1944, p. 76). This is no evidence that Polanyi was aware of Vaihinger's theory of fictions, or his "as if" theory, although there are resonances here (Samuel, 2021).

presumes the market; placing its "black box" where it is no longer available to sociological analysis or reinterpretation. Accordingly, the problem is more one of terminology giving rise to a misleading concept than vice versa; "[w]e can't have it both ways" (Randles, 2003, p. 423). Instead, a "richly *interdependent* mixture of social and economic inter-play exists", echoing Krippner's assertion that "every transaction [...] is *social* in the broader sense of the term" (Randles, 2003, p. 423; Krippner *et al.*, 2004, p. 112).

Finally, the economistic nature of Polanyi's reasoning has been identified as problematic, in that Polanyi relied on his understanding of the neoclassical economics of the time in order to construct his critique (Gemici, 2015). In relying heavily on his own interpretations of marginalist theory of value and neoclassical equilibrium analysis, we are locked into arguments based on market mentalities (Mann, 1986; Gemici, 2015). As a result, the reduction of the market to an "automaton" is problematic in a similar way to that in which criticisms of mainstream economics orthodoxy sometimes build up a straw man of the discipline in order to justify knocking it down. Any "one dimensional view" of the market, delineated with neat boundaries stands in opposition to contemporary sociology's demonstration "that the market's contradictions arise from how its symbols, values, rationalities, and organizational patterns affect the coherence, stability, and reproduction of other institutions in society" (Gemici, 2015, p. 126).

Critiques of micro-level embeddedness

Such intractable dichotomies in the literature (micro/macro, social or economic embeddedness) have prompted some writers to throw in the towel. Mark Granovetter has pessimistically noted that embeddedness has come to mean "all things to all people so that it is meaningless" (Krippner *et al.*, 2004, p. 113). Kerry Rittich has described embeddedness as "devoid of all meaning" (Rittich, 2014, pp. 323–4). Greta Krippner has noted that the concept is "paradoxical", leading economic sociologists to "take the market itself for granted" and leaving it unavailable to sociological analysis (Krippner *et al.*, 2004; Dale, 2011, p. 328). Embeddedness is so central to economic sociology and consequently ESL that, for Krippner, it would be virtually impossible to discard the term even if we wanted to (Krippner *et al.*, 2004, pp. 110, 125). This is a relatively common position, along with the belief that while embeddedness is useful for "tackling the absolutization of the market", "the idea of embeddedness itself is embedded in a context or system of cultural and social structures" (Barber, 1995, p. 388).

Reconciling macro- and micro-level embeddedness?

If we don't throw in the towel or concede that Polanyian and Granovetterian embeddedness are "two distinct intellectual projects", we are left with the task of reconciling them (Krippner and Alvarez, 2007, p. 219). There is a consensus that embeddedness has had one, albeit confusing, career in economic sociology and ESL as a metaphor, as a theoretical lens, and as a methodological tool (Portes and Sensenbrenner, 1993; Barber, 1995; Hart, 2004; Beckert, 2009; Mckeever, Anderson and Jack, 2014, p. 222). However, the implications of this fudge can be seen in more recent literature where embeddedness is frequently used without definition or delineation (Earle, Moran and Ward-Perkins, 2017; Raworth, 2018; Mazzucato, 2021). Once we understand that embeddedness is a generative metaphor, perpetuating the separation of law, economy, and society, and reproducing neoclassical economic rationalities, we can begin to appreciate that the concept has direct implications for how we respond to crashes and crises; how we understand the role and relationships between the economy, its regulation, and the society that performs these.

It is helpful to rehearse attempts to reconcile Polanyian (macro-level) and Granovetterian (micro-level) iterations of embeddedness, starting with a return to the diagram in Figure 3.1 on page 76 which sets out the key iterations of embeddedness according to Frerichs' four levels of social interaction that were introduced in Chapter 2 and set out initially in Figure 2.2 on page 54.

While schema seeking to reconcile both micro- and macro-level applications of embeddedness have been proposed, and these are explored in the following chapter, more recent scholarship has proposed alternative approaches.

Firstly, we might note at least two meanings of Polanyian "embeddedness" that can be drawn from *The Great Transformation*, with a third, Granovetterian, interpretation added later (Ashiagbor, 2014, p. 267). This approach sees that, firstly, "all economies and economic behaviour are embedded to the extent that markets are constructed rather than being natural" while secondly, the "idea that embeddedness differs from one economic system to another", leading to variations in the "*degree* of enmeshment" (Ashiagbor, 2014, p. 267). Alternatively, we might impose a conceptual superstructure that overarches the micro to macro levels, encompassing all interpretations that then sit within it. This approach understands the relations between law, economy, and society across four layers of interaction; micro, meso, macro, and meta (Frerichs, 2011). By superimposing an overarching structure onto the two forms of embeddedness, Granovetter's actors in networks occur at the micro and meso levels of interactions between actors and institutions as seen in Figure 3.1 on page 76. Similarly, Polanyi's embeddedness of markets occurs at the macro level of regimes where we see the interconnections between institutions. Additionally, we can place Evans' "embedded autonomy" at the macro level, while Ruggie's "embedded liberalism" sits more comfortably at the metalevel of rationalities, or the basic principles located in the deep structure and culture of society.

Reconciling the implications: cognitive and normative embeddedness

But there is more. This fourfold ranking, or structure, then offers us the notions of cognitive and normative embeddedness which can then reconcile theories of *dis*embedding at both macro (Polanyian) level and micro (Granovetterian) level (Frerichs, 2011). By *dis*embedding, we can imagine those financial crashes, social crises, and environmental catastrophes that lurk as the ominous backdrop to this discussion: those contexts where we wonder if the economy is really serving society's goals and aspirations, and where we ask whether all voices are being heard equally. For Polanyi looking back to the Industrial Revolution, the market could never become fully disembedded because the social havoc this would wreak on the population was too great. The state would always have to step in to temper the worst impacts of the self-regulating market and regulate to re-embed the economy.

But, using the example of an ESL lens set out in Chapter 2 that combines elements of Roger Cotterrell's community lens with Sabine Frerichs' four rankings of social interaction, we can identify two aspects to any *dis*embedding, although, consistent with other ESL notions, different terms have been applied to similar concepts throughout the literature. While Sabine Frerichs gives us cognitive and normative disembedding, Amanda Perry-Kessaris uses the terms analytical and normative disembedding (Frerichs, 2011; Perry-Kessaris, 2011). By moving the analytical in line with the cognitive, we can then see that there is a distinct argument here about what happens when our ways of doing and thinking come to be dominated by the economic, and when both shift out of alignment with the reality of market interactions.

Cognitive (or what Perry-Kessaris terms "analytical") embeddedness describes the meta level of rationalities and its epistemic effect on actors, relations, and regimes (Frerichs, 2011, p. 7). A cognitively disembedded approach, then, is one "that thinks of *society as economy*" (Perry-Kessaris, 2011, p. 405). Here, then, neoclassical economic concepts and relationships become the mould into which all other types of social relations are poured, meaning that affective, traditional, and belief-based (inter)actions are understood through a mainstream economics lens. They are understood, but then also performed and become re-co-constructed through this lens.

The flip side to this coin is normative embeddedness, which relates to the macro level of regimes and its normative impact on micro- and meso-level phenomena. A normatively disembedded approach, then, is one that "puts economy *be(for)e society*" (Perry-Kessaris, 2011, p. 405). It produces regimes that privilege economic values and interests, "claiming this to be for the good of all", but once again (re)moulding all other types of action in its own image (Perry-Kessaris, 2011, p. 405).

Both cognitive embeddedness at the meta level and normative embeddedness at the macro level can, and frequently do, shift around independently. The problems begin to arise when our levels of cognitive and normative embeddedness no longer align; what Polanyi (and Frerichs) term a "state of crisis" (Frerichs, 2011). This might be when our ways of thinking and our ways of doing are out of kilter, or we perceive that the economy (or, for the purposes of the discussion here, the law) is no longer serving the goals that society aspires to. At this point, there is usually a need for the state to step in and use the law to bring our regimes and rationalities back into line with each other: to make sure that the market economy is serving society and meeting those shared expectations a society holds. For Frerichs, while cognitive embeddedness can be described as ubiquitous, normative embeddedness is contingent, and subject to these state interventions to reshape regimes, to decide what markets can and cannot do, and to ensure that boundaries protect us all from what Polanyi identified as the worst excesses of the free, self-regulating market (Frerichs, 2011, p. 7).

ACADEMIC ANN

Ann looks over her diagrams again at the macro and meta levels. She wonders what cognitive embeddedness might mean for her investors and the state in which they have chosen to build business relations. Then her mind wanders to the investment bank that suggested (rather strongly, and with strings attached) that the state carries out legal reforms in order to make the country more attractive to foreign investors. This had, of course, been common practice 20 years ago, but more questions were now being asked.

For Ann, it seemed like cognitive embeddedness referred to the mental models – the rationalities or those concepts and relationships – that the bank used to issue advice to developing states. By advising legal reform, the bank was implementing rationalities that were based on the economic value of law and its potential to catalyse the economy of the host state. Other factors and unintended consequences that might fall on other sectors or groups within society were rarely considered, and this had had some unfortunate implications for local communities and domestic businesses that Ann had witnessed first-hand over the years. Yes, she thought, cognitive embeddedness was those mental models that privileged economic voices above all others.

By the same token, then, normative embeddedness identified the degree to which these concepts and relationships were constructed at a macro level in the form of regimes. She realized now that regimes such as "the economy" or "the law" could only be performed if actors shared similar mental models and had similar goals. But if these were overwhelmingly those of neoclassical economics, the regimes produced at the macro level would resemble neoclassical economic institutions. So, economic voices – those of foreign investors – would be prioritized above those of non-economic voices such as local communities and those who might have other (affective, traditional, or belief-based) priorities.

Suddenly, the riots a few years ago became clear through this lens. The local community had seen their ancestral lands taken with little in the way of compensation. On what had once been shared land with community buildings now stood a shiny new export processing zone. A lucky few had secured jobs, but the promises of schools and hospitals had never materialized. Shouts of "over our dead bodies" and striking images of police beating down protestors had briefly made the international news headlines, but then the world's attention had moved on. Ann realized that this had been a clear case of a conflict of regimes and rationalities. Both cognitive and normative disembedding had occurred here: the government wanted to follow the advice of the investment bank and had wanted to attract increasing amounts of foreign investment through the construction of export processing zones. The laws had been amended, both to appropriate the land, but also to create economic zones where tax was lower and employment rights less onerous for employers. The regimes and rationalities of the central government had been overwhelmingly economic. By contrast, the protesters cared for their affective, traditional, and belief-based attachment to the land. And yet, the only way they could express this was in economic terms… and then, when that didn't work, in violence.

There are two advantages of using cognitive and normative embeddedness to understand how regimes and rationalities coalesce and coexist over time. Firstly, this approach allows us to ask "how much": how much economy is shaping the way we do, talk, and think? To what extent are our mental models and our ways of performing aligning, and how much are they being shaped by neoclassical economic theory? Being able to ask "how much" means we can compare groups within society – so Ann can understand the needs of investors as well as those of civil society groups, local and central government, local businesses, and so on. Additionally, we can compare how our ways of thinking and doing change over time. Secondly, cognitive embeddedness, or the manifestation of our rationalities or mental models, identifies sites at which meaning is attributed and shared within and between groups. This is the phenomenological dimension, and allows us to focus on how we understand, and how these sites of shared expectations can be communicated, or how, in the case of the protestors that Ann read about, these communication channels might fail when one group seeks to communicate goals that simply do not fit into the dominant regimes or rationalities. Additionally, this inclusion of rationalities, or the epistemic categories that organize our perceptions of reality, offers a space for addressing the incompatibility of embeddedness with constructivism.

But, while conceptually neat, this approach requires a good deal more terminology. In conflating Frerichs' and Perry-Kessaris' suggestions for the sake of streamlining the terms, some nuance might have been elided. The cognitive and normative embeddedness thesis succeeds in fleshing out Ashiagbor's interpretation, and superficially places Polanyian and Granovetterian notions of embeddedness on the same page. For Ann, this provides a valuable conceptual tool for understanding the riots that occurred in the country she is travelling to and the processes that brought about the unrest. Polly, on the other hand, is busy and unsure what a deep understanding of cognitive and normative disembedding brings to her understanding. She can see that rationalities and regimes have become internally dominated by economistic thinking, to the detriment of other voices and values, and that some rebalancing might be beneficial. She can see that such a rebalancing exercise might allow different voices and the values and interests of a plurality of groups to be held in focus equally.

Finally, Lillian, by contrast, wonders why Ann had to make everything so complicated. Lillian could already see that the economy was privileged in mainstream discourse and in the way we think – she could see this just by looking for clues in how we talk, those metaphors and little fictions that seep into our consciousness and mould our thoughts and actions. She could appreciate that our cognitive and linguistic tools were somewhat separate from what was happening in real life, and could understand that when our ways of doing, talking, and thinking were misaligned, the potential existed for misunderstandings to occur, or worse. While the chapters that follow take a step back from embeddedness, and therefore avoid getting tangled up in cognitive or normative disembedding, there are two examples of embeddedness-talk from the fields of political economy and international industrial relations respectively that are worth exploration. Both have been more successful, or perhaps less controversial, in applying the concept of embeddedness than approaches in ES (economic sociology) and ESL and offer us clues as to how embeddedness might be deployed in certain contexts.

POLICY POLLY

Polly put the phone down after a long conversation with Ann about the literature linking legal reform with economic development. They had agreed that the literature tends to establish correlation rather than causation between law and economic development. Even then, it tends to use proxy indicators for both law and development.

At the time, Polly had filled Ann in on an RCT (a randomized controlled trial) that she had been overseeing. This method had much to commend, and RCTs could a begin to address causation. But the various RCT methods had drawbacks too. The results tended to be localized and it was often difficult to generalize from one region to another or extract general principles. Their internal validity (biases and assumptions) could be estimated, but their external validity often posed greater challenges. Thirdly, it was simply impossible to run an RCT in the real world without politics getting involved, either at a government level, a stakeholder level, or a participant level.

Chatting with Ann, Polly explained that she thought that experimentalism in development was a great leap forward, but that the most robust approaches at the moment combined experimental with non-experimental approaches. As such, she thought aloud, some of the structure and taxonomies of an ESL might help her to address and balance some of the non-economic considerations: the political, the moral, the spiritual, and the ethical considerations that all played a part, but which had a tendency to be masked by supposedly scientific, neutral approaches.

How might we make embeddedness more consistent?

If we zoom out a little from economic sociology and ESL literature, there are two iterations of embeddedness that give us clues as to how the concept can be used more successfully. Granovetter's revival of embeddedness came hot on the heels of John Gerard Ruggie's proposal of "embedded liberalism" in the field of international relations in 1982 which sought to marry Polanyian embeddedness with constructivist approaches to law. Then, in 1995, American sociologist Peter B. Evans published his account of the role of state institutions in enabling development. He proposed a theory of "embedded autonomy" that, like Ruggie's embedded liberalism, juxtaposed embeddedness with an equal-and-opposing force to create an oxymoronic descriptor of dynamic relations. It's worth saying a little about each before drawing conclusions about the career of embeddedness.

Embedded liberalism

In 1982, John Ruggie published his study of the post-war international trade and monetary regimes, *International Regimes, Transactions and Change: Embedded Liberalism in the Postwar Economic Order.* This challenged the assumption that the international economic order was "orthodox liberal", instead proposing that "it was characterized by a political commitment to what he called 'embedded liberalism'" (Lang, 2006, pp. 81–2). Ruggie has stated that he "adapted this term from Polanyi [1944]" in an initial bid to "reconcile the efficiency of the markets with the broader values of social community – 'embedding' markets, in short" (Ruggie, 2016, p. 2). His choice of term recalled Polanyi's thesis of the "disembedding of economic from social life", while reflecting the fact that "in the postwar GATT [General Agreement on Tariffs and Trade], the liberalism of freer trade was embedded in a deeper commitment to an interventionist programme of governmental social action" (Lang, 2006, pp. 87–8). The essence of embedded liberalism is set out by Ruggie as "devis[ing] a form of multilateralism that is compatible with the requirements of domestic stability" (Ruggie, 1982, p. 399). This pull of opposing forces – multilateralism versus domestic stability, international openness versus domestic cushioning, economic efficiency versus social stability – presents the "Grand Compromise" of embedded liberalism as an oxymoron, carefully balancing the dynamic and flexible relationship between markets and the state–citizen dyad. These balancing acts are set out in Figure 3.2.

Ruggie's theory echoes Polanyi's original thesis and, in its careful definition and selective application to the international economic order, stands up to the first challenge to our conceptual commitment to embeddedness: its internal inconsistency. So, careful and precise definitions are crucial here, as is Ruggie's avoidance of overarching statements of applicability. Then, the continual flux between the opposing forces maintains a dynamism that echoes Polanyi's thesis. Ruggie's theory of embedded liberalism challenged hegemonic stability theory and the narrative that the post-war order was one of orthodox liberalism. Instead, it argues for attention to be paid to the state–society dyad and the role this has in balancing, regulating, and re-co-constructing the economic sphere. We might visualize it as image (c) in Figure 3.2.

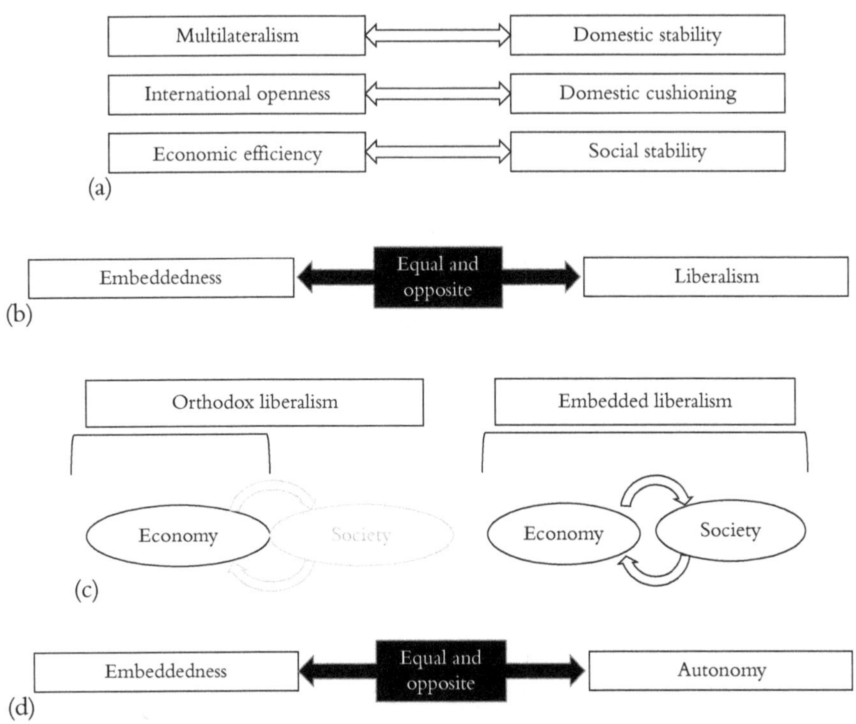

Figure 3.2 Images (a), (b), and (c) visualize dimensions of Ruggie's "Grand Compromise" of embedded liberalism, with opposing forces that counterbalance each other, acting flexibly, dynamically, and responsively. Image (d) visualizes the similar oxymoron that we find in Evans' theory of embedded autonomy.

The constructivist point, or the phenomenological dimension, is also central here – the site at which shared experiences and expectations occur, or the site at which our rationalities or mental models are shaped. Ruggie explicitly confirms this as a constructivist approach, borrowing notions from Giddens' theory of structuration and applying them to his analysis of international economic relations (Ruggie, 1998). This, then, attempts to marry Polanyian embeddedness with social constructivism in the specific context of international regimes in a similar, albeit more straightforward, account to Frerichs'.[9] While "the concept[s] of embedded liberalism and the analytical perspective of social constructivism soon gained currency among international relations scholars", they were slow to be taken up by policy makers (Ruggie, 2016, p. 3). However, embedded liberalism as an idea was also taken up by more mainstream economists and others interested in the impact of economic globalization on domestic social protection, and this is, perhaps, the vessel in which Polanyi's notion of embeddedness has travelled the furthest.

Embedded autonomy

A decade later, Peter Evans' *Embedded Autonomy: States and Industrial Transformation* explored the role of the state in enabling or facilitating economic development in Brazil, India, and Korea. Evans challenged the narrative that the economic successes of these countries had been the result of the operation of free markets. Evans noted that the internal organization of the archetypal developmental state approximated to the Weberian ideal of bureaucracy (Evans, 1995, p. 12). However, contrary to Weber's suggestion that bureaucracies be isolated from the rest of society, Evans notes that "they are embedded in a concrete set of social ties that binds the state to society and provides institutionalized channels for the continual negotiation and re-negotiation of goals and policies" (Evans, 1995, p. 12). "Embedded autonomy" stands up to the first question set out here of the internal inconsistency of embeddedness.

In Evans' "embedded autonomy", the "apparently contradictory combination of corporate coherence and connectedness" itself "provides the underlying structural basis for successful state involvement in industrial transformation" (Evans, 1995, p. 12). Evans cites Polanyi's keen sense of the extent to which markets are dependent on state action, writing that "the life of the market has

9 An alternative reading of Ruggie's constructivist embeddedness is possible, whereby the approach is one of a constructivism *of embeddedness itself*. So, the phenomenological dimension of markets and societies is taken to be embedded, rather than the actual social phenomena themselves. Thus, trade liberalization as a shared notion or set of shared experiences, and domestic social protectionism as a set of shared expectations, might be seen as shifting from being embedded the one in the other, to a state of floating free. This is in contrast to Polanyi's, and later Raworth's, Earle's, and Mazzucato's, uses of embeddedness, and, echoing Frerichs' and Perry-Kessaris' reading of Polanyi, offers a more nuanced approach.

been intertwined not just with other kinds of social ties, but with the forms and policies of the state" (Evans, 1995, pp. 22, 29). Moreover, "[a]n effective state was not simply an adjunct to the market", but "it was an essential prerequisite of the formation of market relations" (Evans, 1995, p. 29).

Evans' use of embeddedness has been praised for avoiding some of the pitfalls outlined in this book, raising the importance of the "context in which certain ideas are deployed and developed" (Krippner *et al.*, 2004, pp. 131–2). Nevertheless, Granovetter questions Evans' static use of the term, noting that he "lacked a dynamic argument" as to how and why bureaucracies became autonomous, become embedded, or change over time (Krippner *et al.*, 2004, p. 124).

Once again, like Ruggie, Evans sets "embeddedness" against an equal-and-opposite force. This acts as an oxymoronic descriptor of relations between industry and bureaucracy that is both dynamic and flexible. Embeddedness and autonomy are understood to pull in opposite directions, with embeddedness providing sources of intelligence and channels of implementation and autonomy protecting the state from piecemeal capture and creeping clientelism. Again, the context is carefully defined, and Evans is at pains to emphasize that he is not proposing a theory that has general applicability or that might scale up. The lens concretizes the structural relations that lie behind the efficacy of the ideal-typical developmental state, but it does not fully capture variations in state involvement across sectors and circumstances.

However, the second charge of external incompatibility (the black box conundrum) still raises some questions. If investor–state relations are described as "mutually reinforcing", it is reasonable to suggest some degree of constructivism here (Evans, 1995, p. 63). If embeddedness assumes the conceptual distinction of the phenomena under consideration, and if these mutually reconstruct themselves, there is a mismatch. This is alleviated to a certain extent by the inclusion of "autonomy" and the dynamism of the oxymoron. However, the spectre of the black box has not entirely been avoided.

Reconciling the insights?

There are some takeaways from the works of Ruggie and Evans, however, that are summarized in Table 3.1 on page 88. Firstly, when juxtaposed with an equal-and-opposite force (either liberalism or autonomy), embeddedness can regain some of the dynamism and flexibility originally implied by the term. Secondly, when concepts and terms are carefully defined, empirically grounded, and applied conservatively to a specific set of circumstances, the concept of embeddedness can be applied to great effect. Nevertheless, while these can assist the concept of embeddedness in overcoming the first criticism levelled in this book – that of internal inconsistency – they remain vulnerable to the second challenge – incompatibility with constructivist approaches. This is despite Ruggie's carefully defined, explicitly constructivist frame that he

Table 3.1 Lessons from Ruggie and Evans on using embeddedness as a metaphor

Embeddedness +	*Example*
Equal-and-opposite force	Liberalism Autonomy
Careful definition	The "what are we talking about?" question that requires a careful and precise response that refrains from sweeping or general statements
Empirical grounding	Based on careful observation of real-world phenomena

argues is necessary as a way of approaching the phenomenological dimension of law, or the understanding of law's reproduction at sites of shared expectations and meaning.

Both Evans' and Ruggie's approaches can be understood as "Polanyian-*inspired*" rather than "Polanyian-*given*", and both Evans and Ruggie rely on empirical analysis rather than any "taken-for-granted" entry point (Randles, 2003, pp. 409–10). We might then see both Evans and Ruggie, as well as Granovetter, as three "pathways out of Polanyi" (Hart, 2004, p. 123).[10] The first of these is the argument that the "developmental state" was the decisive factor in the East Asian "miracles", challenging the neoliberal market narrative of the economic growth (Hart, 2004, p. 123). The second sees embeddedness as a "neo-Weberian" perspective that requires a "kinder, gentler" capitalism, in particular associated with the World Bank, and echoes Ruggie's "embedded liberalism" (Hart, 2004, p. 123; Dale, 2011, p. 326). The third sees the term taken up by Granovetter in 1985 and translated into the core concept of economic sociology and ESL, developing into a conceptual commitment to the term.

The embeddedness conundrum is reinvented

ACADEMIC ANN

When they had spoken, Polly had described an RCT (a randomized controlled trial) that was in progress. Polly had been excited about the potential for the study but had listed some of the limitations and drawbacks. Mulling these over, Ann wondered what an ESL lens could add to experimental approaches in economic development.

Ann didn't want to make any grand, definitive claims. The combination of experimental and non-experimental methods in development had grown up so that each could (try to) compensate for the perceived methodological weaknesses

10 Hart suggests only two pathways. The third pathway here echoes Ashiagbor's "third interpretation" (Ashiagbor, 2014, pp. 268–9).

of the other. But, in combining methodologies, Ann did wonder if a sociological approach embodied in an ESL lens could offer structures and taxonomies for comprehensively considering the non-economic on an even footing with the economic. Might an ESL lens, she wondered, offer a way of highlighting Block's moral or spiritual commitments, or Weber's affective, traditional, and belief-based interaction ideal-type aspects? And, if so, could this be beneficial for the contextualization, analysis, and wider generalizability of experimental data?

There was a consensus in literature reflecting on the 2008 financial crash that the relationships between the economy, its regulation, and the society that these were supposed to serve had become dysfunctional. To recap briefly, the arguments noted that the economy (and its regulation) has become "disembedded" from society. Therefore, the economy (and its regulation) should be "re-embedded" in order to make the economy (and its regulation) work better for society. In identifying the relationships between the spheres of law, economy, and society as the site of one problem that led to the financial crash, the concept of embeddedness offered a superficially helpful descriptive tool to identify, and remedy, the problem. Indeed, the concept continues to function as a universal coat hook on which the distance between law, economy, and society could be hung. In so doing, it also suggests an equally superficially attractive and accessible solution: re-embed the economy (and its regulation) in society and voilà; problems of inequality, injustice, unfairness, and so on will disappear. This has become such a popular mechanism for debating the future relationship between law, economy, and society, heightened in the light of additional social crises and looming environmental catastrophes, that the concept and the heavy lifting we are asking it to do have become invisible. Yet, in the context of a drive to reintegrate the disciplines – one of the goals of an ESL lens – an ongoing conceptual commitment to embeddedness becomes problematic.

To appreciate the depth of confusion surrounding our ongoing use of the concept, Chapter 4 zooms in to compare in detail two analyses of specifically Polanyian embeddedness, namely those of Fred Block and Gareth Dale. It then shifts to compare how these analyses have been reincarnated in literature that responds to the 2008 financial crash, namely Kate Raworth's *Doughnut Economics* and Earle *et al.*'s *The Econocracy*. Then, by comparing and contrasting Raworth and Earle with the theoretical insights of Ruggie's "embedded liberalism" and of Evans' "embedded autonomy", we can appreciate that broader discourse in the wake of the 2008 crash remains vulnerable to both challenges mounted in this book. Lessons from Ruggie and Evans help us to respond to the first criticism levelled at embeddedness in this book: the "what are we talking about?" conundrum. But neither Ruggie nor Evans can rescue embeddedness from the second limitation: the "how are we talking about it?" dilemma.

To explore how and why this matters, and the extent to which we should care, Chapter 4 turns to the details of the differences that result when different interpretations of embeddedness are used.

Bibliography

Ashiagbor, D. (2013) 'Unravelling the Embedded Liberal Bargain: Labour and Social Welfare Law in the Context of EU Market Integration', *European Law Journal*, 19(3), pp. 303–324.

Ashiagbor, D. (2014) 'Embedding Trade Liberalisation in Social Policy: A Research Agenda on Social Regionalism and the Global South', *Northern Ireland Legal Quarterly*, 65(3), pp. 265–281.

Ashiagbor, D., Kotiswaran, P. and Perry-Kessaris, A. (2013) 'Introduction: Moving towards an Economic Sociology of Law', *Journal of Law and Society*,40, pp. 1–6.

Barber, B. (1995) 'All Economies are 'Embedded': The Career of a Concept, and Beyond', *Social Research*, 62(2), pp. 387–413.

Beckert, J. (2009) 'The Great Transformation of Embeddedness: Karl Polanyi and the New Economic Sociology', in Chris Hann and Keith Hart (eds) *Market and Society: The Great Transformation Today*. New York: Cambridge University Press, pp. 38–55. Available at: https://papers.ssrn.com/sol3/papers.cfm?abstract_id=2465810.

Block, F. (2001) 'Introduction', in *The Great Transformation, Karl Polanyi*. Boston: Beacon Press, pp. xviii–xxxviii. https://inctpped.ie.ufrj.br/spiderweb/pdf_4/Great_Transformation.pdf.

Block, F. (2003) 'Karl Polanyi and the Writing of the Great Transformation', *Theory and Society*, 32(3), pp. 275–306.

Christensen, J. (2018) 'Economic Knowledge and the Scientization of Policy Advice', *Policy Sciences*, 51(3), pp. 291–311. https://doi.org/10.1007/s11077-018-9316-6.

Cotterrell, R. (2013) 'Rethinking Embeddedness; Law, Economy, Community', *Journal of Law and Society*, 40(1), pp. 49–67.

Dale, G. (2010) *Karl Polanyi: The Limits of the Market*. 1st ed. Cambridge and Malden: Polity.

Dale, G. (2011) 'Lineages of Embeddedness: On the Antecedents and Successors of a Polanyian Concept', *The American Journal of Economics and Sociology*, 70(2), pp. 306–339.

Dale, G. (2016) *Karl Polanyi: A Life on the Left*. 1st ed. New York: Columbia University Press.

Earle, J., Moran, C. and Ward-Perkins, Z. (2017) *The Econocracy: On the Perils of Leaving Economics to the Experts*. Kindle Edition. Penguin Books. https://www.penguin.co.uk/books/307289/the-econocracy-by-joe-earle-cahal-moran-and-zach-ward-perkins/9780141986869.

Evans, P. (1995) *Embedded Autonomy: States and Industrial Transformation*. Princeton: Princeton University Press.

Frerichs, S. (2011) 'Re-Embedding Neoliberal Constitutionalism: A Polanyian Case for the Economic Sociology of Law', in C. Joerges and J. Falke (eds) *Karl Polanyi, Globalisation, and the Potential of Law in Transnational Markets*. Oxford: Hart Publishing (International Studies in the Theory of Private Law, Vol.8), pp. 65–84.

Gemici, K. (2015) 'The Neo-Classical Origins of Polanyi's Self-Regulating Market', *Sociological Theory*, 33(2), pp. 125–147.

Giddens, A. (1979) *Central Problems in Social Theory: Action, Structure and Contradiction in Social Analysis*. Berkeley and Los Angeles: University of California Press.

Granovetter, M. (1985) 'Economic Action and Social Structure: The Problem of Embeddedness', *American Journal of Sociology*, 91(3), pp. 481–510.

Hart, G. (2004) 'The Career of the Concept of Embeddedness', in Krippner et al. (eds) *Polanyi Symposium: A Conversation on Embeddedness. Socio-Economic Review*, 2(1), pp. 109–135.

Krimsky, S. and Golding, D. (eds) (1992) *Social Theories of Risk*. New York: Praeger.

Krippner, G. (2001) 'The Elusive Market: Embeddedness and the Paradigm of Economic Sociology', *Theory and Society*, 30(6), pp. 775–810.

Krippner, G. et al. (2004) 'Polanyi Symposium: A Conversation on Embeddedness', *Socio-Economic Review*, 2, pp. 109–135.

Krippner, G. and Alvarez, A.S. (2007) 'Embeddedness and the Intellectual Projects of Economic Sociology', *Annual Review of Sociology*, 33, pp. 219–240.

Kuhn, T. (1970) *The Structure of Scientific Revolutions*. 2nd ed. Chicago: University of Chicago Press.

Lakoff, G. and Johnson, M. (1980) *Metaphors We Live By*. Chicago: University of Chicago Press.

Lang, A. (2006) 'Reconstructing Embedded Liberalism: John Gerard Ruggie and Constructivist Approaches to the Study of the International Trade Regime', *Journal of International Economic Law*, 9(1), pp. 81–116.

Lie, J. (1997) 'Sociology of Markets', *Annual Review of Sociology*, 23, pp. 341–60.

Mann, M. (1986) *The Sources of Social Power: Volume 1: A History of Power from the Beginning to AD 1760*. Cambridge: Cambridge University Press.

Maucourant, J. and Plociniczak, S. (2013) 'The Institution, the Economy and the Market: Karl Polanyi's Institutional Thought for Economists', *Review of Political Economy*, 25(3), pp. 512–531. https://doi.org/10.1080/09538259.2013.807675.

Mazzucato, M. (2021) *Mission Economy: A Moonshot Guide to Changing Capitalism*. Penguin. https://www.penguin.co.uk/books/315191/mission-economy-by-mazzucato-mariana/9780141991689.

Mckeever, E., Anderson, A. and Jack, S. (2014) 'Social Embeddedness in Entrepreneurship Research: The Importance of Context and Community', in pp. 222–236. https://doi.org/10.4337/9781849809245.00022.

Park, R.E. (1924) 'The Concept of Social Distance', *Journal of Applied Sociology*, 8, pp. 339–344.

Perry-Kessaris, A.J. (2011) 'Reading the Story of Law and Embeddedness Through a Community Lens: A Polanyi-Meets-Cotterrell Economic Sociology of Law?', *Northern Ireland Legal Quarterly* (Special Issue on *Socialising Economic Relationships*), 62(4), pp. 401–413.

Perry-Kessaris, A.J. (2012) 'What Does it Mean to Take a Socio-Legal Approach to International Economic Law?', in *Socio-Legal Approaches to International Economic Law: Text, Context, Subtext*. Routledge. Available at: https://papers.ssrn.com/sol3/papers.cfm?abstract_id=2085007.

Polanyi, K. (1944) *The Great Transformation: The Political and Economic Origins of Our Time*. 2nd ed. Princeton: Beacon Press.

Polanyi, K. (1957) 'The Economy as Instituted Process', in Karl Polanyi, C.M. Arensberg and M.W. Pearson (eds) *Trade and Market in the Early Empires*. New York: The Free Press. Available at: http://irows.ucr.edu/cd/courses/281/readings/polanyi.pdf.

Portes, A. and Sensenbrenner, J. (1993) 'Embeddedness and Immigration: Notes on the Social Determinants of Economic Action', *American Journal of Sociology*, 98(6), pp. 1320–1350.

Randles, S. (2003) 'Issues for a Neo-Polanyian Research Agenda in Economic Sociology', *International Review of Sociology*, 13(2), pp. 409–434. https://doi.org/10.1080/0390670032000117353.

Raworth, K. (2018) *Doughnut Economics: Seven Ways to Think Like a 21st-Century Economist.* ebook (Kindle). Random House Business. https://www.penguin.co.uk/books/429710/doughnut-economics-by-kate-raworth/9781847941398.

Rittich, K. (2014) 'Making Natural Markets: Flexibility as Labour Market Truth', *Northern Ireland Legal Quarterly*, 65(3), pp. 323–345.

Ruggie, J.G. (1982) 'International Regimes, Transactions and Change: Embedded Liberalism in the Postwar Economic Order', *International Organization*, 36(2), pp. 379–415.

Ruggie, J.G. (1998) 'What Makes the World Hang Together? Neo-Utilitarianism and the Social Constructivist Challenge', *International Organization*, 52(4), pp. 855–885.

Ruggie, J.G. (2016) *Embedding Global Markets: An Enduring Challenge.* London: Routledge.

Samuel, G. (2021) 'The Epistemological Challenge: Does Law Exist?', in S. Glanert, A. Mercescu and G. Samuel (eds) *Rethinking Comparative Law.* Cheltenham: Elgar Online (Rethinking Law Series), pp. 1–30.

Simmel, G. (1950) *The Sociology of Georg Simmel.* Translated by K. Wolff. New York: The Free Press.

Uzzi, B. (1997) 'Social Structure and Competition in Interfirm Networks: The Paradox of Embeddedness', *Administrative Science Quarterly*, 42(1), pp. 35–67.

Weber, M. (1946) 'Class, Status, Party', in H. H. Gerth and C. W. Mills (eds) *From Max Weber: Essays in Sociology*, 1948, but transferred to digital printing in 2007. Abingdon, Oxon: Routledge, pp. 180–195

Chapter 4

Embeddedness

The internal inconsistencies

The internal inconsistency of embeddedness: "what are we talking about?"

ACADEMIC ANN

Having been through the literature on embeddedness, Ann knew that there were many and varied interpretations of this metaphor, and that the arguments ranged in complexity from the bold assertions to the subtle nuances. So far, embeddedness had offered a convenient way of talking about the relationships between different regimes and rationalities, between the legal and the economic.

Explaining it to Polly, though, hadn't been a great success. Shades of nuance that work well in academic inquiry don't always translate well to real-world policy contexts. But, Ann muses, when the nuance is removed, and we talk of the embeddedness (or otherwise) of the economy and the law in society, too much is lost. Ann can see her neighbour, Lillian, rolling her eyes again at the "fancy words" and smiles to herself, making a silent promise to both Polly and to Lillian to keep her empirical application of the embeddedness literature as straightforward and real-world-ready as possible while retaining as much nuance and colour as she can.

In January 2008, Cyprus and Malta joined the euro, while in the US, the presidential primaries were getting underway. The international price of gold reached new heights, whilst territorial, political, and ideological disputes played out in countries including Sri Lanka, Kenya, and Pakistan. All of these have since been eclipsed by the snowballing events of late January that spiralled into one of the most significant market shocks in a generation: "the financial crash". Technically, this title is misleading – other regions had had, and have had since,

DOI: 10.4324/9781003354819-4

financial crashes to rival that experienced by "the West" (aka Wall Street).[1] But, only three weeks into 2008, stock markets began tumbling as the full extent of the subprime lending crisis became clear. While hopes, dreams, and even lives were ended over the following 24 months, and promises of regulation flurried across Western news outlets, the upheaval also sparked a wave of literature analyzing the causes of the crash. Many of these identified one of the problems as the (metaphorical) distance between the (metaphorical) economy and society – one had become "disembedded" from the other. Accordingly, the answer was deceptively, and yet seductively, simple: we ought to re-embed the economy in society.

So far, we have seen how an economic sociology of law (ESL), as a sociological lens that can be useful for research at the interface of law and economy, developed in response to the limitations of overly narrow doctrinal legal and neoclassical economics frames, especially in fields such as development. Then, we noted how embeddedness, coined by Karl Polanyi, came to be the core concept of ESL, but with many and varied interpretations and applications. Yet ESL's ongoing commitment to the concept of embeddedness is vulnerable on two charges; firstly, on grounds of its internal inconsistency and secondly on its external incompatibility with the social constructivism that ESL aspires to. This chapter explores in detail the first charge both in the context of ESL but also in the wider context of the 2008 crash. In essence, "what is embedded, and in what", is the guiding question for the discussion that follows (Cotterrell, 2013). The wider context of why this matters is also considered.

While the previous chapter mapped out the varied career of embeddedness, noting its macro and micro level applications, the discussion here focuses on one single branch of the embeddedness family tree, namely macro-level, Polanyian embeddedness. We can compare interpretations of Polanyian embeddedness by two notable scholars of Polanyi's life and work: Fred Block and Gareth Dale. By taking the same starting point and contrasting the outcomes, the full extent of disagreement over "what is embedded and in what" it is embedded becomes clear (Cotterrell, 2013). Then, by applying both interpretations to the same set of research questions, we can, through Ann's eyes, appreciate the difference this makes on the ground. To oversimplify, while Block reads Polanyi as saying that the economy is embedded in society, Dale's interpretation argues that society has become embedded in the economy. These were visualized in Figure 1.2 in Chapter 1 (see page 9).

1 The 1997 Asian financial crisis is perhaps the most obvious example, although there have been financial crashes in Russia and Argentina and other countries around the world. The 2007–9 financial crash tends to lump together a series of events including the subprime mortgage crisis and US housing bubble, the Icelandic financial crisis and the Irish banking crisis, as well as problems in Russia, Latvia, and Venezuela amongst others. Brazil, Turkey, and China are some of the countries that have seen financial crises in the years that followed, meaning that any claim of the 2008 crash to be "the" financial crash of recent years risks accusations of Global North-induced myopia.

And yet, in the literary wave following the 2008 crash that analyzed the relationship between the economy (and its regulation) and society (and its regulation), similar claims were made. The financial crash was, the literature claims, made possible because of the dysfunctional relationships between the economy, the law, and society. The economy, it said, had become disembedded and, in response, should be re-embedded (or, as we shall see, vice versa). In popular discourse then, the concept of embeddedness grew in popularity as a convenient concept capable of capturing the problematic relationships between law, economy, and society. In the academic literature, a more subtle reading of the situation noted that our regimes and rationalities had shifted out of alignment, and that our conceptual and linguistic tools no longer reflected the reality that markets are socially constructed and performed (Frerichs, 2011; Perry-Kessaris, 2011). Embeddedness offered a catch-all term for describing suboptimal or inadequate ways of doing, talking, and thinking about economic, legal, and social relations. It even offered a superficially simple solution: re-embed the economy (and its regulation) in society.

Two works are exemplary of this literature: Kate Raworth's *Doughnut Economics* which states that the economy is embedded in society, and Joe Earle *et al.*'s *The Econocracy*, which states that society is embedded in the economy. Keen-eyed readers here will note that these two arguments map neatly onto Block's and Dale's interpretations of Polanyi. Is the economy (and its regulation) embedded in society (and its regulation)? Or is society (and its regulation) embedded in the economy (and its regulation)? This was visualized in Figure 1.3 in Chapter 1 (page 21). To explore what difference this makes, and why we should care, an exploration of ESL's ongoing conceptual commitment to embeddedness can be instructive for how we respond to crashes, crises, and catastrophes more broadly, and how we might do so better. To begin, then, we turn to Fred Block's reading of Polanyian embeddedness.

Block's interpretation of Polanyian embeddedness

ACADEMIC ANN

Ann had been mulling over her interview questions for months, but delving into the embeddedness conundrum had made her increasingly aware that the way she defines the relationships between law, economy, and society might have an impact on her research findings. Never usually one to worry too much, Ann is now anxious to get this right.

Her definition of embeddedness seems to have the effect of shifting which actors are relevant for her research, as well as the questions that might be useful.

As a starting point, she jots down some of the questions that Fred Block poses in his 2008 paper "Swimming against the Current". These, she thinks, will make a good jumping-off point for exploring the extent of the variations that result from different interpretations of embeddedness. She notes down:

- *Who are the relevant actors?*
- *What are the most relevant research questions?*
- *In what ways are transactions or contracts embedded in social relations such as family ties, friendships, or longer-term supplier–contractor relations?*
- *To what extent do non-economic goals such as moral or spiritual commitments shape economic decisions?*

Putting her pen down, Ann then realizes that the way she asks about the non-economic – including the legal – is going to be crucial and could also affect the answers she gets. In other words, Ann realizes that different definitions of embeddedness prompt her to consider the variable extent to which non-economic goals shape economic behaviour.

Noted American sociologist Fred Block has written widely and persuasively on politics and political economy, engaging frequently with the ideas and life of Karl Polanyi. Indeed, Block's work on Polanyi extends across several volumes and papers, notably taking an overview of Polanyi's historical analyses with particular emphasis on the Speenhamland system.

Block is of the opinion that embeddedness can be useful and should be retained but strengthened. To do this, he proposes a two-dimensional interpretation of Polanyian embeddedness, with the axis of high- and low-marketness intersecting that of thin and thick embeddedness. For Block, the contradictions across Polanyi's work represented an "epistemological break". While Polanyi "discovered the lost continent" of the "always-embedded economy", he didn't know quite what to call it. As such, we are left with the term "embeddedness" which fails to do the concept justice (Krippner *et al.*, 2004, p. 117).

Block's sliding scale of high- to low-marketness gives us a concept of the market as a variable or continuum, along which we can think of the market as more or less present (Block, 1990; Krippner *et al.*, 2004, p. 111). High-marketness describes a competitive market where pure (presumably neoclassical) economic theory is in operation. Low-marketness, by comparison, corresponds to "organizational hierarchies" and situations where "nonprice considerations take on greater importance" (Block, 1990, p. 53; Krippner *et al.*, 2004, p. 111). Figure 4.1 on page 97 visualizes this.

Thus, "Block notes: 'The term *market* should be reserved for situations in which relatively independent actors come together to make economic transactions of limited duration'" (Krippner *et al.*, 2004, p. 111). This removes from consideration the social aspects of all economic transactions however, and Greta Krippner notes that "[t]he strategy of economic sociology – exemplified

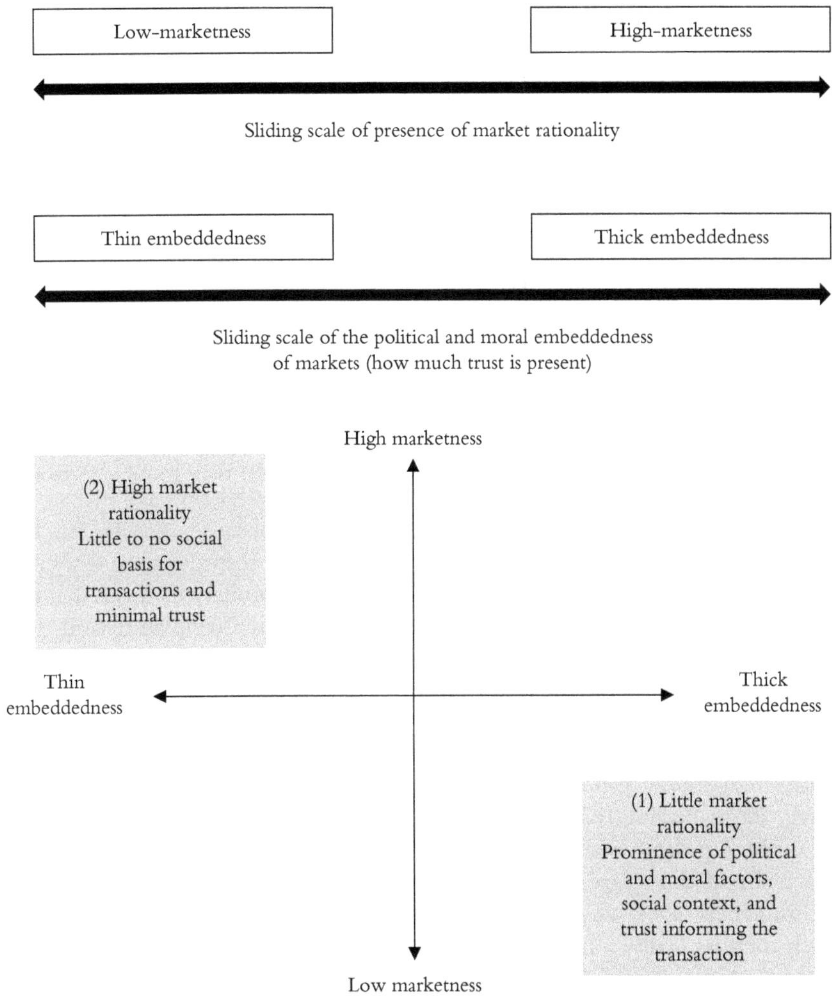

Figure 4.1 Block's low- to high-marketness (top) and thin to thick embeddedness (second). By combining these axes we can plot various types of market exchange (bottom), with the first (1) indicating little market rationality, and the second (2) with high market rationality but limited social basis for transactions.

here by Block's construction of 'marketness' – has been to whittle away at the market construct, revealing that an ever-greater share of transactions are enacted through social relationships", ignoring their intrinsic coexistence (Krippner *et al.*, 2004, p. 112).

However, we can expand this reading of embeddedness, adding a second dimension to encompass "thick" and "thin" interpretations of the term. Block's proposal is to take the concept of the "always embedded market economy" and reinvigorate it with a "thick" reading of embeddedness that takes for granted that the market is always politically embedded (Block, in Krippner *et al.*, 2004, p. 118). This can be taken as read because of the reliance of the market on legal rules, and politically designed and created institutions, and so on. But Block also goes on to state that markets must also be seen as morally embedded, for better or for worse, and that it is the "market society's guilty secret that it is fundamentally dependent on a moral order" (Krippner *et al.*, 2004, p. 118). The rationale is that the market must be morally based, but this dependency has been eclipsed over the past couple of centuries by the story that the market is a rational expression of natural evolution, and that choices made by actors are not morally-based but the mere expression of rationality. Block's contention here is that without moral embeddedness, the market would simply not function, as seen in post-Soviet Russia, and at any point where trust has evaporated and the market grinds to a halt. This addressed head on the fiction of the self-regulating market, asking us to recognize its political and moral foundations, and we might visualize this set of variables set out at the top of Figure 4.1 on page 97.

Thus, the market must be "always embedded" because it relies on the state to function. It is, therefore, always embedded in institutions and society (expressed through state action and regulation). The corollary to this is that the idea of the self-regulating market is nothing more than a utopian fiction. But in addition to being politically embedded, the market is also morally embedded because it relies on trust and a knowledge of basic human interaction to function. So, "given that a moral and institutional framework is invariably present, this approach directs attention towards the different degrees and characteristics of 'marketness' and of 'embeddedness' in different economic structures" (Block, 1991; Dale, 2010a, p. 200).

Combining these two scales, then, of low- to high-marketness and thin to thick embeddedness, gives us the axes seen at the bottom of Figure 4.1.

Using these axes we can visualize where we might plot a transaction in which there is little to no market rationality but where there are significant amounts of moral and political embeddedness and perhaps a high level of trust. We might imagine, for example, a (non-profitable) business deal with a family member in which the trust in family relations and the obligation to do business with friends and family overrides the market imperative to seek out the highest profits. This is indicated as (1) in Figure 4.1. By contrast, (2) in Figure 4.1 plots a transaction with high-marketness and thin embeddedness on the same axes in the upper-left quadrant. This might, for example, be a situation in which market rationality is high and trust is low, and we can imagine the purchase of an item from an unfamiliar seller with no prior knowledge of their reputation, where they are located, or the quality of the item. The purchase is made because the price is the lowest, indicating that this could offer the best value for money, satisfying the market rationality criteria.

For most transactions, for example buying a second-hand car, we look to balance the extremes on both axes. Some element of market rationality plays a part – we do not want to pay over the odds. But some degree of trust, and therefore political and moral embeddedness, also comes into play. We want to know that the dealer is registered, insured, and relatively trustworthy (for a second-hand car salesperson), for example, so we rely on the regulatory structures and mechanisms mandated and/or administered by state bodies. We might ask around amongst friends and acquaintances for a recommendation, thereby engaging the moral and trust elements. In short, the majority of transactions are likely to avoid either extreme of either axis.

ACADEMIC ANN

Ann takes the questions set out by Fred Block and begins to sketch out what this means for her research. The free market is a fiction because it relies on the State and is therefore always embedded in institutions and therefore society. According to this definition, Ann notes down in her sketchbook, economic behaviour must always be embedded in social relations, morally and politically, and she needs to look for these aspects of interactions.

As a result, Ann's small pool of interviewees (foreign investors and a couple of Board of Investment employees) suddenly looks much larger. Ann realizes that she needs to consider local communities, community leaders, charities and civil society groups, local and central government, and local and national business representatives as well if she wants to understand the extent of the impact of the legal reforms. If the economic is always morally and politically embedded, and if she wants to understand the role of the law in facilitating the investment process, she realizes she might have to zoom out and take a broader perspective. Ann is now worried. She doesn't have time to interview half the country! She wonders if she can acknowledge these additional actors in her research and interpret her prearranged interviews in the light of this realization.

Ann decides to follow Fred Block's research questions in her fieldwork, planning to explore the difference that interpretations of embeddedness might produce. She sets out lists of questions such as "In what ways are transactions and contracts embedded in social relations such as family ties, friendships, or long-term supplier–contractor relations? To what extent do non-economic goals such as moral or spiritual commitments shape economic behaviour?"[2] Ann soon notices that different iterations of embeddedness can bring about subtle shifts in research questions, actors identified as relevant, and the data that she

2 (Dale, 2010a, p. 200) For further exploration of these issues, see (Block, 2008).

might collect, analyse, and interpret. The definition of embeddedness, for Ann, is therefore a determinant of her findings.

While Block's Polanyian programme for economic sociology is "generally more successful", it still "falters on the market concept" which is a "stripped down version of the market" (Krippner, 2001, p. 784). This means that social considerations come into play only as we move away from a situation of high-marketness, "preserving intact the asocial market construct" (Krippner, 2001, p. 784). Indeed, as Block himself notes, "[a]s the marketness of transactions diminishes, economic behaviour tends to become embedded in a more complex web of social relations", denying the possibility that markets themselves can represent "complex social relations" (Block, cited in Krippner, 2001, p. 784). This tends to conflate the extent to which an interaction is "social" with the length of time the relationship has endured, while simultaneously taking the existence of the market as a given. While Krippner notes that these critiques are shared by much economic sociology literature, for Cotterrell, networks of community do indeed develop and solidify over time, given the right set of conditions to enable the development of trust (Cotterrell, 1997; Krippner, 2001, p. 785). However, the conflation of time with trust is not a foolproof assumption, and does not, for instance, cover ratings and reviews on websites, which act as a proxy for social trust relations, administered via the platform and enabling transactions between strangers which we might still consider "trusting" (MacKenzie and Millo, 2003, p. 117; Pavlou and Gefen, 2004; see, *inter alia*, Hardin, 2006).[3]

ACADEMIC ANN

Returning to the questions that Block set out, Ann realizes that her interview questions might need to be rephrased in the light of Block's reading of Polanyian embeddedness. As the economy is always embedded in social ties, there will be some degree of focus on trust between actors, as well as their moral or spiritual commitments. To understand this, she realizes that she needs to understand far more about the relationships between the actors she is interviewing, such as the length of the relationship and frequency of contact. She also thinks it would be a good idea to find out about other (non-economic) aspects of the relationship.

She wonders how to find out "In what ways are transactions embedded in social relationships?" and "To what extent do non-economic goals shape economic behaviour?" Given that she now has a larger pool of actors, Ann anxiously jots down some ideas: how can she get to know her interviewees better, how can she find out about their lives, interests, and interactions with other groups of actors she has identified? She realizes that the non-economic is starting to play a much larger role in shaping her questions and, she suspects, her findings.

3 The problematic practice of fake reviews and the ability of sellers to game the system has the potential to undermine the role of reviews in online sites or market exchanges conducted at a distance.

Greta Krippner laments the way that sociologists have stripped markets of their social essence in order to study them. She concludes that "we will be unable to grasp markets fully as constitutive of and constituted by social relations until the concept of embeddedness is liberated from intellectual antecedents that presuppose the separation of economy from broader realms of social life" (Krippner, 2001, p. 798). But while Krippner maintains that "the state, culture, and politics are *contained* in every market act", it might be instructive to invert this, as the following chapters here do, arguing instead that economic and legal phenomena are performed within and throughout each and every social interaction (Krippner, 2001, p. 785). This starts from the other end, focusing on the social essence of each interaction – namely that there are two or more people interacting – and acknowledging that in each and every interaction economic and legal aspects come into play. This avoids the difficulties that arise from continua of marketness, while sidestepping the differentiation that occurs when we use the term "embedded". This idea is developed throughout Chapters 4 and 5.

Dale's interpretation of Polanyian embeddedness

ACADEMIC ANN

Ann then repeats the process using Dale's interpretation of Polanyian embeddedness, but she retains Block's questions, hoping to compare the results. She starts off by identifying her groups of actors. Originally, she had planned to interview foreign investors and Board of Investment employees. Dale's interpretation of Polanyian embeddedness, that society is embedded in the economy and its regulation, doesn't change Ann's pool of actors all that much. But it does prompt a shift in how she looks for where and how social ties might be embedded in economic rationalities. Ann thinks that these economic rationalities might be clear in the language actors use, so she decides to focus on how her interviewees respond to her research questions, looking carefully for the vocabulary of economic rationalities in the descriptions of relations given by her interviewees.

She decides that she needs to pay attention to how actors frame their arguments. Then, she needs to look at if and how non-economic arguments are framed in economic terms. For example, if a local community leader advocates for retention of ancestral lands, is the argument framed in terms of rational economic value (a cost–benefit analysis) or in terms of their moral or spiritual ties with that piece of land?

By contrast, Gareth Dale, also a prolific scholar on Polanyi's life and work, has interpreted Polanyian embeddedness differently. While Block sees the market as "always embedded", Dale argues that society is now embedded in the economy (Dale, 2010a, 2010b, 2016; but cf. Beckert, 2009). For Dale, the free markets of the twentieth century have hollowed out a section of interactions which serve the imperatives of the free market. Accordingly, all normative systems fall in line with free market mentality and rationalities, resulting in the reverse embedding of society in the economy.[4]

While Block's framework reinforces the construct of the asocial market, Dale notes that at this level of abstraction the "institutional and normative embeddedness of free market capitalism" is difficult to dispute (Stanfield, 1986, p. 107; Dale, 2011, p. 331). "The novelty of the market economy is that its institutional embedding involves its diremption from non-economic institutions in manner [sic] that negates both social control over economic institutions and moral behaviour within them" (Dale, 2011, p. 331). By stepping into Polanyi's "mental universe", Dale argues that saying that "the liberal market is 'embedded' in the sense of 'instituted' then, does not negate its 'disembeddedness' at other levels" (Dale, 2011, p. 332). He continues that the "term does not denote the economy's separation from society but from non-economic institutions, a separation that produces a rift between individual and society and a resulting moral degeneration" (Dale, 2011, p. 332). Thus, as Stanfield describes, the self-regulating market has its own "logic [...], process of control [...], and teleological momentum [...]", meaning that it is "necessarily superordinate to society" (Stanfield, 1995, p. 116; Dale, 2011, p. 332). As Dale concludes, this is why "it does make sense to speak of a disembedded economy, and even to conceive of it as one in which society is embedded" (Dale, 2011, p. 332).

Dale bases his reading of Polanyi's use of the concept through an historical appreciation of embeddedness. He notes that Polanyi was influenced by Marx, Weber, and Tönnies, and that, over time, the concept has become central to sociology.[5] Dale contends that Polanyi drew on the Weberian *Gemeinschaft–Gesellschaft* distinction in formulating his ideas, with *Gemeinschaft* corresponding most closely to the embedded economy, while *Gesellschaft* represented the atomization of society and the disembedding of the economy (Dale, 2010a, p. 191). Hence, while Polanyi's earlier usages of embeddedness referred to a Marxian–Tönniesian incarnation of the term, by the time Polanyi was writing *The Great Transformation*, his thinking had grown closer to that of Weber, and this is reflected in his formation of embeddedness (Dale, 2010a, pp. 191–2).[6]

4 This interpretation is echoed in Perry-Kessaris' interpretation of Frerichs' reading of embeddedness explored in Chapter 3 through the categories of cognitive and normative embedding and disembedding of regimes and rationalities.

5 As earlier chapters noted, there is evidence that Thurnwald was one of the first to coin the phrase in 1932, and that Polanyi was familiar with Thurnwald's work. See (Beckert, 2009, p. 40)

6 Polanyi's first use of the term "embeddedness" is in a 1934 essay which explains that no system of labour ("*Arbeitsverfassung*") can be understood without first making sense of "the social system in which it is embedded ('eingebettet')". See Dale, 2010a, pp. 191–2.

But what does a disembedding entail? And can a counter movement re-embed the economy? Dale's analysis of Polanyi brings us no closer to answers to these questions. Nevertheless, the concept has provided a neat way to capture "those social and psycho-social features of human behaviour that are ignored or marginalized in orthodox economic analysis" (Dale, 2010a, p. 195). What we gain through this approach is "a categorical instrument for describing those ordering processes that lead to a reduction of the uncertainty of the action situation and the social structuring of decisions in market contexts" (Beckert, 2009; Dale, 2010a, p. 196).

While acknowledging the lack of internal coherence or meaning of the concept in economic sociology, Dale has considered and critiqued other approaches to it. This includes Greta Krippner's assertion about the paradox of the term, and "desociologiz[ing]" it, as well as John Lie's description of Polanyi's concept of market exchange as "disembedded" (Lie, 1991, p. 219; Krippner *et al.*, 2004; Dale, 2010a, p. 198). If embeddedness equates market exchange with commodification, this renders invisible the underlying social relations through which commodity exchange is organized (Lie, 1991). Additionally, if we see embeddedness as a "gradational concept", and secondly as a holistic principle that "all economies are embedded", we end up, according to Dale, "reif[ying] the market economy" by assuming that life consists of separate spheres (Gemici, 2008, pp. 25–8; Dale, 2010a, p. 198). Ultimately, this approach leaves the market a social sphere "devoid of all social content" (Gemici, 2008, p. 26).

Dale's contention is that none of these critiques holds much water. The charge that the concept reifies society into spheres is, according to Dale, misleading. Polanyi, Dale argues, uses the term not only analytically, but also to allude to "the political goal of ensuring a stable democratic society through the regulation of markets in land, labour and money" (Dale, 2010a, p. 198). In other words, Polanyi was not focused on the economy so much as the larger social systems in which the economies are located (Beckert, 2009, p. 50). Therefore, any sociological theory of the economy that looks to Polanyi "cannot limit itself to examining the preconditions for designing economic institutions adapted to 'efficiency' but must also attend to the effects of the organization of the economic system on society at large" (Dale, 2010a, p. 199).

While recognising Block's interpretation as "probably the most influential" position, Dale places Block's analysis firmly between Polanyi's and Granovetter's, almost as if Block were trying to bridge the two positions and thereby unify economic sociology (Dale, 2010a, p. 199). Yet, by the same token, Block's reading has the effect of obscuring the freshness and theoretical richness of Polanyi's case. "The novelty of the market economy is that its institutional embedding entails a diremption from non-economic institutions in a manner that negates both social control over economic institutions and moral behaviour within them" (Dale, 2010a, p. 201). In other words, a link can be drawn between embeddedness and the social obligation to act in a morally dutiful manner, which gradually dissolves in proportion to the purely functional character traits imposed by the market (Dale, 2010a, p. 201). Thus, "to say that the liberal market is 'embedded' in the sense of 'instituted', then, does not negate its 'disembeddedness' at other levels. The term does not denote the economy's separation from *society* but from non-economic institutions." (Dale, 2010a, p. 202).

Ultimately, Dale's reading of Polanyi gives us an alternative to Block's, especially concerning the subplot of "the 'disembedding' consequences that arise when 'economy' comes to dominate 'society'" (Dale, 2010a, p. 249). If Block's approach can be summarized as attempting to bridge Polanyian and Granovettarian readings of embeddedness, Dale's can be taken as a Polanyian concept in a Marxist context. This makes it vulnerable to the same criticisms as neoclassical economic approaches in the way that both see the economic sphere as separate from the social. In turn, this also entails the black boxing of the market, leaving it unavailable to sociological analysis or reconceptualization. Both are, then, incompatible with a social constructivist understanding of the economic.

In simple terms, Block's and Dale's interpretations can be condensed down to antithetical propositions.[7] They represent opposite ends of the spectrum within the general commitment to the concept of embeddedness. Block argues for an interpretation of Polanyi that sees the economy as embedded in society, while Dale sees the reverse embedding of society in the economy. This was visualized simply in Figure 1.2 in Chapter 1 (page 9).

ACADEMIC ANN

Ann compares her actors and research questions with Block's and then with Dale's interpretation of Polanyian embeddedness. There is a subtle but significant shift in focus between the two. Block's matrix of high–low marketness and thick–thin embeddedness, emphasising that the free market is a fiction, broadens her pool of actors and focuses her research questions on trust and the non-economic.

By contrast, Dale's reading of Polanyian embeddedness, that society had become embedded in the economy, did not expand her pool of actors to such an extent but focused the research on how the non-economic comes to be framed in economic terms.

Ann was aware that the framing of a research project would shape the data and conclusions she was able to draw. But she was surprised at the extent that one small shift in the interpretation of one metaphor could have on her questions, her actors, the sites of enquiry, and potentially her findings.

7 A caveat is necessary here to acknowledge the dangers of reductionist reasoning. Both Block's and Dale's theses are nuanced and multilayered, and in counterposing them in this way much of the detail is necessarily lost. However this exercise is necessary to highlight the broader observations made.

Doughnut Economics *versus* The Econocracy

In 2008, at the height of the financial crisis, the Queen visited the London School of Economics. Quizzing economists there, she asked why nobody had seen the financial crash coming. The awkward pause that followed laid bare the lack of foresight. Some years later, on a visit to the Bank of England, and asking the same question again, the Queen was told that people "had got a bit lax" and had believed that regulation of the markets was no longer really necessary. The Duke of Edinburgh, perhaps speaking for the nation, replied "Don't do it again" (Pierce, 2008; Neate, 2012).

Getting "a bit lax" is one way of saying that our collective mental models and shared beliefs about the markets – how they work and how they should work – along with our ways of talking about them, had shifted. The phrase implies hindsight, criticising previous mental models for failing to appreciate the role of market regulation. But the run up to the financial crash in 2008 might be understood, in neo-Polanyian terms, as the "floating free" of our conceptual and linguistic tools from the social realities of market construction in real life, and the dominance of an ideological belief in the abilities of markets to self-regulate (Perry-Kessaris, 2011). Polanyi saw that market liberals wanted to – and believed they could – embed society in the self-regulating market. He argued that this could not happen because markets were always embedded in society – in the very fabric of social interactions. Additionally, state intervention was always required sooner or later to regulate to protect society from the worst excesses of the free market. The free market did not, and never could, perform as legend would have us believe. Nevertheless, the pervasive myths of the naturally occurring, self-regulating free market persist, indicating that our regimes and rationalities, including our conceptual and linguistic tools, remain somewhat misaligned from the reality of the social production of market interactions.

Whereas a reductionist reading of Block's interpretation sees markets as embedded in society, a similarly reductionist reading of Dale argues that tacitly, and invisibly, we have reached a point where society has become embedded in markets, echoing John Gray's discussions about whether the market economy has become a market society (Gray, 2009). At the heart of the debate is the extent to which economic norms and narratives have come to structure other aspects of society, explicitly or implicitly. We can begin to explore this question by following the career of the concept of embeddedness which, as a rationality or mental model, has become more ubiquitous following the 2008 financial crash, but less meaningful. Like those neoclassical economic models referred to in Chapter 2, despite being able to do less and less, the concept is applied to more and more. In the case of embeddedness, this expansionist application has been in ways that map neatly onto the Block–Dale dual interpretation of Polanyian embeddedness. Kate Raworth's *Doughnut Economics* echoes Block's interpretation, while Earle *et al.*'s *Econocracy* echoes Dale's. By examining the wider conceptual commitment to embeddedness and placing it within the context of well-worn conceptual battles in economic sociology and ESL, we can appreciate that this is not a new phenomenon, but it is one with serious implications for our abilities to respond innovatively to crashes, crises, and catastrophes.

Since the financial crash, there has been a renewed interest in the role, position, and purpose of both the economy as an institution and economics as a discipline. Some steps have been taken to stabilize the global financial system and some (re-)regulation has occurred (Lund *et al.*, 2018). Despite the rise of pluralist economics (Gräbner and Strunk, 2020), and the rise of think tanks promoting alternative economics approaches, mainstream mental models that assume how, where, when, and why regulation should be applied to markets remain remarkably stable.[8] In the literature that appeared in response to the 2008 crash, a common theme emerged: is the economy embedded in society, or is society embedded in the economy? What is the role of the law? And, then, how can we do better?

Doughnut Economics

Kate Raworth's thesis, as set out in her book *Doughnut Economics*, is that we, as a species as well as a society, must learn to live within the ecological limits set by our planet, reconstructing economics to achieve this. She helpfully illustrates what this might look like, simply proposing two concentric circles (the doughnut of her book's title) that represent the lower and upper bounds of societal economic engagement. At the lower end, the needs of every person must be met. At the upper end, we must take care not to pursue economic gains that harm our surrounding environment. The book is a tour de force that has had a notable impact on the engagement of mainstream economics with the climate crisis.

And yet, throughout the book, Raworth describes the economy as "embedded" in society, which is in turn "so evidently embedded in the biosphere" and "within nature" (Raworth, 2018, p. loc.420, 1052). Raworth urges us, in no uncertain terms, to "forget the free market: think embedded market" (Raworth, 2018, p. loc.1219). She continues that "strange though it sounds, [...] there is no such thing as deregulation, only *reregulation* that embeds the market in a different set of political, legal and cultural rules" (Raworth, 2018, p. loc.1219). The "evidence" of the embeddedness of the economy is so strong that it needs no explanation. We are left at the first challenge to embeddedness in this book, the "What are we talking about?" question, with no clear answer.

8 Some of the more notable think tanks and third-sector organizations that have emerged in the wake of the financial crash include Promoting Economic Pluralism, Rethink Economics, and ECNMY.

Raworth's innovation is in her diagrams, and her ability to boil down complex points to a simple visual comprising no more than a couple of circles. In this way, she makes the point that economics as a discipline is in need of a rethink. Her "Circular Flow Diagram" and "Embedded Economy […] ends the myth of the self-contained, self-sustaining market, replacing it with provisioning by the household, market, commons and state – *all embedded within and dependent upon society*, which in turn is embedded within the living world" (Raworth, 2018, p. loc.1387 (emphasis added)). The idea of "nested systems" are proposed as an alternative way of talking about the interface and interdependency of the economy with society but are not developed further (Raworth, 2018, p. loc.2423). Nevertheless, Raworth's focus on how we talk about this is prescient. She notes the importance of the language we use to describe ourselves, our society, and our institutions, remarking that "[f]inding the words to say it may turn out to be more important than we can imagine in determining whether or not we as a species can learn to thrive with others" (Raworth, 2018, p. loc.1730). This notion, that our language not only describes but gives rise to our mental models, our multiple "logics", and "unthought knowns" is central (Rittich, 2014a; Bernstein *et al.*, 2015; Koch, 2018). The language used has the potential to shape the reality it describes, becoming a "self-fulfilling prophecy" (MacKenzie, Muniesa and Siu, 2008).[9]

The Econocracy

The Econocracy, another popular work emerging in the wake of the 2008 crash, was penned by three students at Manchester University who had enrolled on an economics degree hoping to understand the crisis. Nevertheless, the authors found their course a far cry from events happening in the real world, and dismayed by the discipline's refusal, or inability, to engage with the real world, the authors found themselves "frustrated by the failings of the [economics] profession to make sense of this very crisis" (Earle, Moran and Ward-Perkins, 2017, p. x). Duly, they set about reforming the field, starting with those who shape the mental models and conceptual tools that filter down, as Giddens describes through his "double hermeneutic", to the rest of us (Giddens, 1984).

Angered at the "methodological monoculture" within economics, the authors set up a network of economics students around first the UK and then internationally to "widen and deepen the curriculum" (Haldane, in Earle, Moran and Ward-Perkins, 2017, pp. xi, 10). They sought to broaden viewpoints and approaches explored and taught from a "technological discipline to a public dialogue" (Haldane, in Earle, Moran and Ward-Perkins, 2017, p. xi).

9 The Black–Scholes example is commonly cited here as a "theory" of market behaviour that then influenced market traders who altered their behaviour to "perform" the theory. This is also cited by (Raworth, 2018, p. loc.1519).

However, having established the worthy premise of the book, the authors go on to claim, without explanation or definition, that "[w]e are all embedded in the economy" (Earle, Moran and Ward-Perkins, 2017, p. 8). The absence of any definition or clarification about who, when, how, and why raises questions. It is sufficient to note, though, that the implication appears to be the embedding of society in the economy, or the antithesis of Raworth's use of the term.

These two bestsellers exemplify the problem neatly and are visualized in Figure 1.3 in Chapter 1 (see page 21). Is the economy embedded in society, echoing a simplified version of Fred Block's reading of Polanyi (as in Raworth's *Doughnut Economics*), or is society embedded in the economy, echoing Gareth Dale's interpretation of Polanyi (as in Earle *et al.*'s *The Econocracy*)? Which is right? Could the economy be embedded in institutions, structures, or a whole range of possibilities mentioned earlier that serve to further complicate the discussion? Is this imprecise use of terminology having an impact on our conceptions of society, the economy, and the law? And why does this matter?

Emblematic of a wider approach

LAY LILLIAN

Lillian put down the book she was reading and put the kettle on. Is that what had caused the financial crash? Had the economy really become disembedded from society? She thought back to Margaret Thatcher's declaration that there was no such thing as society and frowned. What was the ideal relationship between economy and society, then, and what was the role of the law in navigating this relationship? Were they simply spheres that could be shifted closer together again? Lillian liked the idea of bringing the economy closer in line with the goals and aspirations of society – the society that she knew to be very real indeed.

Before attempting to answer these questions – Lillian or the previous section's – it is worth noting that the two books introduced above are not alone in their use of embeddedness as a central concept. There are myriad examples of a broader commitment to the concept of embeddedness that echo beyond the confines of the debate within ESL. These use the term explicitly, although without definition and generally without precision.

In her latest book, Mariana Mazzucato notes that markets are "embedded in rules, norms and contracts" (Mazzucato, 2021, p. 20). She then goes on to explain that markets are embedded in "institutions and norms and are co-created by different actors" (Mazzucato, 2021, p. 21). Thus, while the hint of constructivism in the co-creation of markets by actors is welcome, we are left wondering if the economy is embedded in the law (contracts) or in society (institutions and norms, understood through a constructivist lens). Delivering the Reith Lectures in 2020, outgoing governor of the Bank of England, Mark Carney noted that "the market is a social construct" before going on to state that "markets are living institutions embedded in the culture, practice and tradition and trust of their day" (Carney, 2020).

Orrell's *Introducing Economics* is a graphic exploration of modern economics which states that a "new kind of economics" is beginning to emerge that "considers the behaviour of real people [... to be] embedded in non-linear dynamic networks" (Orrell, 2014). Robert Skidelsky references Polanyi's work briefly in his most recent book, citing Polanyi's "sociological economics" and his "stress on the 'embeddedness' of individual behaviour" (Skidelsky, 2018). Haskel and Westlake cite research by Corrado *et al.* which talks of "knowledge embedded in firm-specific human and structural resources", while Taleb refers to the employed person as "embedded in an industry" (Corrado, Hulten and Sichel, 2005, p. 23; Haskel and Westlake, 2017; Taleb, 2018). Tapscott and Tapscott, discussing cryptocurrency and technology, state that their story becomes "even more interesting when you consider that billions of agents will be embedded in the physical world" while in discussions of poverty, Desmond notes that some Milwaukee renters are "embedded in networks of below average disadvantage" (Desmond, 2016; Tapscott and Tapscott, 2016).

This revival of embeddedness as a useful relational descriptor for the nexus of relations between law, economy, and society is, on one hand, to be welcomed. There is an implicit recognition here that one of the roots of current problems is in the relationships between these spheres and how we talk and think about these. At the same time, as a brief rehearsal of some of the more prominent uses of embeddedness makes clear, there is little consensus on what is embedded, and in what it is embedded. This is problematic enough by itself. But what few note is that our ongoing conceptual commitment to embeddedness, in all its guises, maintains the metaphorical fiction of the ontologically separate law, economy, and society. Both Mazzucato and Carney hint at the mutual re-co-construction and reproduction of the three spheres, yet entrench their conceptual separation through their commitment to embeddedness.

Furthermore, even when not stated directly, the concept of embeddedness continues to both highlight the problems of existing regimes and rationalities while masking alternatives. A general commitment to the concept of embeddedness functions as an unthought rationality, restricting our range of responses to the current dominant frames that allowed the 2008 financial crisis. By maintaining a commitment to the concept of embeddedness, we deny ourselves the opportunity to reconceptualize the economic, the social, and the legal in a way that includes the non-economic (non-rational, or "differently rational") (Cotterrell, 2011, pp. 9–10). At the same time, we also miss out on an opportunity to ask as a society what we require from economics and from law, and what role we want them to play – as knowledge constructs and sites of contestation, debate, and dialogue – in society. While the moral superiority of capitalism may have been tacitly relinquished in favour of a discourse that presents neoliberal capitalist policies as "just the way of the world", any discourse that seeks to re-embed the economy within society promises to perpetuate the moral and political status quo (Lanchester, 2018).

Perhaps even more crucially, re-entrenched disciplinarity and the dominance of neoclassical economic frames and discourse can shape our preferences and interactions. In other words, when we think *as homo economicus*, we begin to act *as homo economicus*, whether we are aware of this or not. Imprecise use of language deriving from a conceptual commitment to embeddedness tangibly shapes our regimes and rationalities; what we are able to perceive, conceive, and imagine. This, in turn, shapes our expectations of the economy, the market, of the state to intervene, and of society to tolerate the full ramifications of the utopian fiction of the free market. If we are accustomed to talking about society being embedded in the market, are we more likely to think like consumers rather than citizens, and tolerate greater levels of job insecurity, inequality, and poverty than we would if we agree that the market was (analytically) or should be (normatively) embedded in society (Clarke *et al.*, 2007)? If we think more like citizens than consumers, and decide that the economy should be (re-)embedded in society, what could we decide to prioritize and which interests could be highlighted (Law, 2009)? If we think and talk with the language of *homo economicus*, and his lawyerly cousin *homo juridicus*, how can we possibly conceive of other ways of being? And, if we were to ponder how we might act, talk, and think more like a morally constructed, socially situated *homo sociologicus*, how might we begin to imagine a vocabulary and grammar – the conceptual and linguistic tools – that enable alternative approaches?

POLICY POLLY

Polly has kept an eye on some of the work on ESL lenses. She has also received regular updates from Ann, who is overjoyed at having an audience to share some of her insights, musings, and dilemmas with. In one phone call, Polly had explained to Ann that embeddedness was bothering her, too. She explained that there was a disconnect between the way in which the World Bank described the law as socially constructed, but then simultaneously described it as embedded in society in annual World Development Reports from 2017, 2018, 2019, and so on. Polly hinted that this was common among development banks, and that there was no clear definition of the relationship of the law or the economy to society that was conceptually coherent and consistent.

Polly wonders out loud what is really embedded, and in what. She also begins to wonder what the impact of this is, and if acknowledging the disconnect might enable the bank to consider how it understands law and economy in general. Ann's experiments in framing her current research project makes Polly think that there could be something quite important at play here. What if the bank's hints at the social construction of the law (and, she presumes, the economy) and assertions as to their embeddedness were entrenching one particular way of thinking about the relationships between law, economy, and society?

What is embedded? And in what?

Roger Cotterrell's two seminal questions of what is embedded, and in what, are good points of reference. While Fred Block and Gareth Dale disagree on answers to these questions, they have both chosen to continue using the concept and there is a consensus that embeddedness is such a ubiquitous term that, even within the economic sociology community, "it would be hard to get rid of it even if we wanted to" (Krippner *et al.*, 2004, p. 125). There is some agreement that while embeddedness "is problematic, [...] it is still very useful" (Krippner *et al.*, 2004, p. 125). However, approval is not universal, and does not imply that embeddedness should be given a free pass.

In choosing not only to commit to embeddedness but to clarify and strengthen it, Block, Dale, and later ESL writers tend to favour a substantive ("oversocialized") view over the formalist (classical economics, "undersocialized") approach, challenging the dominance of mainstream, neoclassical-doctrinal frames (Granovetter, 1985). Within the ESL tradition, Ashiagbor has also argued for a strengthening of the concept as it "may retain a utility, provided we do not assume it predetermines or encodes the specific characteristics of modern capitalist economies, or the specificity of market organization" (Ashiagbor, 2014, p. 269). Instead, embeddedness can capture an understanding of "the *interdependence* of market and society, to conceive of *varieties* of institutional regulation, with different market societies embedded in diverse configurations of ideas, rules and institutional structures" (Ashiagbor, 2014). The ability and flexibility to recognize historical and structural contingency is one advantage of embeddedness, however frequently this is lost in the deployment of the concept.

As Chapter 3 explored, Ruggie's "embedded liberalism" and Evans' "embedded autonomy" offer us lessons about how embeddedness can be used effectively and with minimal internal inconsistencies. By comparing the approaches in both, we saw that a careful, localized, definition based on empirical observation, eschewing generalizable statements of principle could enhance embeddedness, and that when paired with an equal-and-opposite force, some of Polanyi's original dynamism could be recaptured. There have been more "concrete, empirical [and] institutionally specific interpretations or manifestations of the term" which have built on Ruggie's and Evans' theories (Ashiagbor, Kotiswaran and Perry-Kessaris, 2014, p. 262).

However, the current fashion for talking about the economy and its regulation as (dis)embedded from the society they are supposed to serve shows us that these lessons are generally not followed. Embeddedness tends to be thrown in for metaphorical effect, urging a solution to a misdiagnosed problem. In the process, the internal inconsistencies increase, and little attention is paid to its incompatibility with more constructivist understandings of law, economy, and society. Ultimately, if constructivist approaches to relations between law, economy, and society offer us effective means of responding to crashes, crises, and catastrophes, entrenching the separation of economic, legal, and social silos through the metaphor of embeddedness places any possible solutions beyond reach.

It is worth, then, asking the difficult question: what might we accomplish if we stop using embeddedness? What might we achieve if we choose alternative ways of doing, talking, and thinking about the law, economy, and society? And what might become possible if we follow constructivist thinking to remould the relationships between economy, law, and society – and possibly ourselves in the process? Others, accepting the "diminishing utility and traction" of embeddedness, have proposed alternatives to embeddedness, with relational work and the community lens among two suggestions (Rittich, 2014b, pp. 323–4). Drawing on these bodies of work, along with notions from sociology, socio-legal scholarship, economic sociology, economic history, and psychology, the following chapter offers an alternative. In explaining why we might stop talking about the law or economy as embedded in society, Chapter 5 shows that talking, instead, about legal and economic *aspects of social interactions* offers us a way of referencing legal and economic phenomena as they are socially constructed. In turn, the chapter explores what difference this might make to our abilities to respond to those crashes, crises, and catastrophes demanding our attention.

Bibliography

Ashiagbor, D. (2014) 'Embedding Trade Liberalisation in Social Policy: A Research Agenda on Social Regionalism and the Global South', *Northern Ireland Legal Quarterly*, 65(3), pp. 265–281.

Ashiagbor, D., Kotiswaran, P. and Perry-Kessaris, A. (2014) 'Continuing towards an Economic Sociology of Law', *Northern Ireland Legal Quarterly*, 65(3), pp. 259–264.

Beckert, J. (2009) 'The Great Transformation of Embeddedness: Karl Polanyi and the New Economic Sociology', in Chris Hann and Keith Hart (eds) *Market and Society: The Great Transformation Today*. New York: Cambridge University Press, pp. 38–55. Available at: https://papers.ssrn.com/sol3/papers.cfm?abstract_id=2465810.

Bernstein, R. et al. (2015) 'There is No Local Here, Love', in D. O'Brien and P. Matthews (eds) *After Urban Regeneration: Communities, Policy and Place*. Bristol: Policy Press at the University of Bristol, pp. 95–110.

Block, F. (1990) *Postindustrial Possibilities: A Critique of Economic Discourse*. University of California Press. Available at: http://www.jstor.org/stable/10.1525/j.ctt1pp619.

Block, F. (1991) 'Contradictions of Self-Regulating Markets', in Marguerite Mendell and Daniel Salée (eds) *The Legacy of Karl Polanyi: Market, State and Society at the End of the Twentieth Century*. Macmillan.

Block, F. (2008) 'Swimming against the Current: The Rise of a Hidden Developmental State in the United States', *Politics & Society*, 36(2), pp. 169–206. https://doi.org/10.1177/0032329208318731.

Carney, M. (2020) 'The Reith Lectures 2020: How We Get What We Value-Lecture 1: From Moral to Market Sentiments'. Available at: https://www.bbc.co.uk/programmes/b00729d9/episodes/player (Accessed: 5 February 2021).

Clarke, J. et al. (2007) *Creating Citizen-Consumers*. Sage Publications. Available at: https://uk.sagepub.com/en-gb/eur/creating-citizen-consumers/book229035#preview.

Corrado, C., Hulten, C. and Sichel, D. (2005) 'Measuring Capital and Technology: An Expanded Framework', in Carol Corrado, John Haltiwanger and Daniel Sichel (eds) *Measuring Capital in the New Economy*. Chicago: University of Chicago Press, pp. 11–46.

Cotterrell, R. (1997) *Law's Community: Legal Theory in Sociological Perspective*. New Ed. Oxford: Clarendon Press.

Cotterrell, R. (2011) *Community as a Legal Concept? Some Uses of a Law-and-Community Approach in Legal Theory*. SSRN Scholarly Paper ID 1971610. Rochester: Social Science Research Network.

Cotterrell, R. (2013) 'Rethinking Embeddedness; Law, Economy, Community', *Journal of Law and Society*, 40(1), pp. 49–67.

Dale, G. (2010a) *Karl Polanyi: The Limits of the Market*. 1st ed. Cambridge and Malden, MA: Polity.

Dale, G. (2010b) 'Social Democracy, Embeddedness and Decommodification: On the Conceptual Innovations and Intellectual Affiliations of Karl Polanyi', *New Political Economy*, 15(3), pp. 369–393. https://doi.org/10.1080/13563460903290920.

Dale, G. (2011) 'Lineages of Embeddedness: On the Antecedents and Successors of a Polanyian Concept', *The American Journal of Economics and Sociology*, 70(2), pp. 306–339.

Dale, G. (2016) *Karl Polanyi: A Life on the Left*. 1st ed. New York: Columbia University Press.

Desmond, M. (2016) *Evicted: Poverty and Profit in the American City*. Penguin UK. https://www.penguinrandomhouse.com/books/247816/evicted-by-matthew-desmond/.

Earle, J., Moran, C. and Ward-Perkins, Z. (2017) *The Econocracy: On the Perils of Leaving Economics to the Experts*. Kindle Edition. Penguin Books. https://www.penguin.co.uk/books/307289/the-econocracy-by-joe-earle-cahal-moran-and-zach-ward-perkins/9780141986869.

Frerichs, S. (2011) 'Re-Embedding Neoliberal Constitutionalism: A Polanyian Case for the Economic Sociology of Law', in Christian Joerges and Josef Falke (eds) *Karl Polanyi, Globalisation, and the Potential of Law in Transnational Markets*. Oxford: Hart Publishing (International Studies in the Theory of Private Law, Vol.8), pp. 65–84.

Gemici, K. (2008) 'Karl Polanyi and the Antinomies of Embeddedness', *Socio-Economic Review*, 6(1), pp. 5–33. https://doi.org/10.1093/ser/mwl034.

Giddens, A. (1984) *The Constitution of Society: Outline of the Theory of Structuration*. Oxford: Polity.

Gräbner, C. and Strunk, B. (2020) 'Pluralism in Economics: Its Critiques and Their Lessons', *Journal of Economic Methodology*, 27(4), pp. 311–329. https://doi.org/10.1080/1350178X.2020.1824076.

Granovetter, M. (1985) 'Economic Action and Social Structure: The Problem of Embeddedness', *American Journal of Sociology*, 91(3), pp. 481–510.

Gray, J. (2009) *False Dawn: The Delusions of Global Capitalism*. London: Granta Books.

Hardin, R. (2006) *Trust*. Cambridge: Polity Press (Key Concepts).

Haskel, J. and Westlake, S. (2017) *Capitalism without Capital: The Rise of the Intangible Economy*. Princeton University Press. https://press.princeton.edu/books/hardcover/9780691175034/capitalism-without-capital.

Koch, I. L. (2018) *Personalizing the State: An Anthropology of Law, Politics, and Welfare in Austerity Britain*. Oxford: Oxford University Press. https://doi.org/10.1093/oso/9780198807513.001.0001.

Krippner, G. (2001) 'The Elusive Market: Embeddedness and the Paradigm of Economic Sociology', *Theory and Society*, 30(6), pp. 775–810.

Krippner, G. et al. (2004) 'Polanyi Symposium: A Conversation on Embeddedness', *Socio-Economic Review*, 2, pp. 109–135.

Lanchester, J. (2018) 'After the Fall: John Lanchester on the Decade of Doom that Followed the 2008 Financial Crash', *The Sunday Times*, 9 September. Available at: https://www.thetimes.co.uk/article/after-the-fall-john-lanchester-on-the-decade-of-doom-that-followed-the-2008-financial-crash-cxscrmmj9 (Accessed: 13 July 2019).

Law, J. (2009) 'Seeing Like a Survey', *Cultural Sociology*, 3(2), pp. 239–256.

Lie, J. (1991) 'Embedding Polanyi's Market Society', *Sociological Perspectives*, 34(2), pp. 219–235. https://doi.org/10.2307/1388992.

Lund, S. et al. (2018) *A decade after the global financial crisis: What has (and hasn't) changed?* McKinsey & Company Financial Services. Available at: https://www.mckinsey.com/industries/financial-services/our-insights/a-decade-after-the-global-financial-crisis-what-has-and-hasnt-changed (Accessed: 13 July 2019).

MacKenzie, D. and Millo, Y. (2003) 'Constructing a Market, Performing Theory: The Historical Sociology of a Financial Derivatives Exchange', *American Journal of Sociology*, 109(1), pp. 107–145.

MacKenzie, D., Muniesa, F. and Siu, L. (2008) *Do Economists Make Markets? On the Performativity of Economics*. Princeton and Oxford: Princeton University Press.

Mazzucato, M. (2021) *Mission Economy: A Moonshot Guide to Changing Capitalism*. Penguin.

Neate, R. (2012) 'Queen Finally Finds Out Why No One Saw the Financial Crisis Coming', *The Guardian*, 13 December. Available at: https://www.theguardian.com/uk/2012/dec/13/queen-financial-crisis-question (Accessed: 8 October 2018).

Orrell, D. (2014) *Introducing Economics: A Graphic Guide*. London: Icon Books Ltd.

Pavlou, P.A. and Gefen, D. (2004) 'Building Effective Online Marketplaces with Institution-Based Trust', *Information Systems Research*, 15(1), pp. 37–59.

Perry-Kessaris, A.J. (2011) 'Reading the Story of Law and Embeddedness Through a Community Lens: A Polanyi-Meets-Cotterrell Economic Sociology of Law?', *Northern Ireland Legal Quarterly* (Special Issue on *Socialising Economic Relationships*), 62(4), pp. 401–413.

Pierce, A. (2008) 'The Queen Asks Why No One Saw the Credit Crunch Coming', *The Telegraph*. Available at: https://www.telegraph.co.uk/news/uknews/theroyalfamily/3386353/The-Queen-asks-why-no-one-saw-the-credit-crunch-coming.html (Accessed: 1 July 2018).

Raworth, K. (2018) *Doughnut Economics: Seven Ways to Think Like a 21st-Century Economist*. ebook (Kindle). Random House Business.

Rittich, K. (2014a) 'Making Natural Markets: Flexibility as Labour Market Truth', *Northern Ireland Legal Quarterly (Symposium: Economic Sociology of Law)*, 65, p. 323.

Rittich, K. (2014b) 'Making Natural Markets: Flexibility as Labour Market Truth', *Northern Ireland Legal Quarterly*, 65(3), pp. 323–345.
Skidelsky, R. (2018) *Money and Government: A Challenge to Mainstream Economics*. Allen Lane, Penguin.
Stanfield, J.R. (1986) *The Economic Thought of Karl Polanyi: Lives and Livelihood*. New York: Palgrave Macmillan.
Stanfield, J.R. (1995) *Economics, Power and Culture: Essays in the Development of Radical Institutionalism*. New York: Macmillan.
Taleb, N.N. (2018) *Skin in the Game: Hidden Asymmetries in Daily Life*. Penguin UK.
Tapscott, D. and Tapscott, A. (2016) *Blockchain Revolution: How the Technology Behind Bitcoin and Other Cryptocurrencies is Changing the World*. Penguin UK.

Chapter 5

Embeddedness

The external conceptual incompatibilities

How we tend to think (our default conceptual tools)

POLICY POLLY

Polly's realization that the bank's theories of the law as "socially constructed" and yet at the same time "socially embedded", bothered her. There was a contradiction here, and, if what Ann was saying was right, this had real-world implications for the policies she was designing at the interface of the law, the economy, and society.

She began to wonder if embeddedness was even as helpful a metaphor as she had first thought. It was easy to use, and fashionable. Everyone knew what she meant when she said that the economy should be re-embedded in society – or at least, she thought everyone knew what she meant. She wonders now whether everyone heard and understood something slightly different.

Switzerland has a reputation for being green. But the country has been hugely impacted by climate change (Soguel-dit-Picard, 2021). Famous for its bucolic farming landscapes and mountainous scenery, Switzerland has traditionally prioritized its environment and ecology. But in a 2021 referendum, the Swiss electorate rejected proposals for carbon tax measures, bringing into doubt the country's ability to meet its climate commitments under the Paris Agreement on Climate Change (Foulkes, 2021; O'Sullivan, 2021; Soguel-dit-Picard, 2021). Measures that would ban certain pesticides and improve the quality of drinking water were also voted down. This, perhaps, should not have been such a surprise. After all, the campaigns had been framed in economic terms, pitting the environment against the economy. Responding to the vote, Guy Parmelin, Switzerland's head of the Department of Economic Affairs, Education, and Research, hailed voters for choosing the "rational and pragmatic" option by focusing on price considerations rather than other values and interests (O'Sullivan, 2021).

DOI: 10.4324/9781003354819-5

If I ask you not to think of an elephant, you will, inevitably, think of an elephant (Lakoff, 2014). This is an important insight in terms of our metaphors and the mental models they craft. In asking someone not to think of an object or a concept, the human brain automatically defaults to that mental image. The implication for us is that in arguing that X is wrong, or that we should stop doing X, we implicitly perpetuate thoughtways associated with X. We entrench X and strengthen it. What we ought to do instead is explain – hammer home even – that we should be doing Y. The lesson, then, is that to successfully challenge an argument or a mental model, we need alternatives expressed in different vocabularies and grammars. In short, we must reframe. By repeating the arguments of the opposition – even if only to show how wrong they are – we perpetuate and repeat those very arguments, augmenting their impact (Lakoff, 2014). So, drawing on examples set out in earlier chapters, the politically right-wing framing of "tax relief", whereby tax cuts are painted as relief from the affliction of tax, could be reframed as "tax cuts", or, perhaps more dramatically, "reduced investment in future generations or the environment".[1] Similarly, "taxpayers' money" might be reframed as "public money", "the government's money", or "shared investments in communal resources".

In Switzerland, the referenda might be boiled down to a conceptual competition between the economy and the environment. Our dominant frames, those we class as mainstream or orthodox, as well as our dominant conceptual and linguistic tools, are those of neoclassical economics. As the most easily quantifiable of social systems, economics has the upper hand here (Teubner, 2021). Whilst framing moral, political, ethical, ecological, or other legal arguments in economic terms does not automatically mean that the economy will be prioritized, it can forefront economic preferences and concerns in the mind of the voter. In Switzerland, by framing the arguments in economic terms, the economy enjoyed a preferential position, and this may have been one factor that resulted in economic interests being given priority over environmental interests. Even the result was described as "rational": the core characteristic of the ideal-typical *homo economicus*.

This is not always a deliberate act though. Economic frames of reference have not always been consciously prioritized. But economics is far more convenient in its ability to simplify complex social phenomena from many shades of grey down into binaries of black or white. Neoclassical economics, with its empirical, conceptual, and normative preferences for quantification, mathematization, and comparison respectively, offers us the ready-made tools for giving us simple, clean answers to complex problems (Hirsch, Michaels and Friedman, 1990). And in many scenarios, this is extremely useful. But when these tendencies co-opt and shape the mainstream, and crucially when they do so invisibly, problems can arise.

1 See Chapters 1 and 2 for further discussion of these examples.

We can see this narrative capture – the invisibilization of the mainstreaming of neoclassical economics rationalities – in the law, too. Earlier chapters noted that court judgements claiming to be nothing more than "pragmatic, doctrinal" reasoning relied heavily on the language of neoclassical economics ("efficient" rather than "effective") to justify the optimal use of a resource (Burrows, 2016). No further explanation was needed by the Court, as the most efficient use of a resource was sufficient justification to be a solution to the issue. Our default thoughtways, those shaped by neoclassical economic preferences, know that the most "efficient" use of a resource is, economically speaking, the most preferable outcome. We no longer need to state the obvious that we are engaging in economic analysis here. After all, what alternative is there?

Justices of the Supreme Court, just like the rest of us, think, talk, and act *as homo economicus* owing to the many and varied ways in which mainstream economics has co-opted and shaped our regimes and rationalities, primarily through our conceptual and linguistic tools. This implies, then, that even *homo juridicus* mirrors some of the behaviours and preferences of his more outgoing cousin *homo economicus*, indicating the ways in which mainstream economics comes to co-opt the law. If you start looking out for these tell-tale clues, you will begin to spot signs of the vocabularies, grammars, and mental models of neoclassical economics almost everywhere. And, as with asking you not to think of an elephant, asking you *not* to act, talk, or think like *homo economicus* is simply an inadequate strategy. We need an alternative.

How we might think differently (challenging default conceptual tools)

An exploration of embeddedness in the context of ESL (economic sociology of law) shows how one metaphor can entrench and reproduce default conceptual and linguistic tools, or mainstream regimes and rationalities. As we have seen, these may or may not be serving us well, but, frequently, we lose sight of their function to the extent that they operate below the radar, channelling our thoughts subconsciously. As we zoom out to appreciate our ongoing conceptual commitment to embeddedness in wider social discourse, we can see how the concept prevents any constructivist or integrationist challenge to our dominant regimes and rationalities. While we carry on talking about "re-embedding" the economy and the law in society, mainstream conceptual and linguistic tools are activated, channelling our thoughtways along doctrinal legal scholarship and neoclassical economics.[2] The inherent conceptual separation prevents us asking what might happen if we shift perspective.

2 With thanks to Davina Cooper and Flora Renz for coining the term "thoughtways" (Cooper and Renz, 2022).

The previous chapter unpacked some of the contradictions we see in the internal (in)consistency of embeddedness. Even if we agree *what* is embedded and *in what* it is embedded (which we generally do not), we are still left with a second, more fundamental, contradiction. An economic sociology of law lens has integrative goals, in the sense that it seeks to draw the understanding of law, economy, and society closer together, viewing both legal and economic phenomena as two sides of the same, social, coin. As Chapter 3 proposed, we might say that ESL is a pseudo-constructivist lens, or at least aspiring towards constructivism.[3] We must decide, then, whether law, economy, and society are separate spheres of activity, ontologically and epistemologically, or whether they are all social phenomena. And if we decide in favour of the latter, we might then analyze them *as socially constructed phenomena*. In arguing that legal and economic phenomena are socially constructed, we can move the three spheres closer together in terms of how we research and understand the economic life of the law. But the way we talk then becomes problematic. On the other hand, if we wish to maintain that law, economy, and society are discrete spheres of action and understanding, then our metaphorical fictions of "law", "economy" and "society" work well. As Chapter 1 set out, these primary-level ontological metaphors do an excellent job of referring to collections of social behaviour. This is unproblematic as long as we remember that we are talking about fictions.

Yet, as the past century or so has demonstrated, we frequently forget this detail. We collectively act, talk, and think *as if* the "law" and "economy" were real: tangible entities that we can touch, see, and feel. We personify them, imbuing them with thoughts, feelings, and desires of their own. Notice the trend, when talking about the financial markets, to use active personification implying intention for gains (the markets have climbed) while using passive personification implying no intention for losses (the markets have fallen)

3 Constructivism, or the "social construction" of regimes and rationalities is itself a metaphor (Sismondo, 1993, p. 516). While various definitions have been offered, constructivism is taken here to challenge the agency–structure duality while denying the possibility of pre-existing regimes and rationalities independent of social interaction. The use here is differentiated from the works of Sismondo, Knorr-Cetina, Berger and Luckmann, and Latour, in that it is a loose, relatively broad application of the term (see inter alia Latour, 1983; Berger and Luckmann, 1991; Cetina, 1993; Sismondo, 1993).

While we're all here, a quick word about the difference between construc*tivism* and construc*tionism*. Some authors use the terms interchangeably without apology (Crotty, 1998; Lynch, 1998; Schwartz, 2007), while others find a small but significant distinction between them. Generally, constructionism focuses on the artefacts, or "knowing", created through shared production. Social constructivism, on the other hand, places the individual at the centre of meaning-making within any particular context, with the focus on the individual's learning that occurs through their interactions (Crotty, 1998, p. 58). For the purposes of our discussion here, regimes (what we do) and rationalities (how we understand what we do) are said to be re-co-constituted, or constructed, through social interactions. I call this a constructivist approach, but distinguish this from the strict, sometimes contradictory, descriptions in other literature.

(Geary, 2011, l. loc.534). In constructing these layers of fiction, we bring into being metaphors that begin to take on lives of their own. In the process, these metaphors feed back into our ways of talking and thinking, shaping how we understand our own social positionality and ways of interacting. As our regimes and rationalities become similarly real, we perform, think, and talk about legal phenomena *as homo juridicus*, and we perform, think, and talk about economic phenomena *as homo economicus*.

But these mainstream ways of doing, talking, and thinking that comprise the dominant regimes and rationalities tend to be instrumental, focusing on shared, narrow objectives. The non-economic, or the differently rational, tends to be sidelined and undervalued. We are left, like the Swiss voters, trying to shoehorn other values and interests, such as environmental preservation, into models that were never designed to accommodate the totality of human social experience.

So, in an attempt to avoid thinking about that elephant, what might happen if we were to imagine alternative regimes and rationalities? Might we discover a way of performing *homo sociologicus*, the morally constructed, socially situated cousin of *homo economicus-juridicus*? And what might this mean for how we understand and respond to the financial crashes, social crises, and environmental catastrophes facing society?

Before setting off on the journey that follows though, it is important to avoid making a straw-man of embeddedness as a metaphor, or of our conceptual commitment to it, or of our language in general. As an everyday term, we understand embeddedness as a visual metaphor that describes the relationship between two phenomena. We say that "X is embedded in Y" and understand that X and Y are conceptually distinct but have a close or proximal relationship, potentially sharing the same space and time, as might be visualized in Figure 1.2 in Chapter 1 (see page 5). It is important to recall that, used appropriately, in a setting that recognizes structural and historical contingencies as well as the underlying metaphorical fictions on which the discourse rests, the concept of embeddedness can be immensely helpful. If we are describing conceptually distinct entities, like the coal in the walls of a mine, "embedded" is an unproblematic description. As Chapter 1 noted, the collective leap of faith that we all take when talking about "the law" or "the economy" does not prevent common meaning from being communicated. Instead, the problems appear when embeddedness is overused, becoming invisible through its own ubiquity. And once we lose sight of these metaphorical fictions, we lose sight of the assumptions and concepts that are baked into them, and that are intrinsic to our disciplinary ways of thinking about the relationships between law, economy, and society.

Thinking about embeddedness as a black box

Chapter 2 introduced the concept of a "black box". We tend to encounter references to a black box in relation to the flight recorder on a (usually unfortunate) plane. The point is that we cannot see the internal workings but have to infer what is happening inside the box from external inputs and outputs. Embeddedness-talk constructs a similar black box effect in relation to economic and legal phenomena. When we describe the economy as embedded in society, we conceal the internal, social workings of the market. Similarly, when we describe the law as embedded in society, the linguistically activated black box conceals the social dimensions and intricate function of the law. The "black box" phenomenon is a product of our metaphors, our linguistic short cuts that rely on fictions. When we say that the law (or the market, or the economy) is embedded in society, we entrench the conceptual separation between the law and society. But at the same time, the concept of embeddedness places the law (or the market, or the economy) in a "black box", rendering it unavailable to sociological analysis (Krippner *et al.*, 2004; Cotterrell, 2013, p. 52).

Greta Krippner concludes that "the basic intuition that markets are socially embedded [...] has led economic sociologists to take the market itself for granted" (Krippner, 2001, p. 776; Randles, 2003). Granovetter's roots in Parsonian sociology mean that his approach also sees actors atomistically in much the same way as neoclassical economics. This results in both extremes sharing a vision of the world that is "sharply demarcated into neatly bounded and essentially separate realms" (Krippner, 2001, p. 777). The approaches that have come to characterize economic sociology, even the "New Economic Sociology", have not escaped the sharp separation of the economic from the social, resulting in "an impoverished analysis of both poles" (Krippner, 2001, p. 777).

This raises more fundamental consequences though, given that Polanyian (macro level) and Granovetterian (micro level) versions of embeddedness are both subject to the same criticisms about embeddedness but are setting out to achieve different goals. Krippner and Alvarez point out that by focusing on one particular aspect of the neoclassical paradigm as its primary target, each approach "tends to exacerbate the problem resolved by the other", making the reconciliation of the two broad embeddedness interpretations at the heart of an economic sociology and ESL actually counterproductive (Zukin and DiMaggio, 1990; Krippner and Alvarez, 2007, p. 231).

A Granovetterian perspective starts with atomistic actors more or less embedded in networks that are then scaled up. A Polanyian perspective sits at the macro level, describing the relationship between economy and society; between economic and non-economic phenomena. Somewhat pessimistically, Krippner and Alvarez, note that "embeddedness references a very different relationship between the economic and the social for each of these traditions", making the field incoherent almost beyond repair (Krippner and Alvarez, 2007, p. 232). Agreeing with them, Cotterrell suggests that Granovetter "has run the ship aground on a conception [...] that insists on the separate nature of economy and society" (Cotterrell, 2013, pp. 51–2). Ironically, "the effort to embed economy in society has ended with an entrenchment of *their separation*" (Cotterrell, 2013, pp. 51–2). While acknowledging that this argument is open to challenge, Cotterrell states that it is important not only as a potential flaw in embeddedness, but also as an argument that parallels a serious challenge to sociology of law and socio-legal enquiries. This states that much sociology of law literature can be criticized for:

> failing to analyse *the idea of law itself* sociologically; for failing to "get inside" legal ideas and doctrines and reinterpret them sociologically, so as to understand how and why they have taken particular forms and developed in certain directions rather than others and how they embody particular understandings of the nature of social life and exclude others.
>
> (Cotterrell, 2013, p. 52)

The problem here stems from the limitations of embeddedness. It makes no difference whether we are talking about the embeddedness of the law, markets, the economy, or any other (social) phenomenon. It makes no difference whether we claim that the law is embedded in society, or whether society is embedded in the law – the first of these, (the "X" in Figure 5.1) is left unavailable to any serious sociological review. This presents a far more serious conundrum for ESL than the matters of internal inconsistency that Chapter 4 explored.

It should be noted that this black box problem is not a criticism confined to economic sociology or ESL. Douglass North and Ronald Coase are both quoted as lamenting the fact that neoclassical economics "contains so little discussion of the central institution that underlies neoclassical economics – the market" and that "discussion of the marketplace itself has entirely disappeared" (North, 1977; Coase, 1987, cited in Callon, 1998a, pp. 1, 54). Nevertheless, a sociological perspective needs to be able to analyze *all* aspects of social interaction sociologically, including the aspects that economists refer to as "the market" and that lawyers refer to as "the law". Several solutions to the black box problem have been proposed, and some of these are incorporated into the proposed lens that is set out in the following discussion.

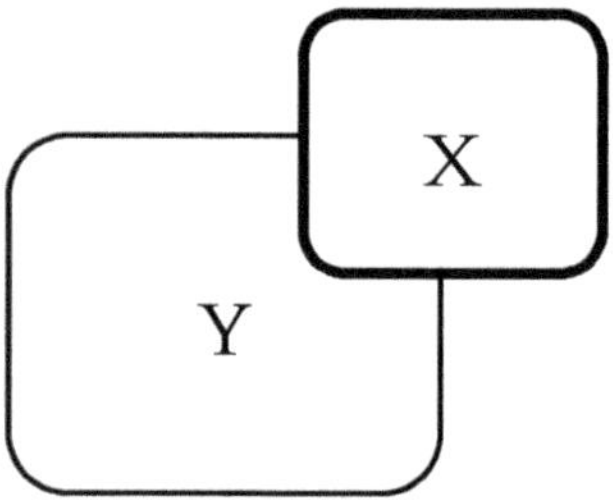

Figure 5.1 When we say that "X is embedded in Y", we place X in a black box, placing it beyond the reach of sociological analysis.

It is important not to lose sight of the empirical nature of the phenomena and how legal and economic aspects of interactions are produced in the real world. While the black box places phenomena beyond the reach of sociological analysis, Roger Cotterrell reminds us that empirical analysis is also essential for understanding these social phenomena. Embeddedness focuses our attention so much on what is embedded, in what, and how the disciplines interface, that we ignore (at our peril) "how the phenomena themselves are structured (as social entities)" (Cotterrell, 2013, p. 52). This is crucial for developing work that enquires into the formulations of social interactions that are currently described as "the law" or "the market". To this end, Cotterrell insists that "*what* is embedded (law and economy) must be explained by sociological enquiry" that addresses its "moral-political" aspects (Cotterrell, 2013, pp. 52, 49).

Proposing an alternative ESL lens: beyond embeddedness

So far, we have established that embeddedness is both the core concept of ESL and a widespread linguistic phenomenon for describing the relationships between law, economy, and society. Sometimes it can be useful. Sometimes not so much. We have seen that there is little internal consistency, and no real consensus about what is embedded, and in what. But, with a few rules and definitions, this is fixable. What is less easy to remedy, in the context of ESL's aspiration to reconcile the three spheres of enquiry, is the conceptual incompatibility between embeddedness and constructivism and the "black box" effect.

Given this conceptual incompatibility, the proposition here is that ESL should move beyond embeddedness. This might seem utopian, especially given the admissions that our conceptual commitment to embeddedness runs so deep that we could not dispense with embeddedness even if we wanted to. So why propose an alternative?

There are two reasons. As Chapters 2 and 3 set out, an economic sociology of law is a timely and useful approach for giving us ways to consider, sociologically, the economic life of the law. The lens suffers from a core conceptual inconsistency which might be ironed out by moving beyond embeddedness. This, in turn, might increase its utility and applicability as a lens for research and policy. In other words, moving ESL beyond embeddedness might be useful for Academic Ann and Policy Polly in their work.

For Lay Lillian, though, the issue is wider discourse – how we are talking about the relationships between law and economy, and how these mould and shape our thoughtways and mental models. Specifically, how our metaphors, acting generatively, guide us to act as *homo economicus-juridicus*. An ESL lens can act as a microcosm for our wider conceptual commitment to embeddedness. If we can resolve the linguistic and conceptual incompatibilities in ESL, this might give us clues as to how these incompatibilities can be resolved in wider and more popular discourse. In short, if we can imagine an alternative in the context of an ESL, we might be able to apply this to our wider ways of doing, talking, and thinking about the relations between legal and economic phenomena. This might give us alternative and innovative responses to those crashes, crises, and catastrophes that continue to loom large.

So why not use Teubner's focus on communicative acts, bridging Habermas' development of a Husserlian phenomenological sphere that sits across from the sociological action frame of reference? Or Giddens' theory of structuration in its mediation between, and reconciliation of, recursive interactions and the reproduction of structure? What about Fineman's more flexible vulnerability theory? In proposing the lens below – a modified ESL approach – I have attempted to both remain at the mid-level, retaining an empirical focus, while offering a lens that is accessible and that avoids the paywall of impenetrable terminology. It also incorporates elements from linguistics and psychology that suggest that contrary to Chomsky's Universal Grammar thesis our mental models are very much shaped and honed by the vocabularies and grammars we have available to us (Russell, 2003; Boroditsky, 2009; Dermendzhiyska, 2021). The way we talk matters, and if we can agree that mainstream legal and economics concepts have "leaked in" to mould and shape everyday social realities, we can see the effect that these concepts have on the language we use, the mental models we are able to construct, and the interactions we perform (Giddens, 1984). In short, mainstream ways of legal and economic *talk* leads us to perform *as homo juridicus* and *as homo economicus* (Teubner, 2021) as the Swiss electorate and Supreme Court judges demonstrated.

So, while we cannot observe conceptual tools, thoughtways, or mental models, we can see how, why, when, where, and with whom actors interact, and the linguistic tools they use to do so. An ESL lens then, in the context of an academic research project, can balance the spheres of doing, talking, and thinking, imputing mental models through the language used. It can offer an understanding of how legal and economic aspects of interactions are performed, the shape these take, and why. Not just the reasons given by actors or what the actors think they are doing, but also deeper levels of cultural awareness and reflexivity, depending on the nature and focus of the research. In a broader context, though, an ESL frame can then ask more leading questions about how and why we might perform as *homo economicus* or *homo juridicus*, and pinpoint sites at which change might be brought about to enable a socially networked, morally constructed *homo sociologicus* to emerge.

Introducing Frerichs' rankings of social interactions (micro, meso, macro, meta), we noted that there were feedback loops between the meta level where we find rationalities (how we think) and the macro level where we find regimes (how we interact). These feedback loops also extend to the meso and micro levels of individual interactions. This includes a cognitive element, and hints at the reflexivity of actors to monitor their situation: do they want to fit in or stand out, to copy or to challenge, to reproduce social behaviour or to change it. Arguably, this offers a degree of constructivism. But the rankings were designed to place micro and macro interpretations of embeddedness on the same page, and in reproducing embeddedness and referring to the regimes of economy and law, and the rationalities of economics and law, the frame is prevented from realizing its full constructivist potential.

Similarly, the existing approach set out in Chapter 2 does not spend much time on how we communicate rationalities, or how interactions are performed. This is problematic given the major role that language has in shaping, and being shaped by, our mental models. In fact, as the following sections pick up, it is in our language where we see those occurrences of cognitive and normative disembedding discussed in Chapter 3. It is in our linguistic tools that we see evidence of the co-option of the non-economic by neoclassical economics because our conceptual tools are those of neoclassical economics. And it is in our language that we find evidence of how we think and perform *as homo economicus*. We need only think of the way we internalize measurements of productivity in the workplace ("I haven't had a very productive day"), or the ways in which the Supreme Court determined best use of a resource ("efficient" rather than "effective" use of a car park) (Burrows, 2016). Or the farcical headline that "Woodland walks save UK £185m a year" through relieving mental health woes; the language, and the mental models we subconsciously default to, and which we assume to be the most persuasive, are those of neoclassical economics (Carrington, 2021).

The remainder of this chapter explores how we might make an ESL-inspired lens conceptually consistent and compatible, moving beyond embeddedness to a constructivist lens that can be applied to empirical research and policy work.

ACADEMIC ANN

Ann wonders if we could shift our focus to interactions and feedback loops. Several of the sociological works she had rifled in the past had referred, in some shape or form, to feedback loops. It made sense to Ann to decentre the actor by focusing instead on interactions as they are performed, and then asking about the various flavours or aspects within each of those interactions. There would be legal and economic elements present in there somewhere – there always were. But there would be lots of other aspects too. Sometimes the actor would be aware of all of these. More often, they would not, with motivations and interests falling well below the radar of conscious awareness. Nevertheless, patterns of behaviour, "being on autopilot", and "acting subconsciously" were all phenomena that, to Ann, seemed an important point to include when seeking an understanding of how people act.

So, then, how might we move beyond embeddedness? The suggestion here is just that; one suggested example rather than a prescription. But it draws on theories from law, economics, sociology, psychology, and linguistics. Two shifts in focus are necessary. Firstly, instead of focusing on actors, we might focus instead on their *interactions*.[4] This allows us to appreciate the performance and reproduction of aspects of these interactions, ubiquitous and quotidian in some cases, shifting and dynamic in others as interactions are repeated across the contingent elements of space and time. This is where the "doing" and the "talking" happens and where we can begin to understand the mental models. So, by focusing on interactions, we are looking for the legal and economic phenomena that are performed throughout and within each social interaction, but we are reminded that these are two aspects among many others that inform how the interaction plays out.

ACADEMIC ANN

Aware of the differences that emerged from subtle alterations to her interpretation of embeddedness, Ann is a little worried that such a significant shift in how she frames her research could have equally significant consequences. Nevertheless, she is now convinced that a constructivist lens could offer the most conceptually cohesive approach, and she sits down with her notebook once again.

She now needs to observe stakeholder interactions, so that she can begin to look out for the performance of legal and economic phenomena. But how can she do this through the medium of interviews? Ann briefly considers switching to ethnography but drops this idea. She realizes that she can still explore the performance of legal and economic phenomena within interactions if she adjusts her interview questions. In the course of the investment and management of the business in the host country, Ann's investors will come into contact and build relationships with a wide range of other actors: local businesspeople, local and central government actors, local civic representatives and community actors, and so on. Ann thinks that, by carefully targeting her questions, she can understand with whom, how, when, where, and why an investor has interacted, and she can begin to understand the relationship in terms of its duration, trust, and any other aspects that are relevant for understanding the development of communal networks.

She jots down: "Instead of asking Investor X about their experience of the legal system, instead ask about their interactions to achieve task Y, and what happened".

Secondly, rather than getting caught up in the embeddedness conundrum, we can look for the *feedback loops* within and throughout each and every social interaction, through which legal and economic phenomena are re-co-constituted.[5]

4 This shift was originally inspired by Giddens' structuration theory which he set out in *The Constitution of Society* in 1984. However, a shift from actors to their interactions mirrors other shifts in various social sciences to decentre the actor.

5 The idea is developed from Giddens' structuration theory, which uses the notion of "homeostatic loops", defined as "causal factors which have a feedback effect in system reproduction". The

These are the mechanisms whereby self-reflective actors monitor their social situation. It is where they (mentally) affirm or challenge the actions of others. It is through these feedback loops that actors choose to use, abuse, or avoid legal and economic phenomena in their interactions. And it is through these feedback loops that actors' perceptions of reality are constantly challenged, honed, and shaped, and mental models formed and reformed; where meaning is attributed and understanding takes place. This reflects the constructivist notion that the legal and economic are *aspects* or "flavours" of social interactions, or that the legal and the economic are two sides of the same, social coin (Ewick and Silbey, 1998, p. 217). This also reflects the understanding that these legal and economic aspects are produced, performed, and re-co-constituted in and through each and every interaction. So, in looking for clues to those feedback loops, we are looking for evidence of the actor's mental models or rationalities, and how these shape the actor's understanding of their role.

ACADEMIC ANN

Having shifted her focus to the interactions between investors and other actors, Ann wonders how she can look for these feedback loops. This is about the investor – or any other actor – reflexively monitoring their position vis-à-vis the other actors: their understanding of the situation. Ann thinks that she can look out for clues in the interview, as well as before it starts and after it ends, about how the investor perceives their own role. Do they pause before answering a question? Do they look uneasy or uncertain, or correct themselves? Do they justify a particular action by reference to the fact that everyone else does the same? In short, are there clues about how the investor sees themselves as a social being, and how they reflexively monitor their situation and their performance of legal and economic phenomena?

By focusing on interactions and feedback loops, and by moving beyond embeddedness, we can avoid placing any aspects in a black box. We can avoid entrenching mainstream mental models, and we can also revisit how we talk about the relationships between legal and economic aspects of social interactions. This approach also allows us to step back from the primary ontological metaphors ("the law" and "economy") and the secondary and tertiary, generative metaphors that sit atop these ("embedded").

The following discussion proposes one way of going about this. It combines the horizontal elements of Roger Cotterrell's community lens with the vertical

feedback loops defined here, though, include intended and unintended effects. See (Giddens, 1984, pp. 27–8, 375).

elements of Sabine Frerichs rankings of principles of social organization that were set out in Chapter 2 (Cotterrell, 1997b; Frerichs, 2011). It then also adds insights from some of the literature on performativity (MacKenzie and Millo, 2003; Callon, 2008; MacKenzie, Muniesa and Siu, 2008). Figure 5.2 (page 56) visualizes the new focus following our two proposed shifts.

Shift 1: from the actor to their interaction

We saw, in Chapter 2, how Weber's interaction ideal types, extended through Roger Cotterrell's community lens, might offer a helpful taxonomy for exploring legal and economic aspects of interactions. Weberian interaction ideal types include the instrumental, the traditional, the belief-based, and the affective, and nudge us to consider aspects of interactions beyond the legal and the economic. It is worth noting though that the flexibility of Cotterrell's community lens can also help us to shift our gaze from actors to their interactions. It encourages us to look beyond the immediate impact of legal (or economic) reform and assess the broader effects as they diffuse throughout society (Perry-Kessaris, 2008a). At the same time, by building "beyond the idea of embeddedness", the community lens allows us to avoid charges of atomization, "oversocialization", or "undersocialization", while encouraging a focus on the content and substance of the interactions (Granovetter, 1985; Cotterrell, 2013, p. 51).

The community lens "is an aid towards understanding, for regulatory purposes, contemporary patterns of social relations in all their fluidity and variety" (Cotterrell, 2002, p. 54). However,

> the idea of "a community" as a distinct social phenomenon that is kind, fuzzy or warm should be avoided. Instead, the focus should be on *social relations of community* of various contrasting types. Community refers to a *quality* of social relationships. It suggests a *degree* of stability and permanence in them, but not necessarily very much.
>
> (Cotterrell, 2013, p. 55)[6]

The language of Cotterrell's communal networks is subtle, offering ways of appreciating relations of community of varying ideal types (instrumental, traditional, belief-based, and affective) that we can extend for convenience over Frerichs' four layers of social interaction (micro, meso, macro, meta). By moving beyond embeddedness but retaining the broad sweep of Frerichs' and Perry-Kessaris' insights, we can reframe the way we talk about legal and economic aspects of interactions and, glimpsed through the language used, how dominant regimes and rationalities are reproduced. We are therefore no longer talking about the extent to which society is embedded in the economy

6 Emphasis in original.

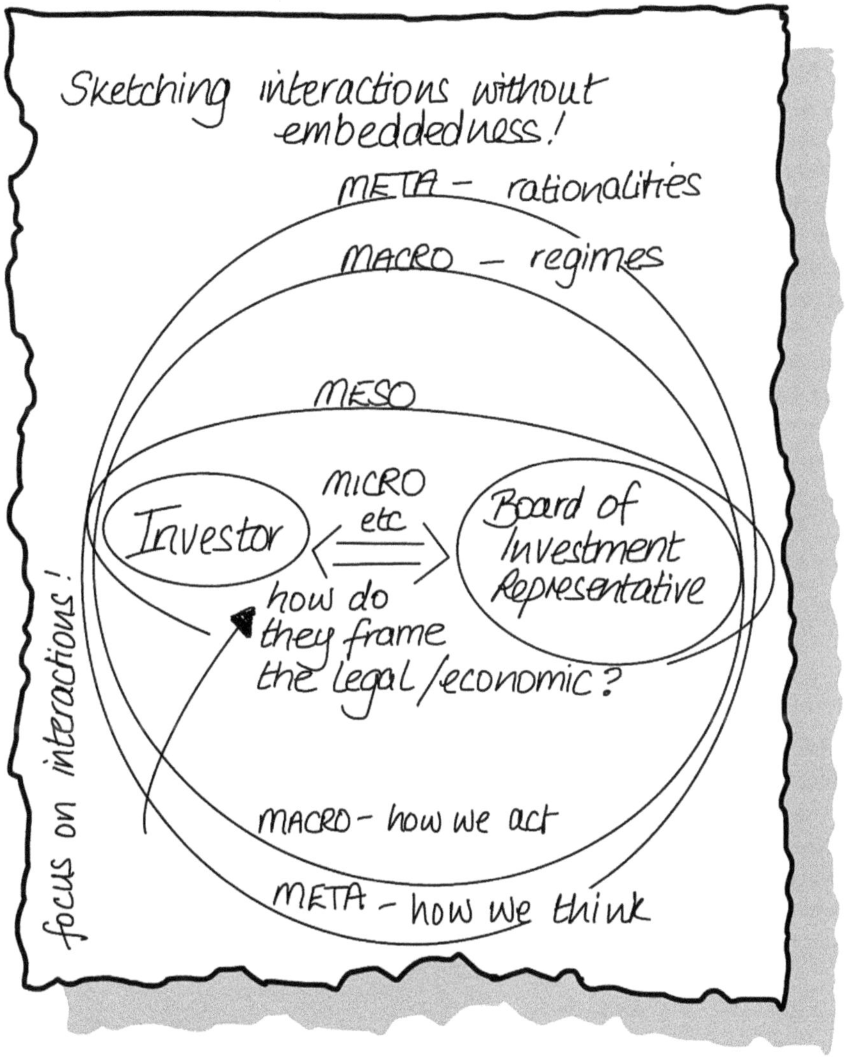

Figure 5.2 A page from Academic Ann's sketchbook, reproduced here with her kind permission. This is Ann's second iteration of her planned fieldwork, as seen through an ESL lens. The first, in Figure 2.3 in Chapter 2 (see page 56), applied an embeddedness-based ESL lens, but having explored the differences that result from different interpretations of embeddedness, Ann has chosen to avoid the concept of embeddedness. This time then, Ann has used an ESL lens that no longer relies on embeddedness. She is focused here on the interactions between the actors, and the feedback loops that operate within those interactions. In practice, she realizes she will have to adjust her interview style and questions to gather data on interactions and feedback loops.

at the level of meta rationalities. Instead, we are asking about the extent to which economic and legal aspects of interactions are performed at the micro and meso levels.

Notably though, this approach lets us understand how aspects (such as the legal or economic) of any interaction are re-co-constructed through each social interaction. We can zoom in to focus on the micro level interactions where these aspects are constructed, and we can zoom out to appreciate the effects of multiple re-co-constructions of legal and economic aspects across space and time, noting the emergence of regimes and rationalities. In so doing, we shift the focus to one in which "the economic appears as an aspect of the social" (Cotterrell, 2013, p. 51). Indeed, Cotterrell specifically seeks to "shift focus [...] away from the idea of law as rooted in the governmental activity, agreements, or relations of *nation states*" and "towards a recognition that law is also rooted in the projects and aspirations of actors operating in networks of community" (Perry-Kessaris, 2012, p. 7). Similarly, the economic has:

> regulatory conditions and requirements that reflect not only the particular characteristics of economic relations but also their situation as part of networks of community that may be held together by a variety of bonds (for example, shared values, allegiances or customary practices, as well as by a convergence of economic interests).
>
> (Cotterrell, 2013, p. 51)

Additionally, though while highlighting the economic, a community lens gives us the vocabulary and grammar for recognizing and valuing the non-economic; the traditional, the affective, and the belief-based relations of community that comprise other aspects of interactions. Weber's fourfold typology of interaction ideal types is "necessary to distinguish carefully different components of law's social environment" (Cotterrell, 2002, p. 53). It is notable here that:

> [p]eople have allegiances, with varying degrees of transience or permanence, at different times and in different ways, and often simultaneously, to different groups and social relations, involving intricate overlapping of the different types of community life – instrumental, traditional, belief-based and affective.
>
> (Cotterrell, 2002, p. 49)

Moreover, "if the law serves one community at the expense of "protecting and promoting the well-being of other kinds of social bonds, other types of community, it fails to meet some important demands" (Cotterrell, 2002, p. 47).

But, you ask, what is different here? Wasn't this all set out in Chapter 2? The lens set out in Chapter 2 that combined Cotterrell's and Frerichs' approaches continued our conceptual commitment to embeddedness, and even sought to strengthen that concept. In setting out the key elements of the lens here, it is helpful to appreciate that the community lens, with its Weberian ideal types, extended across rankings of social interaction, is compatible with a social constructivist reading of legal and economic phenomena. More than that, the combination of elements, along with the trust and performativity that the following sections include, suggests a constructivist reading that moves us beyond embeddedness. This is a subtle shift that suggests a slightly different but more flexibly inclusive focus, avoiding any conceptual inconsistencies between a community-based ESL lens that seeks to strengthen embeddedness as a core concept, and one that seeks to move beyond it.

Trust is important in understanding interactions

The four ideal types exist in complex combinations, varying from actor to actor, and interaction to interaction. Instrumental aspects of interactions are essentially goal oriented and encompass both legal and economic phenomena, and we can observe these as we zoom out from the micro and meso levels to regimes at the macro level and rationalities at the meta level. However, an essential element in the development of networks of community is the mutual interpersonal trust between actors. Again, a need to pay attention to this justifies a shift in focus from the actor to their interaction.

Mutual interpersonal trust is essential for networks of community but, as a nebulous and contested notion, open to interpretation. Each of the four ideal types of collective involvement "imply different kinds of trusting relationships and different regulatory needs" (Cotterrell, 1997a, p. 75). More precisely, such networks of "community [can be] best thought of as a web of understandings about social relations [which in turn] is built on (in a sense codifies) relations of mutual interpersonal trust" (Cotterrell, 1997a, p. 87). Thus, it is necessary to stress that networks of community do not spring up overnight, but rather evolve gradually, consolidated over time. This is imperative for the development of a "high degree of *trust*" to be built on "accumulated experience of past interactions" (Cotterrell, 1997a, p. 86). "Trust encourages future interaction and provides the motivation to engage in relatively free, uncalculated relations with others" (Cotterrell, 1997a, p. 86).

As trust is a subjective matter, the law plays only an indirect role by "*approving and protecting empirical conditions that facilitate trusting relationships*" (Cotterrell, 1997a, p. 88). Like the concept of embeddedness, trust is relational and, along with "networks", comprises "perhaps [one of] the most distinctive terms in the new economic sociology" addressing dimensions of economic organization that most economists choose to ignore (Sayer, 2005, p. 49). Trust can be differentiated from confidence and expectation then, and we can locate it between and straddling the embedded networks of Granovetter's work and Habermas' "systems" (Sayer, 2005, p. 50). It can similarly operate explicitly when stated through linguistic tools, or implicitly acting as an unthought rationality that tacitly shapes both linguistic and conceptual tools.[7]

A trust-based, ideal-typical approach to understanding relations of community is not unproblematic. There are four points to note. Firstly, if you are used to dealing with the certainties, binaries, and quantification of mainstream approaches, a community lens can seem unbearably "woolly", even vague. It is important to keep in mind that "community" does not refer to a cosy theory of neighbourliness but captures the unpleasant side of power relations too. Actors can use the law, as well as abuse and avoid it, and each of these reflects legal aspects of interactions of varying ideal types (Perry-Kessaris, 2008b).

Secondly, as both legal and economic phenomena sit within the category of instrumental relations, some might feel that this blurs the line between them. This is a justifiable critique, and the goal is not to elide the difference between legal and economic phenomena. But, if we agree that a constructivist lens might be useful, our focus shifts to the nature and goals of such aspects of interactions, giving us an alternative perspective on how and why these phenomena are re-co-constituted. We can identify both legal and economic aspects of interactions as instrumental, and still differentiate them.

Thirdly, the approach could be described as purposive in nature in the sense that the goals and aspirations of the actors determine the ideal type. This is the case for instrumental aspects of interactions (is the actor attempting to transact, for example?) but less so with the other ideal types. Once again, this requires an understanding of what the actor understands, and the only tools we have are the actor's words and actions. Nevertheless, as the actor might not be aware of her own motivations – that she is being nudged towards neoclassical economic goals, for example – the categories set out here offer useful reminders for a researcher, such as Ann, to be aware of the wider context in which social interactions unfold. So, we might look for references to and construction of the linguistic and conceptual tools of doctrinal law or neoclassical economics. We then might look for how these contrast with those of other actors, or with the surrounding institutional environment.

Finally, the question of the degree, strength, and sustainability of mutual interpersonal trust is nebulous, relative, and subjective. These grey areas of interpretation sit in contrast to the neat binaries of the mainstream approaches that an ESL lens challenges. The scaling up of social interactions across time and space can mitigate the subjectivity here somewhat as we look for patterns that congeal into regimes and thoughtways that congeal into rationalities. Taken together, this first shift offers a focus on interactions instead of actors.

7 Fineman's vulnerability theory "challenges the dominant conception of the universal legal subject as an autonomous, independent, and fully-functioning adult", emphasising the socially and materially dynamic legal subject in a manner that could be said to echo a shift to a focus on interactions with constitutive elements including trust. See (Fineman, 2022).

The central role of our linguistic tools in both revealing and concealing rationalities and regimes, and their alternatives, can be explored further through notions from performativity.

Shift 2: embeddedness to feedback loops

A second shift is helpful at this point to move us beyond embeddedness. We have already shifted our focus from actors to their interactions, and this gives us the space to ask what aspects comprise those interactions – are there legal phenomena, economic phenomena, or other aspects that we might wish to pay attention to. But within each and every interaction is a series of feedback loops and paying attention to these can give us the tools to explore how behaviours come to be entrenched or challenged. Insights from performativity literature can show us how and why a focus on feedback loops might be instructive.

Understanding feedback loops through performativity

Mistakes happen. But sometimes these small slips can give us interesting insights and can open up new avenues of inquiry and research. The Eurobarometer survey mentioned in Chapter 1 (page 10) of 2007 into animal welfare did just that (Law, 2009; *Eurobarometer Special EB on "Attitudes of Europeans towards Animal Welfare"* (Ref 442), 2016; *Public Opinion – European Commission and the Eurobarometer Surveys*, 2021).[8] The survey had intended to gauge attitudes to animal welfare across Europe, repeating a similar survey that had been carried out a couple of years previously. In the survey, question QB6 asked whether the regulation of animal welfare should be a matter for consumers at the point of purchase, or a matter for all citizens that should be regulated by public authorities (*Summary: Attitudes of Europeans to Animal Welfare*, 2016, p. 14). It would appear that most people believed it to be a matter of general public interest that should not be left to consumers alone.

The survey did not set out to test the performativity of respondent labelling, namely whether they were identified as "European citizens" or "consumers" ("Eurobarometer Survey Reveals European Citizens Have Increasingly Positive Image of EU", 2014). But from subsequent analysis of the data, commentators have noted that those respondents identified as "citizens" appeared to have a higher regard for animal welfare than consumers even when all other parameters remained the same (Law, 2009). This was an unintended by-product. Somehow though, the mistake had occurred, and subsequent data analysis was unable to account for the differences in opinion, save for the different identification of respondents. Pointing out the "creative" enactment of

8 (Law, 2009; *Eurobarometer Special EB on "Attitudes of Europeans towards Animal Welfare" (Ref 442)*, 2016; *Summary: Attitudes of Europeans to Animal Welfare*, 2016, p. 3)

a European consumer-citizen, John Law notes that this appears to raise the question of a difference in the attitudes expressed between a citizen with rights and responsibilities (who cares deeply about animal welfare and thinks the state should intervene regulate), and a consumer with rights (who prefers to let the market determine animal welfare through consumer choice) (Law, 2009).

For Callon, theories of performativity can help to explain the interplay between discourse and the social reality that it both describes and shapes (Callon, 2008). Developing Goffman's notion of social "performance", Butler has noted that identities themselves are constructed in and through social performances (Butler, cited in Callon, 2008). These notions locate the importance of the feedback loops within interactions through which actors are able to perceive, understand, and then affirm or challenge their own self and behaviour as a social being. We should be careful not to over-simplify things here though. We also need to keep in mind the phenomenon of Merton's "self-fulfilling prophecy", whereby actors perform according to the model (MacKenzie, Muniesa and Siu, 2008, p. 3). The most common, and perhaps the original, illustration given for this is the Black-Scholes method.

In 1972, Black, Scholes, and Merton, three economists with an interest in financial markets and trading, developed a model (the BSM model) that applied the principles of modern, orthodox economics to options trading, transforming it in the process and removing the sense that this was, in some way, a form of gambling. Instead, through the application of economics, options trading became a respectable endeavour. The problem, at first, was that their model did not fit all that well. However, as traders quickly caught on to the model and realized its potential value, they began to play to the model and the "fit began to improve" (MacKenzie and Millo, 2003, p. 121). By 1986, further testing by Rubenstein found that deviations from the model had fallen to less than 1 percent (Rubenstein, 1994, p. 74, cited in MacKenzie and Millo, 2003). The model had not changed. What had altered was the behaviour of the traders. They had begun to perform the model.

More recently, this phenomenon has come to plague modellers of the COVID pandemic, whose early models (or what the public tended to refer to as predictions) did not take into account their impact on social behaviour. Responding to criticism of "doom mongering" from those critical of lockdowns, modellers have pointed out that their estimates in effect changed the way people behave, thereby invalidating the model. COVID models themselves have come to perform a pandemic – the archetypal self-fulfilling prophecy (van Basshuysen *et al.*, 2021).

There is a wider point here though. We have seen the extent to which models, predictions, and theories can alter human behaviour. It is not unreasonable then to ask about the extent to which other theories from the social sciences shape the way we think and act. Like the traders in the Chicago Board of Options Exchange, by monitoring our interactions we adjust accordingly. Like our neighbour when faced with predictions of high mortality and sickness, we choose to stay at home a little more or cancel that holiday. This is particularly relevant when we consider ways of doing, talking, and thinking about legal and economic phenomena. If the linguistic tools that we have available to us assume (implicitly and tacitly) *homo economicus* and his lawyerly cousin *homo juridicus*, this will direct our thoughtways, mould our conceptual tools, and shape our actions. To return to the opening sentence of the preface, the way we talk matters.

We have seen how an ongoing commitment to the concept of embeddedness re-entrenches neoclassical-doctrinal lenses, and we have now seen that, in turn, these direct us to perform as *homo economicus-juridicus*. The fictions and metaphors that we use to talk about legal and economic phenomena hide those baked-in assumptions and tacit thoughtways that entrench doctrinal and neoclassical theories. And by performing these linguistic and conceptual tools (as seen in the example of embeddedness-talk), we affirm the mental models to others. Feedback loops within our interactions confirm these to be accepted ways of acting – accepted ways of performing legal and economic phenomena socially. Therefore, to challenge embeddedness-talk and the entrenchment of mainstream theory that it engenders, shifting our grammar and vocabulary beyond embeddedness can assist in creating ways for us to do, talk, and think *as homo sociologicus*.

Performativity, like the works of Karl Polanyi, has become more fashionable lately and therefore suffers from similar contentions and disagreements. While it is hard to find a "clear unambiguous definition of performativity in the literature", there is a general consensus that performativity involves "changing rather than describing behaviour" (Mäki, 2011, p. 2). It is beyond the scope of the present discussion to settle whether actors are "inside" or "outside" of the economy, intrinsic or endogenous to it or to the law (Callon, 1998a, 2008; MacKenzie, Muniesa and Siu, 2008; but cf. Santos and Rodrigues, 2009; and Mäki, 2011). Callon's best-known assertion that the economy "is embedded not in society but in economics" is not universally accepted (Callon, 1998a, p. 30), but there is a consensus that it raises core questions about the power of economics to shape how we think and act, and that as we perform economic theories, we construct "the economy".[9] For Callon, economics refers to the full range of disciplines, specialities, technologies, and forms of knowledge with which economic actors and their markets are equipped, meaning that economics "performs, shapes and formats the economy, rather than observing how it functions" (MacKenzie, Muniesa and Siu, 2008, p. 4). Economics creates the phenomena it sets out to describe, echoing Giddens' notion of the

9 According to MacKeever's three types of performativity, only strictly *Barnesian* performativity has a truly recreative role in shaping economic processes, meaning that these definitions of performativity are, as with most subjects, subject to a great deal of debate and controversy, as cited in (Mäki, 2011, p. 3).

"double hermeneutic", whereby social science ideas "leak" back into the real world, shaping the phenomena they seek to describe (Giddens, 1984). As such, sociology's goal should be to understand the role of economics in producing the agent (MacKenzie and Millo, 2003, p. 108). We can make a similar argument about the law. Legal theory creates principles, ideals, and concepts that shape how we all think. The language of legal theory is baked into everyday vocabularies and grammars (we enter into a contract, we have a right to something, or an interest in something else), shaping not only how we talk, but how we think, and therefore how we (inter)act. In performing as a legally aware, juridical person, we perform *as homo juridicus*. In accepting performativity's suggestion that our conceptual tools might shape our actions, and society more broadly, we can raise an interesting thought experiment in response: what conceptual and linguistic tools might we have at our disposal now if Polanyi's *The Great Transformation* had received more attention than Hayek's *The Road to Serfdom*?

Exploring the performativity of law and economics with a thought experiment

Karl Polanyi wrote *The Great Transformation* in the US in the early 1940s, drawing on a decade of prior work. The book was first published in the US, where, by all accounts, the publishers were so pleased that they commissioned a follow-up. Nevertheless, the book made relatively little impact in the 1940s, and although Polanyi pledged it to the working people of Britain, "whatever they may think of it", it made even less impact in the UK. This is, in hindsight, a shame, and possibly due to the politics of the time. Polanyi, a committed socialist, was not only a foreigner in the UK – repeatedly failing to secure teaching positions at UK universities even later in life despite multiple appointments in the US and stellar references – but was distrustful of American post-war intentions. While "the New Deal had been designed to make America safe for market capitalism", the Bretton Woods institutions "aimed to repeat the trick on a global scale", facilitating US "hegemonic ascendancy by establishing the dollar as the world's paramount currency" (Dale, 2016, p. 195).

As a scholar of the havoc wreaked by the gold standard, Polanyi was worried. Nevertheless, the demands of Wall Street, and the economics of Keynes and Hayek, won through to shape the economic reconstruction of Europe in the shadow – and image – of the US. The McCarthyist and, later, Cold War mentalities doubled down on free market rationalities, presenting Communism as the global threat to American, and by this time European, stability, and setting the stage for the emergence of an extreme version of market society: neoliberalism. The implications of these shifts, based on utopian fictions of self-regulating markets and their co-option of society, continue to define how we understand and respond to current dilemmas: those financial crashes, social crises, and environmental catastrophes that we are grappling with in the third decade of the twenty-first century. Our mental models are those that decades of economic, legal, and social orthodoxy have shaped, mainstreaming particular rationalities while sidelining and invisibilizing others. How we talk, think, and perform legal and economic phenomena is the product of our recent history. So, then, what mental models might we be using now had Polanyi's *Great Transformation* been more widely read, and received greater debate at the time? Might his subtle historical reading of the fictitious commodities and the tendencies of economic liberalism to push the limits of "utopian" free markets that undermined the very fabric of society have given wider pause for thought? What might be the orthodox relationships between law, economy, and society had Polanyi's always (or never) embedded market thesis met with wider acclaim?

This thought experiment brings into play the way that our mental models are continually affirmed or challenged through feedback loops: the reflexive monitoring of our own thoughts and behaviours compared to those of others we interact with.[10] We have seen, above, how our vocabularies and grammars can shape our mental models sysnaesthetically, as we associate combinations of sounds with ideals and concepts, often subconsciously. We have also seen how these mental models then shape the way we act and interact, and that through interactions we can reflexively monitor our behaviour against that of those around us. We make sure that we fit in (or stand out, depending on our wishes), and that we perform legal and economic phenomena appropriate to the context. Given that our language presumes a *homo economicus-juridicus* figure, we perform accordingly, whether we are aware of this reference point or not. But this is dependent on the self-monitoring and reflexivity that each actor engages in, even on the smallest scale, in each and every interaction (Goffman, 1959, 1967). We might say then that the way we do, talk, and think are mutually re-co-constituted within and throughout each and every interaction, as diagram (c) in Figure 5.3 on page 138 visualizes. It is helpful to examine the feedback loops that enable this mutual re-co-constitution in a specific setting.

We could suggest that, as set out in Figure 5.3(a), there are two parts to the feedback loops that comprise reflexive monitoring and behaviour adjustment in the use, abuse, and avoidance of legal and economic phenomena. The first occurs within the interaction, where the actor observes how others behave. Say, for example, you go into a local newsagent to buy a newspaper. There is a queue. You, being in the UK, join the queue and wait your turn to pay, as others are doing, carefully noting the polite amount of distance between

10 Giddens refers to "homeostatic loops", which have more complexity than the feedback loops proposed here. This is in the interest of keeping ESL portable, lightweight, adaptable, and accessible. See Giddens, 1984. Alternatives here, although not directly equivalent, could have included Foucault's *epistemes*, Bourdieu's *habitus*, or Latour's ANT (actor–network theory).

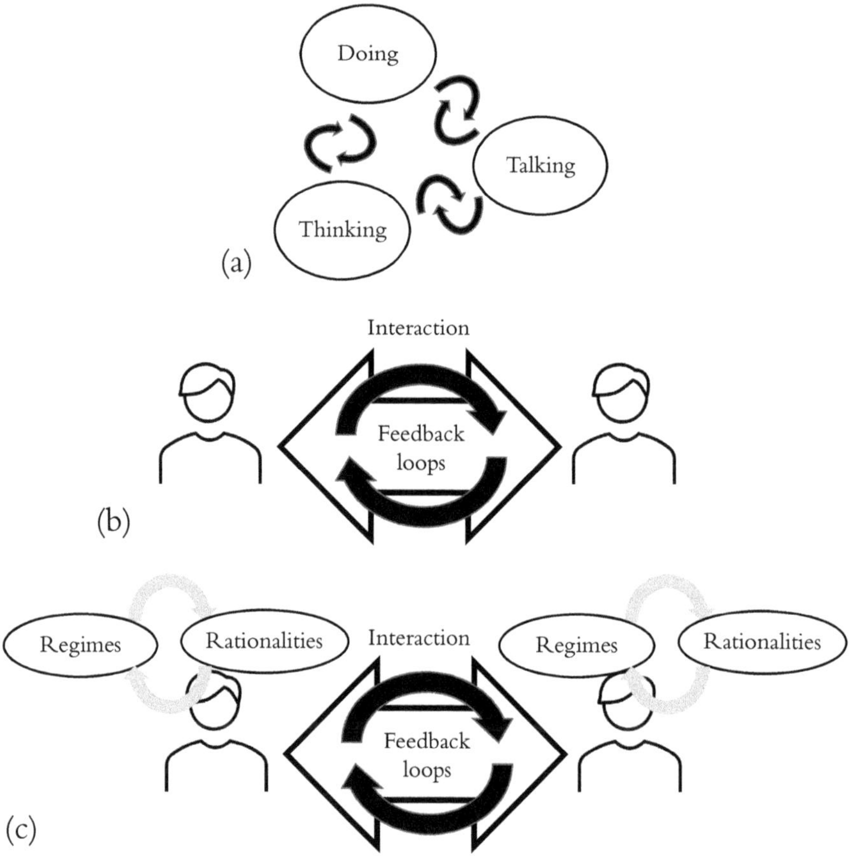

Figure 5.3 The two shifts in focus proposed here place interactions and feedback loops at the heart of any sociological understanding of legal and economic phenomena. In diagram (a) at the top, we can see feedback loops between our ways of doing, talking, and thinking. Then, in diagram (b), we can see that feedback loops operate within and throughout each and every interaction. Finally, in diagram (c), we note that there are additional feedback loops internal to each actor.

you and the next customer. Convention dictates that you wave your intended purchase at the cashier, and then wait for them to ask you for payment before offering a card or cash. All the other shoppers have done this. Anything else, throwing the money down first, or pushing into the line, would meet with tuts of disapproval or even outright approbation.

The second part of these feedback loops occurs in your own head when, having compared and monitored the behaviour of others and adjusted your own accordingly, you then reflect on whether your latest interactions demand shifts in your regimes and rationalities. Have you encountered social clues that suggest a modification to your conceptual and linguistic tools? Perhaps the most obvious example here is, having spent weeks in your own house during lockdown, whether you notice changes in general social behaviour upon re-entering society, and whether these require you to adjust your regimes (how you understand society to act) and rationalities (how you understand society to think). For example, if people used to queue to pay for their morning paper, but now simply throw the money down and walk out, you might be dismayed that standards have slipped, but, seeing the acceptance of this new state of affairs by the cashier, you decide to follow suit and act in the same way. You have monitored the behaviour of others, and adjusted your behaviour to fit in, at the same time shifting your expectations of social interactions (of buying a newspaper) to this new reality.

In purchasing your newspaper, you are engaging in a social interaction with the cashier and, as two sides of the same social coin, you are therefore performing both economic and legal phenomena. You are handing the cashier money in exchange for the newspaper (economic aspects of the interaction), but money is also backed and guaranteed by the state (legal phenomena).[11] You are engaging a business (the newsagent) which is registered as a company, and which employs its staff (company and labour law). The newspaper you are buying (also a company) relies on free speech to investigate and publish its stories (libel and human rights law). Were you to take your newspaper without paying, the analysis would be the same except you are performing economic and legal phenomena through their avoidance or abuse. You know you should pay but decide not to. Similarly, in the example above where post-lockdown standards appear to have slipped, throwing the money on the counter for the cashier to find later does not alter the interaction, your expectations, or your interpretation of those expectations. Nor does it alter the fact that you are performing the same legal and economic phenomena, despite the physical distance in the interaction.[12]

The reflexive monitoring of our context, and our understanding of our position within this context, is continuous. As such, we are not always, or even usually, aware of this process and the "transformative impact which the social sciences can have on their 'subject matter'" can occur both consciously

11 Polanyi's thesis about the fictitious commodity of money is relevant, but not the focus, here. Whether a fiction or not, we act "as if" money were real. This Vaihingerian "epistemological attitude" allows the focus to remain on the fact that money, as legal tender backed by the authority of the state, invokes legal as well as economic phenomena. I'm grateful to Geoffrey Samuel for drawing Vaihinger's work to my attention. See (Kelsen and Kletzer, 2014; Samuel, 2018, p. 231).

12 There is a point to be made here that interactions in situations of non-co-presence can still be understood through this lens. This covers the despondently absent cashier, but also extends to Internet-based transactions where sites of co-presence are rare. Nevertheless, legal and economic phenomena can still be identified in each and every interaction, and our feedback loops continue to be reflexively activated to monitor our behaviour according to our understanding of our surroundings.

and subconsciously (Giddens, 1984, pp. xix, 7). This, again, can happen deliberately or by chance. Noting the power of subtle changes to the context in which interactions occur, the field of behavioural economics, or "nudge" theory, advocates the design of "choice architecture" that directs behaviour towards a particular outcome (Thaler and Sunstein, 2009). The discussion above explored the development of the Black-Scholes options trading formula that became more accurate over time not because the models were honed, but because traders adjusted their behaviours to the model (MacKenzie and Millo, 2003, pp. 121–2). These feedback loops, here the result of deliberate application of social science ideas to the real world, operated to shift both the field of inquiry and the academic research into that field.

But the "double hermeneutic" can also happen by chance (Giddens, 1984). This can occur at a slower pace but can have greater and longer-lasting impact. The absence of intent, however, does leave a potentially larger space for unintended consequences. We might think of the historically "good ideas" that social scientists have had over the centuries (the rule of law, parliamentary democracy, the independence of the judiciary, etc.) to see how an academic idea can seep into the daily functioning and consciousness of society, adjusting shared expectations and socially monitored behaviours accordingly, solidifying over time to become deeply held principles. But we can also bring to mind ideas from economics that have come to shape social regimes and rationalities subconsciously, even without the explicit acknowledgement of economists (Callon, 2008, p. 312). This "double hermeneutic" means that social sciences, unlike the natural sciences, can and do influence the sphere they set out to study (Giddens, 1984, p. 374).

By shifting our focus to interactions and the feedback loops that operate continually and dynamically within and throughout every interaction, we have one way of moving ESL beyond its current conceptual commitment to embeddedness. The alternative set out here is both flexible and dynamic, while capable of capturing multiple levels and ranks of social interactions, voices, and interests. By assessing the centrality of linguistic tools for shaping both the actor and her regimes and rationalities, the proposed lens set out here provides alternative terminology and linguistic tools for discussing legal and economic phenomena sociologically. The shifts in vocabulary and grammar are set out in Table 5.1.

Beyond *homo economicus-juridicus*?

We have already been introduced to the three archetypal caricatures that embody core assumptions and preferences of mainstream doctrinal legal and neoclassical economics approaches. Set out in Chapter 1, these are *homo juridicus*, the rational man of law, and his market-based cousin, *homo economicus*, the typical utility maximizer. The discussion in this chapter has suggested that two small shifts in our focus can offer us an alternative way of talking, and therefore

Table 5.1 Comparing how we might talk about doing and thinking about legal and economic phenomena. Mainstream ways of talking are contrasted with those suggested by an ESL lens

Conventional discourse	*Doing (how we might talk about doing)*	*Feedback loops*	*Thinking (how we might talk about thinking)*
Law	What is the law? What is perceived as legal/illegal?	⇔	What is understood to be legal/illegal, and the thought processes and reference points that inform such decisions
Economy	What is the economy? What interactions are seen to be market-based or market-driven?	⇔	Economic thoughtways that recognize behaviour as market oriented or not market oriented. Draws on neoclassical economics for rationalities (productivity, efficiency, growth, etc.)
Economic sociology of law	What aspects of interactions might we identify and sociologically analyze as legal or economic, and how are these performed?	⇔	What rationalities or thoughtways, conceptual and linguistic tools, might we identify and sociologically analyze as legal or economic? How might we *think* about legal and economic phenomena in a sociological context?

of thinking and of doing, that can challenge orthodox approaches, suggesting a *homo sociologicus*. Insights from performativity and cognitive sciences indicate that our ways of talking might have far greater impact on our ways of thinking and (inter)acting than we realize. Our words channel our thoughtways. The example of embeddedness-talk, the core concept of ESL, suggests that the unthought application of metaphors to a particular context can have unforeseen and unintended consequences on the outcome of research or policy. The suggestion is, therefore, that there is an equally significant impact in wider discourse from the inadequacies of our language and that this might have a direct impact on how we are able to respond to crashes, crises, and catastrophes.

As the discussion on performativity indicates, the close re-co-constitution of theory and reality through interaction works in both directions. Thus, while *homo economicus-juridicus* is not to be found in the wild, he "nevertheless 'really does exist'" (Callon, 1998a, p. 51; MacKenzie and Millo, 2003, p. 109). Moreover, while rational, economic man does exist, it is not as a rule or an ahistorical reality, but rather as "the process of configuration" that pulls together the forces of "material and metrological investments, property rights and money" (Callon, 1998b, pp. 22–3, cited in MacKenzie and Millo, 2003, p. 137). And, referring back to economic sociology and ESL, the cultural and historical context still matters. Even in the most economistic of settings, where actors "perform" *homo economicus*, "reputation and respect" matter, and while a passable version of rational economic man has been "configured cognitively", it remains to be seen whether "he can be configured morally" (MacKenzie and Millo, 2003, p. 141). Or if we would want to. Or whether, indeed, performativity could even extend this far – into the cognitive configuration of actors to the extent that they exclude moral and communal concerns from their actions. MacKenzie and Millo suggest that morally atomistic markets, were they to be created, should be done so out of silicone, as software or algorithms, rather than flesh and blood (MacKenzie and Millo, 2003, p. 141). The balance in approaches and frames used between *homo economicus* and his "classical apparent negation, *homo sociologicus*", remains both elusive and perhaps even illusive (MacKenzie and Millo, 2003, p. 141).

Making some predictions with caveats in 2000, Nobel Memorial Prize winning economist Richard Thaler suggested that *homo economicus* might evolve into something more akin to *Homo sapiens* (Thaler, 2000). The predicted rise of "more realistic conceptions" of economic agents in the two intervening decades has seen some progress. A good lens to appreciate this evolution is through the World Bank's World Development Reports which, year on year, have reflected the trends in economic and legal thinking. A shift towards experimentalism and a recognition of mental models expanded limited conceptions of rational agents, however the stubborn implementation gap suggests that there are still improvements to be made. The proposition is that through alternative ways of talking, specifically sociologically oriented vocabularies and grammars that recognize the social basis of legal and economic aspects of interactions, we might allow ourselves the thoughtways to explore becoming *homo sociologicus*. To return to the opening paragraphs of Chapter 1, we might start hacking a new pathway through that jungle, opening up a range of different destinations to which, having established pathways, we can then default.

There are wider shifts occurring in how we challenge the limitations of our current conceptual and linguistic tools. The law and political economy movement in the US (see, inter alia, Blalock, 2015), the emergence of theories like Fineman's vulnerability theory (Fineman, 2022), and wider calls to decentre and rethink the legal subject in the era of the Anthropocene (Matthews, 2021; Norman, 2022), all indicate that dissatisfactions with our mental models can lead us to conjure something better. An economic sociology of law, like economic sociology and socio-legal literature before it, has identified limitations with mainstream, dominant ways of doing, thinking, and talking at the interface of law, economy, and society. The suggestions put forward in this book have sought to link in with discoveries across a wider range of literature, including the cognitive sciences, linguistics, the natural sciences, and philosophy, where relevant. Hopefully, synergies between these fields can build momentum, as the crashes, crises, and catastrophes facing society demand swift answers.

Simply arguing that mainstream or orthodox approaches are outdated and unhelpful has been done successfully and is not new. But the argument here is more subtle and, despite using the niche area of ESL as an example of how and why the way we talk matters, has greater significance for our everyday discourse and framing of social interactions. In combining the limitations of our mainstream ways of doing, talking, and thinking with insights from sociology, linguistics, and psychology, we can begin to ask how and why interests are minimized or silenced. We can begin to unpick how voices come to be invisibly sidelined, and how dominant thoughtways then channel us straight past any exploration of alternative responses to social dilemmas. One of the arguments this book has tried to make is that when we lose sight of the fictions on which our regimes and rationalities are based, we are unable to recognize how they function, and the voices and interests being elided, minimized, or altogether silenced in the process. So, how can we begin to rebalance these? What of their socially grounded, morally constructed cousin, *homo sociologicus*? Chapter 6 asks how a *homo sociologicus* might act, talk, and think, and what their arrival might mean for how we understand, reproduce, and study legal and economic phenomena.

Bibliography

Berger, P.L. and Luckmann, T. (1991) *The Social Construction of Reality*. Penguin Books.

Blalock, C. (2015) 'Neoliberalism and the Crisis of Legal Theory', *Law & Contemporary Problems*, 77, pp. 71–103.

Boroditsky, L. (2009) 'How Does Our Language Shape the Way We Think?', *Edge*, 6 November. Available at: https://www.edge.org/conversation/lera_boroditsky-how-does-our-language-shape-the-way-we-think (Accessed: 17 November 2021).

Burrows, A. (2016) 'Challenges for Private Law in the 21st Century', *Oxford Legal Studies Research Paper* 3/2016 [Preprint]. https://doi.org/10.2139/ssrn.2710270.

Callon, M. (1998a) 'Introduction: The Embeddedness of Economic Markets in Economics', in Callon, M. (ed.) *The Laws of the Market*. Cambridge, MA: Blackwell, pp. 1–57.

Callon, M. (ed.) (1998b) *The Laws of the Markets*. Wiley-Blackwell.

Callon, M. (2008) 'What Does It Mean to Say that Economics is Performative?', in MacKenzie, D., Muniesa, F. and Siu, L. (eds) *Do Economists Make Markets: On the Performativity of Economics*. Princeton: Princeton University Press, pp. 311–357.

Carrington, D. (2021) 'Woodland Walks Save UK £185m a Year in Mental Health Costs, Report Finds', *The Guardian*, 4 December.

Cetina, K.K. (1993) 'Strong Constructivism - From a Sociologist's Point of View: A Personal Addendum to Sismondo's Paper', *Social Studies of Science*, 23(3), pp. 555–563.

Coase, R. (1987) *The Firm, the Market, and the Law*. Chicago and London: University of Chicago Press.

Cooper, D. and Renz, F. (2022) 'Reimagining Gender through Equality Law: What Legal Thoughtways Do Religion and Disability Offer?', *Feminist Legal Studies*. https://doi.org/10.1007/s10691-021-09481-3.

Cotterrell, R. (1997a) 'A Legal Concept of Community', *Canadian Journal of Law and Society*, 12, p. 75–91.

Cotterrell, R. (1997b) *Law's Community: Legal Theory in Sociological Perspective*. New Ed. Oxford: Clarendon Press.

Cotterrell, R. (2002) 'Seeking Similarity Appreciating Difference: Comparative Law and Communities', in Harding, A. and Örücü, E. (eds) *Comparative Law in the Twenty-First Century*. London: Kluwer Law International.

Cotterrell, R. (2013) 'Rethinking Embeddedness; Law, Economy, Community', *Journal of Law and Society*, 40(1), pp. 49–67.

Crotty, M. (1998) *The Foundations of Social Research: Meaning and Perspective in the Research Process*. St Leonards: Sage Publications.

Dale, G. (2016) *Karl Polanyi: A Life on the Left*. 1st ed. New York: Columbia University Press.

Dermendzhiyska, E. (2021) 'Feeling, In Situ', *aeon.co*, 8 October. Available at: https://aeon.co/essays/what-if-emotions-arent-universal-but-specific-to-each-culture?utm_source=pocket-newtab-global-en-GB (Accessed: 22 October 2021).

Eurobarometer Special EB on 'Attitudes of European towards Animal Welfare' (Ref 442) (2016). Available at: http://ec.europa.eu/commfrontoffice/publicopinion/index.cfm/Survey/getSurveyDetail/instruments/SPECIAL/surveyKy/2096 (Accessed: 24 July 2018).

'Eurobarometer Survey Reveals European Citizens Have Increasingly Positive Image of EU' (2014) European Consumer Centre (ECC) Ireland, 14 May. Available at: https://www.eccireland.ie/eurobarometer-survey-reveals-european-citizens-have-increasingly-positive-image-of-eu/ (Accessed: 24 July 2018).

Ewick, P. and Silbey, S. (1998) *The Common Place of Law*. Chicago: University of Chicago Press.

Foulkes, I. (2021) 'Swiss Voters Reject Key Climate Change Measures', *BBC News*, 13 June. Available at: https://www.bbc.co.uk/news/world-europe-57457384 (Accessed: 25 June 2021).

Frerichs, S. (2011) 'Re-Embedding Neoliberal Constitutionalism: A Polanyian Case for the Economic Sociology of Law', in Joerges, C. and Falke, J. (eds) *Karl Polanyi, Globalisation, and the Potential of Law in Transnational Markets*. Oxford: Hart Publishing (International Studies in the Theory of Private Law, Vol.8), pp. 65–84.

Geary, J. (2011) *I is an Other: The Secret Life of Metaphor and How it Shapes the Way We See the World*. New York: Harper Collins ebook.

Giddens, A. (1984) *The constitution of society: outline of the theory of structuration*. Oxford: Polity.

Goffman, E. (1959) *The Presentation of Self in Everyday Life*. New York and Toronto: New York and Toronto.

Goffman, E. (1967) *Interaction Ritual: Essays in Face-to-Face Behavior*. New York: Routledge.

Granovetter, M. (1985) 'Economic Action and Social Structure: The Problem of Embeddedness', *American Journal of Sociology*, 91(3), pp. 481–510.

Hirsch, P., Michaels, S. and Friedman, R. (1990) 'Clean Models vs. Dirty Hands: Why Economics is Different from Sociology', in Sharon Zukin and Paul DiMaggio (eds) *Structures of Capital: The Social Organization of the Economy*. Cambridge University Press, pp. 39–57.

Kelsen, H. and Kletzer, C. (2014) 'On the Theory of Juridic Fictions. With Special Consideration of Vaihinger's Philosophy of the As-If', in del Mar, M. and W. Twining (eds) *Legal Fictions in Theory and Practice*. Switzerland: Springer International Publishing, pp. 1–20.

Krippner, G. (2001) 'The Elusive Market: Embeddedness and the Paradigm of Economic Sociology', *Theory and Society*, 30(6), pp. 775–810.

Krippner, G. et al. (2004) 'Polanyi Symposium: A Conversation on Embeddedness', *Socio-Economic Review*, 2, pp. 109–135.

Krippner, G. and Alvarez, A.S. (2007) 'Embeddedness and the Intellectual Projects of Economic Sociology', *Annual Review of Sociology*, 33, pp. 219–240.

Lakoff, G. (2014) *Don't Think of an Elephant: Know Your Values and Frame the Debate*. Kindle. Chelsea Green Publishing.

Latour, B. (1983) 'Give Me a Laboratory and I Will Raise the World', in K.D. Knorr-Cetina and M. Mulkay (eds) *Science Observed: New Perspectives on the Social Studies of Science*. London: Sage, pp. 141–170.

Law, J. (2009) 'Seeing Like a Survey', *Cultural Sociology*, 3(2), pp. 239–256.

Lynch, M. (1998) 'Towards a Constructivist Genealogy of Social Constructivism', in I. Velody, and R. Williams (eds) *The Politics of Constructionism*. London: Sage Publications, pp. 13–32.

MacKenzie, D. and Millo, Y. (2003) 'Constructing a Market, Performing Theory: The Historical Sociology of a Financial Derivatives Exchange', *American Journal of Sociology*, 109(1), pp. 107–145.

MacKenzie, D., Muniesa, F. and Siu, L. (2008) *Do Economists Make Markets? On the Performativity of Economics*. Princeton and Oxford: Princeton University Press.

Mäki, U. (2011) 'Economics Making Markets is not Performativity'. Available at: https://www.hse.ru/data/2011/04/05/1211693735/PerformativityMoscow2011.pdf.

Matthews, D. (2021) *Earthbound: The Aesthetics of Sovereignty in the Anthropocene*. Edinburgh University Press.

Norman, J. (2022) *Posthuman Legal Subjectivity: Reimagining the Human in the Anthropocene*. Abingdon and Oxon: Routledge.

North, D. (1977) 'Markets and Other Allocation Systems in History: The Challenge of Karl Polanyi', *Journal of European Economic History*, 6, pp. 703–716.

O'Sullivan, D. (2021) 'Voters Reject Pesticide-Free Farming Proposals', *swissinfo.ch* . Available at: https://www.swissinfo.ch/eng/pesticide-free-farming--can-the-vision-seduce-swiss-voters-/46691640 (Accessed: 24 November 2021).

Perry-Kessaris, A. (2004) 'Use, Abuse and Avoidance: Foreign Investors and the Legal System in Bangalore', Asia Pacific Law Review, 12(2), pp. 161–189

Perry-Kessaris, A.J. (2008a) *Global Business, Local Law: The Indian Legal System as a Communal Resource in Foreign Investment Relations*. Aldershot, Hampshire: Ashgate.

Perry-Kessaris, A.J. (2008b) 'Recycle, Reduce and Reflect: Information Overload and Knowledge Deficit in the Field of Foreign Investment and the Law', *Journal of Law and Society*, 35(1), pp. 65–75.

Perry-Kessaris, Amanda, What Does it Mean to Take a Socio-Legal Approach to International Economic Law? (2012, June 15). *Socio-Legal Approaches to International Economic Law: Text, Context, Subtext*, in A. Perry-Kessaris (ed), Routledge,December 2012, Available at SSRN: https://ssrn.com/abstract=2085007.

Perry-Kessaris, A.J. (2012) 'What Does it Mean to Take a Socio-Legal Approach to International Economic Law?', in *Socio-Legal Approaches to International Economic Law: Text, Context, Subtext*. Routledge.

Public Opinion – European Commission and the Eurobarometer Surveys (2021) *Eurobarometer*. Available at: http://ec.europa.eu/commfrontoffice/publicopinion/index.cfm (Accessed: 24 July 2018).

Randles, S. (2003) 'Issues for a Neo-Polanyian Research Agenda in Economic Sociology', *International Review of Sociology*, 13(2), pp. 409–434. https://doi.org/10.1080/0390670032000117353.

Russell, J.A. (2003) 'Core Affect and the Psychological Construction of Emotion', *Psychological Review*, 110(1), pp. 145–172.

Samuel, G. (2018) *Rethinking Legal Reasoning*. Cheltenham, Gloucester: Edward Elgar.

Santos, A.C. and Rodrigues, J. (2009) 'Economics as Social Engineering? Questioning the Performativity Thesis', *Cambridge Journal of Economics*, 33(5), pp. 985–1000.

Sayer, A. (2005) 'Markets, Embeddedness and Trust: Problems of Polysemy and Idealism', in Stan Metcalfe and Alan Warde (eds) *Market Relations and the Competitive Process: New Dynamics of Innovation & Competition*. Manchester: Manchester University Press.

Schwartz, T.A. (2007) *Dictionary of Qualitative Inquiry*. Thousand Oaks: Sage Publications.

Sismondo, S. (1993) 'Some Social Constructions', *Social Studies of Science*, 23(3), pp. 515–553.

Soguel-dit-Picard, D. (2021) 'Swiss CO2 Law Defeated at the Ballot Box', *swissinfo.ch*. Available at: https://www.swissinfo.ch/eng/switzerland-votes-on-controversial-co2-law-/46695016 (Accessed: 24 November 2021).

Summary: Attitudes of Europeans to Animal Welfare (2016) Special Eurobarometer 442, WaveEB84.4-TNS Opinion&Social. European Commission. Available at: https://ec.europa.eu/commfrontoffice/publicopinion/index.cfm/ResultDoc/download/DocumentKy/71349 (Accessed: 24 July 2018).

Teubner, G. (2021) 'The Constitution of Non-monetary Surplus Values', *Social and Legal Studies*, 30(4), pp. 501–521.

Thaler, R.H. (2000) 'From Homo Economicus to Homo Sapiens', *Journal of Economic Perspectives*, 14(1), pp. 133–141.

Thaler, R.H. and Sunstein, C.R. (2009) *Nudge: Improving Decisions about Health, Wealth and Happiness*. Penguin.

van Basshuysen, P. et al. (2021) 'Three Ways in Which Pandemic Models may Perform a Pandemic', *Erasmus Journal for Philosophy and Economics*, 14(1). https://doi.org/10.23941/ejpe.v14i1.582.

Zukin, S. and DiMaggio, P. (eds) (1990) *Structures of Capital: The Social Organization of the Economy*. Melbourne: Cambridge University Press.

Chapter 6

Beyond embeddedness

The next steps

What remains of ESL without its core concept of embeddedness?

> **LAY LILLIAN**
>
> *Lillian thought back to Ann's lectures about changing the way we do, talk, and think. Ann had said that this could give us different ways of responding to crashes and crises, and she had explained to Lillian that the way we think about law and economy are not predetermined. Nor are they laws of nature. Instead, how we talk and think about legal and economic phenomena are historically and culturally contingent, changeable, and the product of preferences.*
>
> *What's more, these preferences – what we think of as important or not important, valuable or not valuable, relevant and not relevant – are equally up for discussion. At the time, Lillian wasn't convinced about how any of this could work in practice. Besides, she had more pressing worries. Her bills were due, her granddaughter was struggling to rent a room, and her sons were both trying to get re-referred to a food bank. What use did Lillian have for reframing law and economy?*

We cannot universally get rid of embeddedness-talk; nor should we try to. We speak in metaphors and think in metaphors. This is eminently helpful most of the time, offering us linguistic short cuts while revealing and concealing shared concepts, theories, and working mental models. But we "run the ship aground" on a contradiction when our metaphors are not conceptually compatible (Krippner *et al.*, 2004, p. 112). And this fundamental contradiction is, this book has shown, limiting our abilities to respond to financial crashes, social crises, and environmental catastrophes innovatively and imaginatively. Even if you are sworn against constructivism, or the belief that we construct social institutions through our interactions, there is an undeniable and fundamental contradiction in claiming one phenomenon to be embedded in another, when neither exist physically or tangibly.

DOI: 10.4324/9781003354819-6

Should we, as many claim, seek to "re-embed" the economy in society? Should we think of the law as "embedded in" society? Should we claim that both the law and the economy have become problematically "disembedded" from society in recent decades? As the previous chapters have set out in detail, while these might pose valid questions about the relationship between law, economy, and society, in relying on embeddedness-talk, their phrasing leads us into a conceptual cul-de-sac.

We have seen that embeddedness, as the core concept of an ESL (economic sociology of law) lens, suffers from two limitations. Firstly, it is internally incoherent; the "what are we talking about?" problem. The concept has been applied to everything, and therefore no longer means anything (Granovetter, in Krippner *et al.*, 2004). This was exemplified in the application of the concept to responses to the 2008 financial crash, where everything was, at some point, said to be embedded in everything else: economy in society, society in economy, law in society, law in economy, economy in law... Cotterrell's key questions to keep in mind of "what is embedded, and in what", are good starting points but offer few solutions given the complexity of the discourse and what is potentially at stake (Cotterrell, 2013).

Secondly, our conceptual commitment to embeddedness perpetuates the metaphorical fiction of the ontologically separate law, economy, and society. This, in turn, reveals some insights, but conceals other, potentially helpful, constructivist analyses. By this, I mean that talking *as if* the three spheres were separate, and then attempting to integrate them using the metaphor of embeddedness results in the re-entrenchment of their separation. At the same time, it prevents us from thinking about legal and economic phenomena as they are socially constructed. In the light of ESL's aspiration to reunite the disciplines, the perpetuation of their separation is a problematic inconsistency that has far-reaching effects. It sets up a black box whereby one or more of the spheres is placed beyond the reach of sociological enquiry. But it leaves unchallenged the dominant discourses – those ways of talking and thinking – that constitute mainstream approaches in each sphere. For law, this is a narrow, doctrinal approach that assumes *homo juridicus*. For economics, this is an equally narrow, neoclassical approach that assumes *homo economicus*. In perpetuating these assumptions, and the preferences that are tacitly baked in to the mainstream ways of doing, talking, and thinking, we create the conditions in which we then act *as homo economicus-juridicus*. We end up wearing the blinkers of mainstream theories which then mask alternative approaches. We reproduce the same values that are prioritized in these mainstream approaches and privilege the same voices.

An ESL is one response to mainstream approaches that challenges the central assumptions of doctrinal law and neoclassical economics. But its core concept, embeddedness, sits at odds with its reintegrative aspirations for the disciplines it straddles. As an important and timely, albeit niche, lens for structuring sociologically oriented empirical enquiry at the interface of law and economy, the embeddedness conundrum is central to ESL. But it is also fundamental for wider discourses about our responses to financial crashes, social crises, and environmental catastrophes. "Embeddedness-talk" has become increasingly fashionable since responses to the 2008 financial crash appeared, and the lessons we can draw from an exploration of ESL's core concept are equally applicable to our wider ways of doing, talking, and thinking about legal and economic phenomena. Removing the blinkers of mainstream models might involve shifting the way we do, talk, and think, and Chapter 5 suggested one possible way of moving beyond embeddedness.

Focusing on the impact of one tertiary, generative, ontological metaphor might seem overly pedantic, but the impacts of one word are extensive, and our guides, Academic Ann, Policy Polly, and Lay Lillian have explored the effects of reframing for them. Ann, our main guide in the first chapters, was planning a research trip to carry out interviews with foreign investors. She wanted to understand what this group was looking for in a host state legal system, and whether the shape of the legal system would be a deciding factor in their decision to invest, as development banks have claimed. Ann began to explore what an ESL lens might mean for her research, and quickly found that an ESL lens nudged her to consider wider social impacts of legal reform. Additionally, by approaching her research questions through a different lens, a wider pool of actors was identified as relevant for her understanding of legal reform for foreign investment. But, on reading further, she saw that there was a conundrum at the heart of the ESL lens that she was about to apply. How could a lens that sought to reintegrate the disciplines of law, economics, and sociology then separate out these spheres by talking about one being embedded in another?

At this point, Ann decided to compare two interpretations of embeddedness to explore the difference it might make. Using Block's research questions as her starting point, she set out who was involved and what the relationships were between them, and analyzed her fieldwork using two different – opposite – interpretations of embeddedness. Fred Block's reading of Polanyian embeddedness, simplified down, claims that economy (and its regulation) is embedded in society. By contrast, Gareth Dale's reading of Polanyian embeddedness, again in simplified form, claims that society has become embedded in economy (and its regulation). Ann found that these two interpretations of embeddedness resulted in different groups of actors being identified as relevant, and different foci being highlighted in their interactions. Depending on which reading of Polanyian embeddedness she chose, she would need to interview different actors, ask them slightly different questions, and pay attention to different aspects of how each answered. Ann reminded herself that these were two caricatured extremes of reading Polanyian embeddedness and that there were multiple alternatives, including Granovetter's micro level embeddedness, and many more offerings in between. For Ann, while an ESL lens offered a comprehensive and robust means to structure and undertake her research, its core concept undermined the conceptual coherence and consistency of the lens, and she decided to explore an ESL lens that moved beyond embeddedness. She found that this gave her a conceptually consistent lens through which she could sociologically understand the economic life of the law.

Along the way, she had bumped into a friend from university, Policy Polly, who was now working in research and policy development at a development bank. Polly just happened to be focusing on a similar area – both geographically and substantively – to Ann but from the perspective of policy interventions. Polly had been enthusiastic about experimentalism and the growth of randomized controlled trials (RCTs) in the development industry, but she had admitted that the implementation gap remained problematic and had seen the benefits of RCTs. But, what happened in the textbooks and what was happening on the ground still did not always align, and Polly listened intently as Ann rushed through her latest framing exercises and what an ESL lens might mean for her research. While Polly isn't sure that ESL could solve all the Bank's problems, she immediately saw that it posed some interesting questions. She could see that as a way of balancing the diverse, complex, and dynamic needs of multiple communities, the lens could offer an alternative understanding of legal and economic phenomena in the context of economic development. More to the point, she wondered if a sociological lens might help imagine some of the unintended consequences of economically oriented law reform that countries engaged in with the aim of shaping legal systems according to the (perceived) expectations of foreign investors.

Finally, Lay Lillian, Ann's frustrated but perennially optimistic neighbour, over many tea breaks with Ann, listened while Ann explained her research. Lillian wasn't impressed with complicated words and wasted no time telling Ann that the name of the lens, an economic sociology of law, would not catch on. But when Ann started explaining that we need different ways of thinking about legal and economic phenomena, and that this might start with alternative ways of talking, Lillian began to listen. As our guide for the rest of this chapter, Lillian's thought experiments allow us to zoom out from the preceding discussions and look at the wider implications for society that the microcosm of embeddedness-talk in an ESL context have revealed.

LAY LILLIAN

Lillian's heart swelled with pride whenever she looked at her granddaughter's graduation photo – the first in the family to go to university. Now, her granddaughter had moved to another city to start a new job as a nurse. But when she had mentioned the extent of her student debt on the phone, Lillian had nearly fainted. What's more, she needed a guarantor just to rent one room in a shared house, and she had asked

Lillian. But guaranteeing rent for a year was more money than Lillian had ever had in her bank account in her life.

Fretting, but determined not to let her granddaughter become homeless, Lillian thought about the way that her family had clubbed together to purchase the council house in the 1970s, and there was money in that, she thought.

But all that money, just for one small room for a key worker. Lillian wondered what Ann might say to this, and imagined Ann's voice talking about the application of market concepts and language to housing. Lillian couldn't disagree. When she had bought her council house, the application of market principles had benefited her, but "the housing market" was failing her granddaughter now.

Fred Block's quip from 2013, that there was nothing quite like a financial crash to spur developments in critical thinking about the economy and its regulation, is a good reminder of the purpose of the current narrative (Block, 2013, p. 28). However, there is an even more pressing need for research into how we frame legal and economic phenomena, and how we might talk about legal and economic phenomena in the future. Can our conceptual and linguistic tools evolve? What might it take to alter them, and to reframe the narrative? Might this be a way to rebalance the voices and interests that our concepts and words highlight?

Complicating all these questions is the revolution in technology and the implications for our language: the Internet, big data, algorithms, and the growth of artificial intelligence (AI) systems that can engage in natural language processing (NLP). The handful of foundation models (FMs) on which NLP depends are monolithic entities with emergent qualities. In short, these FMs can engage in "self-supervised" learning, and can learn new tasks without needing to be prompted or commanded to do so (Bommasani and Liang, 2021). But they are trained on data from the Internet: data that has, for the most part, been created by a subset of flawed human beings. This data – blog posts, comments, reactions, and so on – encodes the biases and preferences that ordinary humans have. But in encoding these biases into FMs, research indicates that they are not only reproduced, but augmented (Sap *et al.*, 2020; Bender *et al.*, 2021). Thus, neo-liberal preferences for the self-regulating free market and small government are being both encoded and amplified. Political choices and decades of narrative capture by the political right are being translated into future algorithmic intelligence, potentially preserving them in digital aspic (Williams, 2022b). At the same time, this process risks placing our current analytical and normative tools beyond the reach of interrogation of future generations, and beyond the reach of any evolutionary processes.

In setting out an urgent research agenda to understand the extent of the problem and to seek ways of addressing this, later sections in this chapter outline what the example of embeddedness can tell us about AI and the future "of our linguistic tools. Before that, however, it is worth asking what becomes of an ESL lens if we remove its core concept.

Lingering questions about an ESL lens

Before turning to Lillian musings on reframing, it is helpful to address some lingering questions that may have arisen. If we accept that embeddedness-talk introduces conceptual limitations, we might consider moving beyond embeddedness, and Chapters 4 and 5 explored one way (among many) of going about this. But, if we discard the core concept of ESL, what remains? Then, how can we address the linguistic limitations and contradictions in the lens's name? Can an ESL lens really offer a serious challenge to the preference for "clean answers" over the "dirty hands" of complex, messy, sociologically oriented research (Hirsch, Michaels and Friedman, 1990)? And to what extent is an ESL lens a political undertaking – if we advocate moving towards a morally constructed, socially networked concept of the individual, can an ESL lens be anything but political? Before turning to any of these, there are two fundamental questions that need to be addressed. What, or where, or perhaps even who, is "the social"? And "how much" economic or legal "flavours" are discoverable there (Ewick and Silbey, 1998, p. 217)?

What, where, or who is "the social"?[1]

The discussion in the preceding chapters has used "the social" to refer to situations in which two or more actors are present, although this does not mandate physical co-presence; virtual or online interactions can also see the performance of legal and economic phenomena.[2] The point, then, is that legal and economic phenomena might be understood and studied as two sides of the same, social coin, and that each and every social interaction will invoke some legal and economic aspects, whether in the use, abuse, or avoidance of formal or informal legal and economic institutions. This does not confirm or deny the exercise of power or privilege. Nor does it deny domination or control any more than it conveys a woolly sense of what we know to be "society".

And yet, proposing a shift beyond embeddedness by reinterpreting the legal and the economic through a social constructivist lens demands some explanation of what, or where, or even who "the social" is. As Chapter 1 noted,

1 As noted in Chapter 1, a full social ontology is beyond the scope of this book, but see (Searle, 2006).

2 See (Goffman, 1959, 1967). This includes engagement with a device, over a telephone, or where we can imagine that another party is necessary for an interaction to occur. For example, agreeing to updated terms and conditions within an app necessitates interaction with the app on one's device, and this can be understood as a proxy for the company that developed the app which, here, might be understood as the other actor.

"society", like "law" and "economy", is an ontological metaphor. There is no such thing that we can reach out and touch, and yet, somehow, we understand a shared meaning. As a metaphor, then, for collections of actors and social behaviours, the previous chapters tell us that it is important that our metaphors are appropriate, and conceptually consistent. Any definition of society, or social ontology, will depend to some extent on the context. To ask what society is asks, at a micro or macro level, where the boundaries and borderlands are, and where we fall off the map.

When "society" is counterposed against "government", we invoke notions of the political power encroaching into the realm of what might, or ought to, be considered private. When "society" is counterposed against "the economy", we invoke the mental models of neoclassical economics and, usually, a trenchant belief in the power of free markets to offer solutions to social problems. In both scenarios we might think of the legal as straddling the divide, offering channels of movement and counter-movement, where contestation is performed and power plays out.

Perhaps a better question, then, is "what makes the social, social?". For our purposes here, the presence of two or more actors is sufficient for an ESL lens to structure enquiry into the legal and economic. Are there any other structures or qualities that we might note as necessary for enquiry into the social setting of the construction of legal and economic phenomena? For Roger Cotterrell, degrees of mutual interpersonal trust emerge over time, supported by the law. With repeated interactions these coalesce into networks of community. Fukuyama also points to the central role of trust in social relations, and Uzzi's work confirms the importance of trust in facilitating economic aspects of interactions.

But this leads on to a more serious challenge to a constructivist ESL lens: the ability to ask "how much"?

But "how much?": the "sociological fallacy"

There is an argument that in understanding legal and economic phenomena as aspects of the social, re-co-constructed through and within each social interaction, we lose the ability to ask "how much": exactly how much economic or legal aspect is there in this interaction or in that one? Has it increased or decreased over time? And how does it compare with the interactions being performed over there? This has been termed the "sociological fallacy", and can be important for comparing societies, timelines, geographies, cultures, and asking about the regulatory needs of one group vis-à-vis another (Peck, 2013, p. 1542). Skipping back to embeddedness-based ESL momentarily, the argument goes, if we say that all markets are always embedded, we leave ourselves no room to differentiate between different sets of institutions, or for grappling with the specifics of different market systems and societies. There is, further, no way of distinguishing between groups within a society, whether they construct more or less economic or legal aspects within their interactions, and what their precise regulatory needs are.

While we need to be better aware of the fictions baked into our metaphors and the implications of these leaps of faith that we all take, we need ways of distinguishing between performances of the legal and the economic across space and time. If we were to retain our conceptual commitment to the embeddedness metaphor, we might look back to Block's "thick" and "thin" notions of embeddedness and his concepts of "high" and "low marketness" to describe the amount of economic colour or flavour we can discern in any given interaction (Krippner *et al.*, 2004). As the discussion has explored though, this tends to place "the market" firmly back in the black box and outside the reach of sociological analysis, although this is a function of the metaphor of embeddedness rather than of how Block wants us to talk and think about economic aspects of the social. Nevertheless, the sociological fallacy can easily fade into the economistic fallacy whereby the market is placed in a black box and left unavailable to sociological analysis. In effect, by focusing on one, we lose sight of the other, and so the cycle continues. Neither extreme offers uninterrupted views of the totality of the interaction, and with this approach we can only ask "how much" by separating out the spheres of law, economy, and society and recreating those fictions.

If we want to understand or adjust the regulatory requirements of a particular set of interactions, it might be helpful to be able to pick out the extent to which they are economic, and, for example, the type of trusting relations of community that we are dealing with. We have a set of linguistic tools that are compatible with a constructivist lens, set out in Chapter 5, that avoid embeddedness-talk. We can identify the interaction ideal type(s) and can specify if certain ideal types are more or less present. We can also continue to begin at the micro level, focusing closely on how economic and legal phenomena are performed by paying close attention to the language actors use in their interactions. We can begin to zoom out, scaling up the rankings of social interaction but maintaining a focus on the empirical: on the economic and the legal as they are performed, and on the regimes that are re-co-constructed. So, referring back to Block's research questions that prompt consideration of the extent to which non-economic goals such as moral or spiritual commitments shape economic decisions, we might note that the non-economic goals align here with Weber's affective, traditional, and belief-based interaction ideal types (Block, 2008). Thus, we are able to bring in other factors than the economic and, in turn, ask "how much?".

In short, while some find it necessary to separate out the legal and economic aspects of interactions in order to analyze them as discrete phenomena, this is not always necessary and can entrench fictions that lead to misunderstandings. The way we talk and think about legal and economic phenomena should remain as consistent as possible with how these are performed in real life for as long as possible. Retaining their social construction as the foundational backdrop to any sociological analysis is essential for understanding these phenomena as they are performed. Extraction risks losing context, and when we lose context, we lose insights into the meaning attributed and the expectations of actors. In other words, a phenomenological understanding which enables a fully constructivist approach can only occur when social phenomena (like the economic or the legal) are understood in their full context. Then we can identify sites at which shared expectations come into play, and in so doing we can identify – should we choose Cotterrell's community lens – the regulatory requirements that might best support the mutual interpersonal trust that enables networks of community to operate.

This shift in perspective highlights how our language determines outcomes. It also emphasizes that in starting with empirical enquiry we need to start with what we can see, touch, and measure: interactions (rather than abstracted notions of metaphorical fictions like "the law" or "the economy"). As previous chapters have emphasized, the problems begin when we lose sight of the metaphorical fictions that we shape through our language, and which then shape us. By starting with careful observation at the micro level and focusing on interactions, we can remain empirically grounded. If we then choose to bring in metaphor or fiction to enable the analysis later, it is important to keep in mind that these are fictions and will operate as such – as imagined fantasies of our version of the real world, rather than the real world itself.

Removing the core concept: what is left?

An economic sociology of law (ESL) has structured and informed valuable and innovative research and continues to do so (Ashiagbor, 2011, 2013, 2014; Ashiagbor, Kotiswaran and Perry-Kessaris, 2013). At its core are central tenets and questions that are timely and crucial to empirically grounded, theoretically informed, and methodologically rigorous work in the social sciences at a time when this is needed more than ever. These include a commitment to real-world observation, evaluation and critique, and a challenge to orthodox, mainstream, doctrinal, and neoclassical approaches (Cotterrell, 1998). The focus, this book argues, lies then with the lived experiences of people as these are played out in interactions, challenging abstracted models of assumed behaviour. As such, an ESL continues to remind us that the social institutions that we live, work, and perform daily are not a given or the product of received wisdom. The legal and economic structures that we re-co-construct daily did not appear, fully formed, by some act of divine intervention. Rather, the current structures and processes, that is, our existing ways of doing, talking, and thinking, were all products of a good idea – someone's good idea – at some point in time. This applies to concepts like money and the metaphors we use to describe it as much as it does to institutions like the rule of law, the separation of powers, and the independence of the judiciary. Given the right setting, good ideas tend to stick, and are maintained by those who benefit from them or who can see the benefit in them. Nevertheless, this playing field of values is tilted to maintain the status quo, and insights into how this might be subtly shifted in order to accommodate alternative sets of voices, interests, and values therefore constitute a high-stakes game of persuasion, politics, and power as society faces up to challenges on a previously unknown scale.

At the same time, an ESL responds to entrenched disciplinarity within the social sciences and the continental drifts of departmentalization, professionalization, and differentiation that have occurred in the academy over the past half-century. A sociological lens invites both law and economics, as scholarly disciplines, to revisit their origins as the study of social, or socially constructed, phenomena. It thereby challenges the conditions that led economics to ape the natural sciences, and other social sciences to ape economics. It challenges the notion that law is an internally sealed system or that the law can be, or should be, co-opted by economic rationalities. The suggested focus on feedback loops emphasizes the real-world construction of economic and legal regimes, highlighting the ways in which certain voices are privileged while others are silenced as we move between actions (doing), thoughts (thinking), and their expression (talking). Moving beyond ESL's conceptual commitment to embeddedness is unlikely to limit any of these overarching goals, nor will it limit ESL's demands of us to approach questions about the economic life of law critically and reflexively.

Furthermore, removing any commitment to the concept of embeddedness need not entail severing all ties with projects addressing similar problems (Dukes, 2018). Nor need it mean discarding all references to ESL as a neo-Polanyian project should we wish. Karl Polanyi set out to reappraise the historical narrative giving rise to current relationships between law, economy, and society. While the scholarly landscape has shifted since the publication of *The Great Transformation*, solidifying silos of research and practice into distinct, inflexible spheres, Polanyi's analysis of the fictitious commodities of land, labour, and money continue to offer fresh insights that challenge today's orthodoxies, as the previous chapters have shown. The need for constructivist approaches that respond to entrenched disciplinarity in the social sciences, offering us glimpses of unifying themes and common insights, has made our ongoing commitment to the concept of embeddedness problematic. But the avoidance of embeddedness-based discourse need not entail banishing other insights from Polanyi's work into the flexible and dynamic relationship between markets, regulation, and society.

What's in a name? Linguistic limitations

Perhaps one of the greater challenges an ESL lens faces is also the most trivial: that of its name. "An economic sociology of law" is, to borrow Giddens' own criticism of his structuration theory, and as Lay Lillian found, "an unlovely term at best" (Giddens, 1984). Do we reduce it to "ESL" or "ESoL"?[3] Either

3 I'm grateful to Saadat Pirzada for drawing my attention to this and explaining the preference for an acronym that, when pronounced "ee-soul", reflects the social, ethical, moral, and political preferences of those who are studied through the lens.

way, the problem lies in the named separation of the disciplines that an ESL lens sets out to reunite. In naming the three areas of enquiry, economy, sociology, and law, the lens linguistically undermines its aspiration of responding to entrenched disciplinarity within the social sciences. While an ESL seeks to reunite discourse across the three areas, its very name re-entrenches their separation. We might refer to this as ESL's very own black box problem, by which economics, law, or worse, both, are left substantively unavailable to sociological analysis. As this book has argued, by assuming a social constructivist understanding of legal and economic phenomena, we can square this circle and enable ESL to offer a sociological lens on the interface between the legal and the economic as this occurs through (social) interactions.

Additionally, for those unfamiliar with the lens, the name can be deceptive, indicating an engagement with economics that suggests a law and economics approach. As we saw in Chapter 2, an ESL is anything but, and might more accurately be described as an anti-law and economics lens, given its goals of challenging economics imperialism and market fundamentalism. An ESL challenges the co-option of law for economic ends as well as the application of the empirical, conceptual, and normative tools of mainstream economics to legal scholarship or reasoning. Moreover, an ESL lens asserts that scholarship at the interface of law and economics should be studied sociologically, demonstrating its insistence on bringing the disciplines of law and economics back into the social sciences and reorienting them around the social, however this might be identified or defined. Nevertheless, however worthy the lens's aims might be, none of them are clear from its title.

Clean models or dirty hands?

There are still more questions. First among these is the recognition of our preference for clear answers over the messy complexities of reality (Hirsch, Michaels and Friedman, 1990). The attraction of having a clear answer to a complex social question cannot be overstated, even when this answer is wrong, or at least partial. None of us likes uncertainty or imprecision – least of all policy makers tasked with designing regulations or policy that will address a particular social problem. The woolly nature of sociological and socio-legal lenses, and their ability to capture multiple realities and values simultaneously, is both their strength and weakness. Sometimes, preference for a simple, clear answer will win out, and time-pressed policy makers like Polly will tend towards the binaries offered by more economistic models. This is not to make a straw man of quantified and quantifiable research, which can provide invaluable insights into aggregated behavioural patterns. Against this, the inherent vagueness of sociological research must take care to emphasize its value if it is to realize policy and social impact.

In other words, less quantifiable research needs to sell itself better. It can do this through good old-fashioned marketing but also through the way it presents itself. Communication of the "dirty hands" answers of sociological research need not be hidden in walls of text or placed behind paywalls of dense terminology. Recent developments in the application of design to law and socio-legal research show how research and findings can be made "visible and tangible", offering us "enabling ecosystems" in which the research can help us to be "practical, critical, and imaginative" in our responses to pressing social demands (Perry-Kessaris, 2021). By harnessing the potential of the visual, we can identify, interrogate, and then, if necessary, sidestep the inadequacies of our language, complementing and enhancing the textual findings of careful, empirical enquiry (Williams, 2022a). The chapter title page background illustrations in this book are a case in point, illustrating some of the core concepts that are explored in each chapter. While visualizations of socio-legal concepts, methods, and frames might not replace text and verbal persuasion, they can offer another point of entry to the discussion and an alternative perspective.

ESL, politics, and power: can an ESL lens ever be apolitical?

The final question remaining is the extent to which an ESL is a political lens, or the extent to which an ESL lens necessarily engages with the exercise of power. The first question of social ontology touched on this briefly, as "social" does not, in this context, tell us anything about power relations or their expression. Similarly, "community", while sounding soft and fluffy, does not deny or elide the exercise of power, of domination, and of privilege, specifically the opposite (Perry-Kessaris, 2011; Cotterrell, 2006, p. 68).

Firstly, an ESL lens, while aware of the normativity of actors and their interactions, does not propose normative substance beyond its challenges to orthodoxies and entrenched disciplinarity. The lens is just that: a lens rather than a methodology or theory, and the choice of words is crucial here to convey something that we look through to understand the world from a different perspective. Nevertheless, claiming that any approach to social science enquiry could be anormative, apolitical, or amoral sounds disingenuous. After all, an ESL lens reminds us to reflect carefully on our preferences and biases, and to uncover the assumptions baked in to our mental models (of which we are usually unaware). An ESL lens therefore draws attention to existing normativity rather than seeking to add its own preferences.

On the other hand though, ESL specifically sets out to challenge neo-liberal performances of economic and legal phenomena. In challenging disciplinarity and the dominant discourses in law and economics, ESL seeks to balance these voices with those that are typically silenced by neoclassical or neo-liberal discourse. As we noted earlier, the term "community" does not mean some fluffy, warm notion of friendship. On the contrary, understanding relations of community means understanding the exercise of power and of privilege in the way that actors perform legal and economic phenomena. In accepting the contingency of social structures, institutions, and therefore power, ESL cannot be anything other than a political undertaking, even though this may not be the primary focus of the lens, and certainly has not been the primary focus of this book. The discussion here has focused on the impact ESL might realize in carefully defined contexts (academic, policy, and lay, and with regard to economic development) as has been illustrated by Academic Ann, Policy Polly, and Lay Lillian.

So why might we see an ESL as a lens with political implications, if not ambitions? Neo-liberalism, understood here as the political, economic, and cultural incarnation of econo-centrism, sees the free market as "an ideological system that holds the 'market' sacred" (Mudge, 2008, p. 706). It is "built on a single, fundamental principle: the superiority of individualized, market-based competition over other modes of organization" (Mudge, 2008, p. 706). Facing this, scholars are hindered in their responses by being "embedded in disciplinary professions" which have interests and competitive dynamics of their own, as well as the "internationalization of the economics profession" which mirrors the earlier discussion about economics imperialism (Mudge, 2008, pp. 706–9). Moreover, "[n]eo-liberalism's ideological distinctiveness is identifiable in the missions of international political organizations, which mark the political institutionalization of dominant schools of economic thought" (Mudge, 2008, p. 716).

Any ESL lens claims deep reflectiveness on the part of the researcher in contrast to the veneer of scientific neutrality claimed by neoliberal and neoclassical economics. Thus, by posing an ESL-informed lens as a response to the problems with current approaches, it is difficult to argue that an ESL can be anything but political. This is true whether we continue to use the concept of embeddedness or not. For Polanyi, neoclassical economic theory attempts to realize the embeddedness of society in the market, even though his work shows that this is not – and could never be – fully possible. An ESL that looks back to Polanyi and which maintains a conceptual commitment to embeddedness will tend to challenge neo-liberal assumptions through sociological approaches that seek to re-embed the economy in society and reconfigure the relationship between the two, adjusting the regulatory requirements accordingly. Thus, in rebalancing the voices and interests that are considered (relevant) and seeking to accommodate non-economic values, there is a further natural tendency to see an ESL as a response to (political) neoliberalism.

This is problematic, as the previous chapters have shown. An ESL responds to the normative silence and supposed scientific neutrality of orthodox approaches by requiring reflectiveness about the text, context, and subtext of the research. Once again though, the importance of language and the metaphors we use are central here. Neoliberalism, being generally premised on a sharp distinction between market and state (two more ontological metaphors), draws on these metaphors and can be understood as a "set of myths embedded in the institutional environment" that tends to anchor political actors' orientations (Meyer and Rowan, 1991, p. 41, cited in Krippner and Alvarez, 2007; Mudge, 2008, p. 721). In the light of the discussion on performativity this might be restated as a set of myths that construct and perform the institutional environment, shaping actors, their regimes, and their rationalities in the process. Nevertheless, in stepping back from any "objectivity" and "neutrality" that are claimed by the natural sciences and mainstream economics, an ESL relinquishes any moral authority that it might claim, and in comparison to those approaches which do claim unbiased, clear, straightforward answers, becomes a very hard sell, but one that is essential for the future health and well-being of the social sciences. This importance is heightened in the context of the development of AI systems, which the following sections discuss in greater detail.

LAY LILLIAN

Lillian had started to look out for embeddedness as a metaphor and was surprised to see how often it cropped up; on the television, on the radio, in newspapers and magazines too. Whenever they interviewed an expert, it seemed to Lillian that they described the economy as "embedded". She began to pick out frequent hints of neoclassical economic framing too, listening out for behaviour described as "rational", "efficient", or "productive".

Thinking of her granddaughter's student loan and struggle to rent a room, Lillian began to notice some of these words and how debates tend to be framed in terms that privilege values and interests aligning with neoclassical economics. Grudgingly, she begins to wonder if Ann might have a point after all.

Updating Ann over more tea, Lillian wonders aloud whether the latest round of tax relief might be a good thing, because by paying less tax her granddaughter might have more money to spend on rent and essentials.

Ann paused, and then replied "Tax relief? You mean tax cuts? Or, to put it another way Lillian, you mean reduced investment in our public services, environment, and future generations? I'd try framing it differently. Is less investment in shared public services a good thing for your granddaughter's wallet?"

Lillian frowned.

Responding to crashes, crises, catastrophes

Lillian is probably right to be sceptical of our ability to do away with any metaphor. And yet, after a few conversations with Ann, she can see that the way we talk about legal and economic phenomena matters. Ann had explained that the metaphor of embeddedness separated out law from economy and from society, and perpetuated the narrow yet dominant ways of thinking in each of these spheres. Ann had also talked to Lillian about two other ways of using embeddedness set out by John Ruggie and Peter Evans, where they are carefully defined and meet a set of specific criteria. So, Lillian thought, it was not necessarily a case of banishing embeddedness-talk for good. It was a case of being more aware of the context in which it was being used, and the implications of the assumptions that it perpetuated. This meant that the first challenge to embeddedness, the "what are we talking about?" question could be answered by careful definition. The second problem with embeddedness, which Lillian now understood to be the "how are we talking about it?" question, was more problematic.

Ruggie and Evans show us that when we combine the concept of embeddedness with an equal-and-opposite force, "liberalism" or "autonomy" for example, we can reintroduce some of the dynamism and flexibility that Polanyi might have originally intended, given that he was writing in an era of pre-disciplinarity. However, there remains a tension between the ultimate aims of social constructivism, epitomized in the integrative goals of an ESL, and our ongoing commitment to a relational concept that entrenches disciplinarity, separation, and the isolation of certain aspects of social behaviours for separate analysis.

So, Lillian mulls over, the question remains: are the law and economy embedded in society? Or is society embedded in the law and economy? The metaphorical fiction of ontological separation takes us back to the separation of the disciplines that occurred in the second half of the twentieth century and the subsequent aping of the approaches and methods of the natural sciences. The "clean models" of neoclassical economics and doctrinal law remove us from the "dirty", messy realities of social enquiry, where answers are not black and white, and where certainty is not guaranteed (Hirsch, Michaels and Friedman, 1990). But they also remove us from the careful, empirical observation on which social enquiry – for legal and economic phenomena are social – is founded.

Our conceptual commitment to embeddedness continues

More recent literature is illustrative of the ongoing work to reframe how we do, talk, and think about law, economy, and society, and how we understand the relationships between these three spheres as we respond to financial crashes, social crises, and environmental catastrophes.

The 2021 *Dasgupta Review*, *The Economics of Biodiversity*, recognized that our preferences are "socially embedded" and called for "changes in how we think, act and measure economic success" (Dasgupta, 2021, p. 5). The report called for individual choices to be nudged in the right direction through education to bolster institutional changes that might be realized through "sustained commitment" and "hard choices" (Dasgupta, 2021). Nevertheless, these need not be so arduous if we have the conceptual and linguistic tools to enable us to make better choices and to perform as an environmentally aware, socially situated, morally constructed *homo sociologicus*.

Statements that markets are "social construct[s]" and "living institutions [that are] embedded in culture, practice and tradition" look back to Adam Smith and pre-disciplinary conceptualizations of markets (Carney, 2020). They challenge the continental drift of the disciplines that have produced silos of research and discourse. Increasing recognition of the social situatedness of markets indicates an encouraging willingness to shift and reframe. And yet, our ongoing conceptual commitment to embeddedness seems to endure. Arguing that economics might to focus on missions, Mariana Mazzucato, one of the leading thinkers on economic reframing, states that "markets are embedded in rules, norms and contracts" before on the next page stating that "markets are embedded in institutions and norms" (Mazzucato, 2021, pp. 20–1). In the first instance, Evans' theory of embedded autonomy is referenced, but the assertion appears to be that markets are embedded in law. It is unclear whether by "law" Mazzucato means "the state", but by any socio-legal or constructivist understanding this seems unlikely. An alternative reading might understand her argument to be that markets are embedded in "norms" (this is stated twice), implying that markets are embedded in social behaviours. Following this line of interpretation, markets are "co-created by different actors in both the public and private sectors, as well as civil society organisations" (Mazzucato, 2021, p. 21). This understanding of the co-creation of markets by actors also hints at a shift towards a social constructivist understanding of markets and their regulation, indicating the implicit but central role of the social. Nevertheless, the lack of definition reinforces the two limitations of embeddedness-based discourse set out in the preceding chapters: its internal inconsistency ("*what* are we talking about?") and its external incompatibility with constructivist lenses ("*how* are we talking about it?").

Shoehorning concepts into categories: Happy the Elephant, Chucho the Bear, and their friends

The limitations baked in to our conceptual and linguistic tools are worth worrying about. Our conceptual tools both shape and are shaped by our linguistic tools (Russell, 2003; Dermendzhiyska, 2021). When we reproduce inadequate metaphors and fictions in our speech, our actions come to align with the default, mainstream assumed caricatures that have solidified into human form over decades. We perform as *homo economicus-juridicus*. But our values and priorities have shifted. They have had to. Climate change will not conform to the economic models we have developed. Ecological destruction, the zone beyond the outer ring of Raworth's diagram in *Doughnut Economics*, is challenging existing legal and economic models in unprecedented ways and forcing a reappraisal of how we conceive of the human as a legal subject (Raworth, 2018; Matthews, 2021; Fineman, 2022; Norman, 2022). Like a torch shining brightly across a topographical landscape, casting deep shadows whilst highlighting other features, our frames reveal and conceal in equal measure. They highlight partial understandings of crises, suggesting equally partial solutions. Similarly, we can appreciate the effects of our legal and economic framing in the inequalities spotlighted by the COVID pandemic which illuminated the limitations of our existing conceptual and linguistic tools for realizing goals just as justice, fairness, and equality. Two examples of the inadequacies of our mental models and linguistic tools relating to legal and economic phenomena, and the metaphorical fictions these necessitate, are helpful illustrations of the challenge underway to rebalance the values prioritized through our conceptual and linguistic tools.

Happy the Elephant is being held unlawfully by the New York zoo – or so her lawyers argue. Having been trucked and bartered around the world while still a baby, Happy (for that is, unironically, her name) became "trapped in human history" (Lepore, 2021). Happy's legal journey, and her petition of *habeas corpus*, follows on from those of other non-human plaintiffs, including Pablo Escobar's "cocaine hippos", and Chucho, the Andean Bear.[4] Chucho had become "severely depressed" following a bereavement, and a petition of *habeas corpus* allowed the Colombian court to find bears to be "sentient beings" and holders of some rights, although these still fall short of the full bundle of rights a human might expect (Cheng, 2021; Franceschini, 2021).

Courts have not been blind to the ecological devastation that is now threatening humanity. Responding to the wave of non-human rights cases, they have increasingly been willing to recognize the intrinsic value of affording protection in the form of rights, not because a thing is endangered or because it is the property of a human. Koko the Gorilla, in meeting and surpassing human-designed tests, proved beyond doubt that gorillas were "intrinsically worthy beings", deserving of protection. In law, however, the only way of accomplishing this has been to "promote" gorillas to the status of a person, which has been done with varying degrees of success in Western Europe, New Zealand, and Argentina (Smith, 2021). While analogies between gorillas, and even hippos, and humans can be made, and legal personhood justified on their intrinsic qualities, forests and rivers are a completely different matter. And yet, finding these also deserving of protection (from the humans to which analogies are, legalistically, drawn), courts have begun to assign legal personhood. A Colombian court granted some rights to the Amazon rainforest in a decision that urged the government to put an end to the deforestation crisis.[5] In New Zealand, the Whanganui River was given personhood status in 2017 in deference to the beliefs of the Indigenous Māori people (Kramm, 2020).

And yet, equally unironic is the extension of Western legal categories and Western legal consciousness to the things which we currently notice need protection. From us. We can only do this by stretching our own metaphorical fictions to extremes; by finding that a river is a legal person, or that a hippo is a sentient being. At the same time, by shoehorning in places and animals to

4 The hippos were designated "interested persons" by a US court. While the ruling is not enforceable in Colombia, it marked a legal milestone in the assignment of non-human legal rights (Smith, 2021).

5 The Supreme Court in Colombia recognised the Colombian Amazon as an "entity subject of rights", just as last year the Constitutional Court did with the Atrato River. This means that the state has a duty to protect, conserve, maintain, and restore it. In Colombia, an '*acción de tutela*' is a writ for the protection of constitutional rights (Dejusticia, 2018).

Western legal notions, we affirm the dominance of Western legal consciousness, pushing out any space for reconsidering how we conceptualize – and whether the discourse of rights is the most suitable for challenging the damage that Western legal and economic rationalities allows (or positively encourages) (Norman, 2022).

"Earth is a political community composed of all sorts of 'persons' – only some of whom are human" (Smith, 2021). The use of metaphor and fiction in the extension of legal rights to non-human entities is rife. The term "person", deriving from the Latin *persona*, refers to a mask that an actor dons, and therefore refers to the role that they perform in the drama. The fiction of legal personality being extended to artificial persons was set out by Thomas Hobbes in 1651 when he distinguished natural from artificial persons. Over centuries, this has allowed legal personhood to extend to corporations, municipalities, and the state. But to extend this to a river demands an extra leap of metaphorical faith, and ardent belief that despite the limitations of our conceptual tools, that extension of legal personhood is the only means by which we might afford some protection to the environment. When contrasted with certain Indigenous beliefs about the co-constitutive roles of nature and human, Western legal consciousness appears unsatisfactorily narrow, and yet more "borrowing" of Indigenous conceptual tools raises more problematic questions of further appropriation.[6] While Indigenous ways of doing and thinking appreciate a "socio-natural unity", representing this in terms of entrenched legal and economic regimes and rationalities necessitates "legal animism" that "personalizes nature" (Ost, cited in Smith, 2021). New ways of conceptualizing legal personhood and the relation of humans with nature in our legal and economic thoughtways are beginning to emerge, but are far from mainstream (Matthews, 2021; Norman, 2022).

Shoehorning concepts into categories: COVID versus the economy?

Similarly, the COVID pandemic has been pitched in a dialectical battle with the economy, usually in the form of a binary discussion: we either lockdown and save ourselves but destroy the economy, or continue as normal, risking lives, but securing our economic well-being (Casey, 2020; Foucault, Agamben and Benvenuto, 2020; Proctor, 2020). While an oversimplification of the discourse that tends towards the reductionist and the binary risks eliding nuance (see Supiot, 2021), there is little question that, in re-co-constituting the dominant frame of much of the discourse, neoclassical economics ensures the re-co-constitution and maintenance of the privilelge of economic voices, interests, and values. As Chapter 5 asked, if I ask you not to think of an elephant, you

6 I'm grateful to Nick Piška and the Obligations reading group at Kent Law School for drawing my attention to this point.

will, inevitably, think of an elephant. This is just how the human brain is wired, and repetition of unhelpful frames, even to prove how wrong they are, simply reinforces them in the conscious mind (Lakoff, 2014). As the Swiss voters in Chapter 5 illustrated, if you frame an argument in economic terms, you give economic rationalities the upper hand. Moreover, the health of the economy has almost become a proxy for the health of the nation. Our conceptual tools have been shaped by decades of discourse that has painted the free market as the institution that offers a solution to all of society's ills. Liberal, or libertarian, discourse seeks to paint social regulation as anti-free market, indicating that our goal, then, is to be as free as the (fictional) free market that we imagine will save us from incursions into our liberties. This sits in the context of a wider meta level shift in narratives from publicly oriented conceptual and linguistic tools to those of the private sphere, with phrases such as "tax relief" and "taxpayers' money" embodying broader shifts in favour of individual choice and the freedom to contract.[7] There is a tendency to use the conceptual and linguistic tools of mainstream economics to compare options, choices, and outcomes. We quantify so that we can compare, again mirroring the analytical tools and normative preferences of neoclassical economics. In framing the options and outcomes in economic terms, we privilege those economic outcomes and the voices and interests that enjoy a best fit and prioritization within those models, aligning how we think and how we act with the model of *homo economicus*.

Were we to flick back to our ESL lens that has moved beyond embeddedness, we might focus instead on how interactions are performed, the language used within them, and what this tells us about how fictional metaphors construct, and are constructed by, our conceptual and linguistic tools; how we do, talk, and think. Having identified limitations, we can then interrogate their impact and challenge their effects. The lesson of a study of embeddedness-talk in the context of ESL is that we can then begin to imagine and design alternative linguistic tools that enable different sets of voices and values to be prioritized.

Rebalancing voices and values: becoming 'homo sociologicus'?

How might we imagine the socially networked, morally constructed notion of *homo sociologicus*, and what bumps might still lie in the road towards their incarnation? Reframing is key here, and we can look back in time to examples of reframing in Bhutan and that country's focus on gross domestic happiness. Then, more recently, Oslo's example of a carbon budget applies mainstream economic frames to try and shift patterns of thought and behaviour in relation

7 I'm grateful to John Wightman and the Obligations reading group at Kent Law School for drawing this wider shift to my attention. See Chapters 2 and 5 for further discussion of this shift.

to the pressing climate crisis. However, the development and increasing application of artificial intelligence (AI), in particular AI that engages in natural language processing (NLP), raises urgent questions about the perils of preserving our current hegemonic frames and their intrinsic biases in digital aspic. What risks might we be taking by training algorithms to do, talk, and think about legal and economic phenomena as we currently do? What inequalities and biases might we be entrenching permanently, perhaps pushing our frames even further beyond the realm of conscious interrogation? Before turning to these questions, a note is helpful in introducing *homo sociologicus*.

LAY LILLIAN

Lillian was angry. She didn't often admit it, but the situation her family faced – her sons, and now their kids – just wasn't fair. She had raised a family on her husband's salary, and with a bit of help from the government, they had bought their house. But over the years, things had been sold off or privatized. Lillian thought back: she used to own the railways, the electricity infrastructure, the water, the gas, the mines, the ports, the main industries and the big names of UK manufacturing. Not any more.

Her sons both lost jobs in the 2008 crash. They had struggled ever since to get back into work – they just didn't have the right skills, despite being hard workers. She thought about their children, now teenagers and off to university – that used to be free too. Her eldest granddaughter's graduation had made Lillian so proud, but her student debts had Lillian up at night worrying.

But, thanks to Ann, Lillian appreciated that "law" and "economy" were not facts of nature. They were choices made by people that embody preferences and assumptions. She thought, then, that "austerity" had to be a choice too. Lillian now knew how theories from economics had come to structure and mould the way we talk about other areas of social life. Ann had termed it "scientism", or the way that law and economics had copied biology and physics. Lillian was now on the look out for metaphors such as "embeddedness" and found herself noticing the little word more in everyday discussions.

Seeing the effects of framing, it occurred to Lillian that our current frames normalized ways of doing, talking, and thinking that got "the poor to behave well in the world as it is, rather than questioning its justice" (Supiot, 2021).

The third cousin, our socially networked, morally constructed caricature of the archetypal social actor was introduced in Chapter 1. *Homo sociologicus* has less back story in the literature to draw on, and offers much more of a blank slate than *homo economicus* or *homo juridicus*. As *homo sociologicus* is the negation of *economicus* and *juridicus*, we can make a few assumptions, in the spirit of reflexivity and constant reappraisal. To start with, they are freed of the gender binary, they are emancipated from assumptions of ethnicity and race, and they are removed from the structures of socio-economic status. They may be differently able, old or young, and with preferences that shift around depending on who they have just spoken to, or what they have just read.[8]

The importance of how we talk has been extensively explored over the previous chapters. Assuming *homo sociologicus* to be on board with social constructivism, we can therefore expect that they do not see "the economy" or "the law" as distinct ontological phenomena with given ways of doing, talking, and thinking, but instead notice how these social phenomena are performed as aspects of each interaction, constructing regimes and rationalities through repeated performances in social settings across time and space. This character therefore has a different starting point for empirical enquiry (as well as for conceptual musings), and, like our three personas, notices the inconsistencies we reproduce when our vocabularies and mental models are limited, inadequate, or misaligned in some way.

Lillian, by contrast, isn't convinced. She believes Ann and can see that the way we talk has an impact on how we act and interact. But she is sceptical about how widespread this phenomenon really is. Ann has only given her one example: the metaphor of embeddedness. Lillian thinks that even if we could stop everyone using it to describe the relationship between the law, economy, and society what difference might it have more broadly? Paying more attention to the ways in which we describe the relationship between legal and economic phenomena, Lillian begins to notice examples, including how Bhutan measures happiness, and how the city of Oslo is measuring carbon.

"Happy" Bhutan

Gross domestic product (GDP) was originally proposed in the 1930s by economist Simon Kuznets as a way of measuring the impact of the Great Depression. Even Kuznets noted the deficiencies in GDP when it is used as a proxy for the nation's welfare. Nevertheless, GDP has enjoyed an illustrious career.

In 1972, the fourth King of Bhutan, King Jigme Singye Wangchuck declared that "Gross National Happiness is more important than Gross Domestic Product" (Ura *et al.*, 2012; Ura, 2015; OPHDI, 2021). In the decades since, a complex matrix of indicators has emerged measuring the more conventional socio-economic concerns as well as more subjective standards of well-being

8 Analogies with Rawls' original position behind the veil of ignorance should be avoided here, as the focus sits on *sociologicus'* interactions and feedback loops. *Sociologicus*, aware of the baked-in biases and assumptions of their linguistic tools, is careful to interrogate these and deploy them in a way that minimizes such limitations. The ideal of *homo sociologicus* set out here is in the context of an exploration of an economic sociology of law, and therefore reflects the approaches proposed more generally in this book.

such as psychological well-being and culture. Based on the Alkire-Foster method of multidimensional measurement, gross national happiness (GNH) identifies four groups of people – unhappy, narrowly happy, extensively happy, and deeply happy – and focuses on how policies can increase happiness and sufficiency among those identified as unhappy or narrowly happy (Ura *et al.*, 2012). GNH is often explained by reference to its four pillars of good governance, sustainable socio-economic development, cultural preservation, and environmental conservation. These are broken down into nine domains and then 33 indicators which are "statistically reliable, [...] normatively important, and are easily understood by large audiences" (OPHDI, 2021).

The GNH then acts as a policy lens requiring that all relevant dimensions be considered prior to implementation of any policy. There is an overarching aim that government policies and projects work together for the increase of the country's gross national happiness. Given that quantification, mathematization, and comparison are the empirical, analytical, and normative tools, respectively, of neoclassical economics, it is important to note that the aim here is different. Bhutan's GNH is not, therefore, a manifesto about *not* counting, but about looking carefully, critically, at what and how we count, and how we decide what is, and what is not, important. Along with the Human Development Index (HDI), which is a summary measure of average achievement in key dimensions of human development,[9] Bhutan's GNH index offers us a glimpse of how we might seek to accommodate and prioritize alternative voices, interests, and values in what we count and measure. It offers a snapshot of what might emerge should we choose to prioritize alternative interests.

Given their performativity, indicators can shape the behaviour of those they set out to measure, and can come to act as technologies of governance (Davis, Kingsbury and Merry, 2010). Nevertheless, it is unclear the extent to which top-down measures such as the GNH index have reframed popular or broader discourse within Bhutan, indicating that shifts in conceptual and linguistic tools – especially in a global discursive context – reflect an evolutionary rather than a revolutionary trajectory. This mirrors the timescale of the capture of language and interests by the political right that we can see in the US, as Chapter 5 explored (Lakoff, 2014). Shroeder has noted that GNH tools have had "little influence" in

9 The Human Development Index (HDI) was created to "emphasize that people and their capabilities should be the ultimate criteria for assessing the development of a country, not economic growth alone". This index was created to challenge the situation where countries with the same GNI (gross national income) had different human development outcomes, prompting debates around government policy. While an awareness of shifts in goals and outcomes is desirable, a caveat about the use of indicators as a technology of governance is necessary. The HDI relies on indicators, which as previous chapters have set out, have a performative impact on the populations they quantify, and can easily become technologies of governance, meaning that we have simply replaced one small part of the system with an alternative set of interests without challenging the conceptual and normative limitations of the approach. See (UNDP, 2021).

shaping GNH media policy, and that "GNH governance structures and instruments are largely absent in shaping these interactions, yet a common set of values linked to GNH seems to underlie and shape the priorities and practices of all stakeholders" (Schroder, 2012, cited in Ura, 2015, p. 18). There is evidence of the GNH in school curricula with an emphasis on "value education" that extends "beyond a more conventional formal education framework to reflect and respond more directly to the task of creating good human beings" (Ura *et al.*, 2012, p. 21). However, policy changes have seen only incremental adjustments to national discourses.

"Sustainable" Oslo

In 2017, Oslo implemented its first "Carbon Budget" which set out to "count carbon the way we count money" (*Oslo European Green Capital 2019*, 2019). As the 2019 European Green City, Oslo introduced the Business for Climate Network to foster co-operation between the business community, citizens, and NGOs (non-governmental organizations) in addressing the impact of business on the environment. These initiatives not only encourage but demand that environmental impact is factored into policies and business plans, just as profit forecasts might be. The concept has spread, with other cities around the world copying Oslo's Climate Budget as an effective and efficient governance tool that aims to see a 95 percent reduction in greenhouse gas emissions by 2030 from their 2009 levels (*Climate Budget 2020*, 2020). While the Climate Budget pioneered in Oslo has seen some successes and offers a way of incorporating sustainability issues into the wider economic planning of the city, it is notable that the core terms are still those of mainstream economic planning: budgets and targets. The approach does not seek to reinvent the wheel but instead adds additional categories to what is already measured so that existing ways of measuring and comparing progress can be applied to environmental protection and sustainability. This is similar to the "Green GDP" paradigm which measures economic growth but incorporates the environmental consequences of such growth. Of note, however, is that once these categories are given equal weight as the growth of the economy, it enables the design and implementation of government policies to realize these goals.

Lillian is somewhat cheered to have started noticing a more pluralistic approach to the quantification of legal and economic phenomena, along with how and why this takes place. She is not convinced though. Ann had spoken about the impact of indicators on our mental models, and she wonders how much of an impact "happiness" measurements or "green" measurements have had on social regimes and rationalities – on conceptual and linguistic tools – in Bhutan and Oslo respectively. The performativity of the indicators, or the effect they produce in the society they set out to quantify, is one point. Another is the reminder that quantification, mathematization, and comparison are the empirical, analytical, and normative tools of neoclassical economics, and that the use of indicators, even to measure happiness or carbon, might imply that while the unit of measurement might have changed, the processes of measuring, and the rationalities that demand quantification and comparison, have remained resolutely the same. For Lillian, this does not represent a wholesale shift in ways of doing, talking, or thinking about the relationships between the law, economy, and society. But it does indicate a willingness to take small steps to include a more diverse set of values and interests within existing approaches. It does indicate a willingness to consider what, and how, we measure and compare, and the descriptive language we use. The performativity of indicators aside, Bhutan and Oslo allow us to ask whether small shifts in framing might allow alternative regimes and rationalities to develop and *homines sociologici* to emerge. How might they perform? How might they talk? And how might they understand, identify, and shape preferences?

Framing the future? Rebalancing voices and values

LAY LILLIAN

With her granddaughter safely installed in a shared house and starting a new job, Lillian explained the situation to Ann. Taxpayers' money – Lillian's money – was being spent without her having a say in it. Not that she paid much tax, she admitted. But why wasn't it helping her granddaughter?

Ann paused, before pointing out to Lillian that some years ago we used to talk about public money or the government's money. Lillian nodded, agreeing. Now there was a sense of proprietary ownership over the money that Ann hinted might be divisive. Thinking to herself about Lillian's sense of ownership over the money, Ann wondered to herself, in a moment of unbridled cynicism, whether this reframing had been designed to distract voters from everything else they might once have owned but which had since passed into private ownership.

Reframing the policy as "tax cuts", and then as "reduced investment in our future public services", and noticing Lillian's eyebrows shoot up, Ann sipped her tea. She thought through some of the wider shifts in narrative framing that she had noticed, pondering larger shifts from publicly oriented to privately oriented discourse. Were property rights, freedom of contract, and the maximization of individual utility now supplanting notions of shared ownership, public goods, and social resources? And what about the cumulative effects of these micro level shifts for us all?

The political right have been framing narratives for decades (Lakoff, 2014).[10] As mainstream or hegemonic frames, these conceptual and linguistic tools align

10 Lakoff's analysis is based in the US but applies to a greater or lesser extent throughout much of the Global North.

with and highlight the dominant voices and interests prioritized in neoclassical economics and doctrinal law, as well as the embodiment of the political realization of both in the form of neoliberalism. Reframing, or reclaiming some of the narratives, is not a quick fix but rather a longer-term strategy that might level the conceptual playing field so that we are able to imagine alternative ways of doing, talking, and thinking about legal and economic phenomena. There is little question that technology will play a significant role in our future, and the role of artificial intelligence (AI) in shaping society and perpetuating particular frames is therefore of significant relevance to if, and how, we might begin the work of reframing.

In particular, algorithms that engage in "self-supervised learning", or so-called "foundation models" (FMs) on which AI applications can be built, hold enormous promise, along with correspondingly large risks for humanity. But this is a social experiment being played out in real time on a global scale, and AI systems already sit behind many of the social interactions that previous chapters have discussed. Any time you use a search engine, make a purchase, watch television, read a newspaper, or see a doctor, you are benefiting from the development and implementation of algorithms and advancements in machine learning. Neural learning means AI systems can process or "learn", and then copy. Underpinning most AI systems now are a handful of what are referred to as "foundation models" (FMs), which are defined as "any model that is trained on broad data at scale and can be adapted (e.g., fine-tuned) to a wide range of downstream tasks" (Bommasani and Liang, 2021, p. 3).

But the magic happens when these systems do more than copy – they improvise, applying the lessons from their learning to accurately mimic trolls, or predict outcomes of operations, for example, with the power of foundation models coming from their "emergent qualities rather than their explicit construction" (Bommasani and Liang, 2021, p. 6). In other words, the potential of foundation models lies in what they can learn to do, or what they can figure out by themselves from a few so-called 'natural' language prompts.

FMs, as monolithic entities, are time-consuming and expensive to construct from scratch, and the few that exist therefore form the basis for almost all AI systems that take and adapt an FM to produce a more specialized application. This unprecedented level of homogenization has led to a situation in which almost all state-of-the-art natural language processing (NLP) models are adapted from one of a few foundation models. This can have cost-saving benefits, but means that "any flaws in the [foundation] model are blindly inherited by all adapted models" downstream (Bommasani and Liang, 2021, p. 6). Flaws, for our purposes, include anything problematic that might have been included in the data curated to train the algorithm initially, usually meaning data scraped from the Internet. Data curation is an important phase at which normative judgement comes into play, as this represents the point at which choices are made about what is important for the algorithm to learn and what is not; what is relevant and what is not. However, the data taken from the Internet to train the FM is likely to contain not only explicitly and implicitly gendered and racialized language, but might tacitly reproduce the assumptions, values, and norms of a specific culture in a particular time and place. Given the available data, this is likely to reproduce a world-view consistent with dominant conceptual and linguistic tools in North America amongst those with Internet access who speak English. And, as previous chapters have explored in detail, the way we talk matters. We talk and think metaphorically, and our conceptual and linguistic tools have the potential to perform us, just as much as we believe we perform them.

While "[l]anguage has the power to reinforce stereotypes and project social biases onto others" (Sap *et al.*, 2020, p. 5477), there is a growing awareness of "representational bias", defined as "harmful biases resulting from stereotyping that propagate negative generalizations about particular social groups, as well as differences in system performance for different social groups" (Liang, Morency and Salakhutdinov, 2021, p. 1). While there is an awareness that "large datasets based on texts from the Internet overrepresent hegemonic viewpoints and encode biases potentially damaging to marginalized populations", there is still little research into wider questions of framing, especially in relation to law and economy (Bender *et al.*, 2021). Specifically, given that Internet data encodes our dominant conceptual and linguistic tools for law and economy and forms the target of "self-supervised" algorithmic learning, what might the potential consequences be of preserving these tools in digital aspic (Williams, 2022)? Might we be preserving in perpetuity our current ways of doing, talking, and thinking about law and economy? Might we be placing our current metaphors and framing devices beyond reach of interrogation, permanently? And, given the insights of previous chapters, what does this mean for our potential to break free from the preformed assumptions of *homo economicus-juridicus* and imagine *homo sociologicus*?

Given the time and expense in constructing an FM, there is a further recognition that "it is difficult to retrain a new [language model] whenever a new source of bias is uncovered from the data" (Liang, Morency and Salakhutdinov, 2021, p. 2). Indeed, recent work "has focused on defining and evaluating social bias as well as other notions of human-aligned values such as ethics, social bias implications, and toxic speech in generated text" (Liang, Morency and Salakhutdinov, 2021, p. 2). In other words, biases will inevitably be baked into the FMs, and reproduced and amplified in their myriad downstream adaptations and applications. This leaves us with the unsatisfactory solution of remedying unsavoury or discriminatory language *post hoc*. Current approaches to mitigating biases in future generations of foundation models "require retraining the models through adversarial trigger prompts, data augmentation or collection, and different objective functions" (Liang, Morency and Salakhutdinov, 2021, p. 2).

Nevertheless, recent de-biasing initiatives have tended to focus on the more egregious, and more obvious, examples of bias in language, and gendered and racialized language has been the focus of de-biasing initiatives. While more subtle biases and the downstream harms that they can produce are beginning to attract more attention, the richness and complexity of language *in context* as pairings of form and meaning remains somewhat at odds with the decontextualized learning carried out by FMs: the models have access to form only and cannot be said to "understand" or process "meaning". While FMs can replicate and parrot accurately and effectively, leading humans to impute meaning to the text and images generated, the models still cannot be said to understand what they are doing. The only meaning is that imputed by downstream human recipients, to whom the propagation of representational and allocational harm remains a distinct possibility (Bender *et al.*, 2021, p. 615).

More worryingly though, future FMs are likely to be trained on data generated using the current set of FMs that encode and amplify bias and hegemonic framing. The question then begs whether we might be encoding neoliberal frames, neoclassical economics, and doctrinal legal conceptual and linguistic tools into the future algorithms that will educate our children, provide healthcare decisions for us in moments of greatest need, and adjudicate on our legal disputes. This is no more science fiction than the mobile phone or space tourism. Implementation of FMs and NLP in AI is being carried out by private companies and applied to real humans who, for the most part, are unaware that they are being experimented on. Have you, for example, expressly given consent for your data to be preserved online and used to train language models and future AI? While there are many wider points to be made about the risks and rewards of AI,[11] we need a greater awareness and understanding of how our current framing performs us, and how this is being captured and used to train the AI systems of the future.

Moving beyond embeddedness?

Some ten years before this book was written, socio-legal scholars interested in the economic life of the law convened a "caravan" that first "moved" and then "continued" towards an economic sociology of law (Ashiagbor, Kotiswaran and Perry-Kessaris, 2013, 2014). In the intervening decade, that caravan has grown in size and ambition, asking questions about what ESL might be and do, where it might sit, and how it might look. Research undertaken under the banner of ESL has pushed boundaries and challenged assumptions about the relationships between law, economy, and society, and promises productive avenues for future enquiries. In that decade, new generations of researchers have intellectually grown up understanding and applying an ESL as a nascent but well mapped-out lens through which to understand the world and develop exciting research programmes.

11 For more on this, in particular the development of work on bias encoding and the de-biasing of FMs, see (Abebe *et al.*, 2020; Blodgett *et al.*, 2020; Sap *et al.*, 2020; Bender *et al.*, 2021; Bommasani and Liang, 2021; Hellman, 2021; Liang, Morency and Salakhutdinov, 2021).

ACADEMIC ANN

Boarding her flight, Ann was excited. Her exploration of an ESL lens meant that she was approaching her fieldwork from a different perspective. She knew how the previous trip had worked out, and on that occasion she had been far less prepared. Her lens had been narrower, her insights fewer, and her understanding had been shallower, and yet she had made a real contribution. This time, she had a wider and richer conceptual framing through which she could analyze her data, making decisions in real time about which regimes and rationalities she might like to explore further, and how these related to each other. She could follow through and explore how certain regimes and rationalities manifested on the ground, and what the dominant ways of doing, talking, and thinking about law and economy meant for the people whose lives she was briefly going to be a part of.

This book has presented an economic sociology of law as a lens through which empirically grounded, theoretically informed, and methodologically rigorous research might be carried out. However, an ESL lens has far more to give us than simply a way of approaching research sociologically at the interface of law and economy, and the previous chapters have shown that through generations of economic sociology (ES) and ESL scholarship the core concept of "embeddedness" has been contested and refined. This book has reframed ES's and ESL's internal debates about embeddedness in terms of primary ontological metaphors (the law, the economy, society) and one tertiary, generative, relational metaphor (the extent to which we can say that one or more of these is embedded in the other). Seen in these terms, we can appreciate that as a generative metaphor, embeddedness defines both the problem and solutions, revealing and concealing in equal measure. It therefore tacitly maintains the metaphorical fiction of the ontologically separate law, economy, and society, in contradiction to the aims of ES and ESL lenses which seek to challenge entrenched disciplinarity. At the same time, embeddedness forecloses areas of inquiry, placing one or more aspects in a "black box" and therefore unavailable to sociological analysis.

This is problematic enough, but as the book has shown, the implications extend further as we zoom out. Responses to the 2008 financial crash have identified suboptimal relationships between the spheres of law, economy, and society as potential causes of the crash, criticising the way that the economy, in the form of the self-regulating market, was allowed to float free from society and the regulation that had been peeled back by successive governments with decades of deregulatory tendencies culminating in the 2008 crash. While some commentators assert that the "economy is embedded in society", others claim the opposite, arguing that society is embedded in the economy. Debates are ongoing about the extent to which we can claim either, but there seems to be a general consensus that "re-embedding" the economy in society post-2008 crash should be a priority for policy makers, economists, and all with an interest in avoiding a repeat of the financial crash. And yet, there are no definitions of embeddedness to be found, and little in the way of context to understand "what is embedded, and in what it is embedded" (Cotterrell, 2013).[12]

By examining the career of embeddedness in ESL literature, and our ongoing conceptual commitment to the concept, this book has shown that the way we talk has significant implications for our abilities to respond to financial crashes, but also to social crises and to environmental catastrophes. To respond innovatively, we need multiple vocabularies, grammars, and mental models. We need frames that can accommodate myriad, dynamic and diverse interests and values, and that can reorient or tilt the playing field in different directions according to which values we wish to prioritize. And we need an awareness of the metaphors that we use (and that use us) through quotidian ways of doing, talking, and thinking about legal and economic phenomena. We need an awareness of how these metaphors, through invisible ubiquity, come to perform the mental heavy lifting in re-entrenching dominant frames, guiding us to solutions and responses that typically reflect and enact the mainstream. And we also need an awareness of how we might be preserving and augmenting hegemonic frames in AI systems that have the potential to amplify inequalities and shift our conceptual and linguistic tools beyond the reach of future interrogation.

Nevertheless, we are where we are. So, can "re-embedding" the economy and its regulation in society fix the problems that led to the crashes, crises, and catastrophes? The discussion in the preceding chapters suggests that the short answer is no. While this approach leads us in the right direction, the concept of embeddedness renders this a conceptual cul-de-sac that reproduces mainstream frames. Instead, we might consider ways of talking that allow us to think of legal and economic phenomena as collections of social behaviours, acknowledging the metaphors where they appear and the thought processes they invoke. "Re-embedding" might get us part of the way there, but it conceals any truly innovative or imaginative responses to the dilemmas facing society.

Do we banish the word altogether then? McCloskey notes that we would be unwise "to attempt the impossible by banishing [metaphors]" (McCloskey, 1998, cited in Geary, 2011, p. loc767). Even in the generally more circumspect and reflective ESL community there is a consensus that banishing a ubiquitous

12 In the wake of the 2008 crash, the Dodd–Frank Act was passed in July 2010 in the US which was then partially repealed in 2018 by the Economic Growth, Regulatory Relief, and Consumer Protection Act. In the UK the Financial Services Act 2012 formed part of the "sweeping" reforms. See https://bills.parliament.uk/bills/932.

term like embeddedness is unrealistic. Nevertheless, there are three reasons to be optimistic, should we wish to reduce our conceptual commitment to embeddedness. Firstly, this book shows that there are ways of talking about legal and economic phenomena that are consistent with social constructivism, and that eliminating embeddedness when talking about the relationships between law, economy, and society is not as impossible as it might first appear. Two simple shifts in focus offer a way of bringing the legal and the economic back within the purview of, or at least into dialogue with, the social. Secondly, and crucially, the point is that we become aware of the limitations of our current ways of doing, talking, and thinking and how hegemonic biases are baked in to the metaphors we rely on. Finally, should we choose to maintain embeddedness as a tertiary, generative, relational metaphor along with the ontological metaphors it relies on, there are certain criteria that can make the term as consistent and meaningful as possible. With reference to the works of Ruggie's "embedded liberalism" and Evans' "embedded autonomy", we can see that when embeddedness is applied to carefully defined phenomena in specific, narrow contexts, avoiding sweeping statements of principle, and when paired with an equal-and-opposite force, it can function as a helpful linguistic tool.

Interviewed on the *Today* programme in November 2020, Yuval Noah Hariri noted that we are all "living the dreams of dead people" (Hariri, 2020). By this, he meant that the institutions, things, and ideas we take for granted all started out as nothing more than somebody's "bright idea". This is true for the mundane and everyday (like the invention of the microwave) as well as for concepts like the separation of powers and independence of the judiciary. Similarly, our ways of doing, talking, and thinking about legal and economic phenomena are neither inevitable nor permanent, nor are they beyond challenge. They have though, for the most part, slipped beyond view into a twilight zone where they are taken for granted.

Yet these "dreams of dead people", those that we are aware of and those that have passed into obscurity, are bound up in the vocabularies and grammars bequeathed to us by, and shaped over, generations of lawyers and economists. If the history of a language is the accumulation of a cultural experience, we can think of our ways of talking as a "fossil record of changing communication strategies" along with the mental models structured to reflect the mores of society (Shariatmadari, 2019, p. 240). To speak is to "swim in an inherited stream of images and words" that we have neither chosen nor shaped. But those that we do choose in order to invoke our priorities and imagine the society in which we wish to live have never had greater importance. The "liberalism of abstractions and neutrality fails to provide a compelling account of what holds societies together", and elides what can make them thrive (Sandel, cited in Coman, 2020). An ESL lens gives us a microcosm for exploring the impact of just one metaphor, allowing us to see how we might accommodate a plurality of voices with different interests and values. An ESL lens, then, as explored over the previous chapters, shows us the value of framing. It shows us how and why, if we are to move from performing as *homo economicus-juridicus* to a morally constructed, socially situated *homo sociologicus*, we need conceptual and linguistic tools that enable this shift. Embeddedness is just one example of how metaphors (re)frame relationships between law, economy, and society, shaping us as actors in the process. There are countless others, and they continue to tacitly shape how we are able to respond to the dilemmas facing society. In short, the way we talk matters.

Bibliography

Abebe, R. et al. (2020) 'Role for Computing in Social Change', *FAT* '20*, January 27–30, 2020, Barcelona, Spain [Preprint]. https://doi.org/10.1145/3351095.3372871.

Ashiagbor, D. (2011) 'Embedding Trade Liberalization in Social Policy: Lessons from the European Union?', *Comparative Labour Law and Policy Journal*, 32(2), pp. 373–404.

Ashiagbor, D. (2013) 'Unravelling the Embedded Liberal Bargain: Labour and Social Welfare Law in the Context of EU Market Integration', *European Law Journal*, 19(3), pp. 303–324.

Ashiagbor, D. (2014) 'Embedding Trade Liberalisation in Social Policy: A Research Agenda on Social Regionalism and the Global South', *Northern Ireland Legal Quarterly*, 65(3), pp. 265–281.

Ashiagbor, D., Kotiswaran, P. and Perry-Kessaris, A. (2013) 'Introduction: Moving towards an Economic Sociology of Law', *Journal of Law and Society*, 40, pp. 1–6.

Ashiagbor, D., Kotiswaran, P. and Perry-Kessaris, A. (2014) 'Continuing towards an Economic Sociology of Law', *Northern Ireland Legal Quarterly*, 65(3), pp. 259–64.

Bender, E.M., Gebru, T., MacMillan-Major, A. and Schmitchell, S. (2021) "On the dangers of stochastic parrots: Can language models be too big?" FAccT '21, March 3–10, 2021, Virtual Event, Canada ACM, https://doi.org/10.1145/3442188.3445922, ISBN 978-1-4503-8309-7/21/03.

Block, F. (2008) 'Swimming against the Current: The Rise of a Hidden Developmental State in the United States', *Politics & Society*, 36(2), pp. 169–206. https://doi.org/10.1177/0032329208318731.

Block, F. (2013) 'Relational Work and the Law: Recapturing the Legal Realist Critique of Market Fundamentalism', *Journal of Law and Society*, 40(1), pp. 27–48.

Blodgett, S.L. et al. (2020) 'Language (Technology) is Power: A Critical Survey of 'Bias' in NLP', *Proceedings of the 58th Annual Meeting of the Association for Computational Linguistics*, pp. 5454–5476. https://doi.org/10.18653/v1/2020.acl-main.485.

Bommasani, R. and Liang, P. (2021) 'On the Opportunities and Risks of Foundation Models', Centre for Research on Foundation Models (CRFM), Stanford University Human-Centered Artificial Intelligence, available at https://crfm.stanford.edu/report.html (Accessed: 13 April 2022).

Carney, M. (2020) 'The Reith Lectures 2020: How We Get What We Value -Lecture 1: From Moral to Market Sentiments'. Available at: https://www.bbc.co.uk/programmes/b00729d9/episodes/player (Accessed: 5 February 2021).

Casey, B.H. (2020) 'Covid-19: Is There a Trade-Off between Economic Damage and Loss of Life?', *LSE Impact Blog*, 18 December. Available at: https://blogs.lse.ac.uk/europpblog/2020/12/18/covid-19-is-there-a-trade-off-between-economic-damage-and-loss-of-life/ (Accessed: 5 December 2020).

Cheng, A. (2021) 'Pablo Escobar's 'Cocaine Hippos' Are Legally People, U.S. Court Rules', *The Washington Post*, 26 October. Available at: https://www.washingtonpost.com/world/2021/10/26/pablo-escobar-cocaine-hippos-colombia/ (Accessed: 5 December 2021).

Climate Budget 2020 (2020). Chapter 2: Oslo City Government's budget proposal 2020 with appendices. Oslo. Available at: https://www.klimaoslo.no/wp-content/uploads/sites/88/2019/12/Climate-Budget-2020-Oslo.pdf (Accessed: 16 June 2021).

Coman, J. (2020) 'John Rawls: Can Liberalism's Great Philosopher Come to the West's Rescue Again?', *The Guardian*, 20 December. Available at: https://www.theguardian.com/inequality/2020/dec/20/john-rawls-can-liberalisms-great-philosopher-come-to-the-wests-rescue-again (Accessed: 9 February 2021).

Cotterrell, R. (1998) 'Why Must Legal Ideas Be Interpreted Sociologically?', *Journal of Law and Society*, 25(2), pp. 171–192.

Cotterrell, R., (2006) *Law, Culture and Society: Legal Ideas in the Mirror of Social Theory*, Aldershot: Ashgate, at p. 68.

Cotterrell, R. (2013) 'Rethinking Embeddedness; Law, Economy, Community', *Journal of Law and Society*, 40(1), pp. 49–67.

Dasgupta, P. (2021) *The Economics of Biodiversity: The Dasgupta Review*. HM Treasury. Available at: https://www.gov.uk/government/publications/final-report-the-economics-of-biodiversity-the-dasgupta-review (Accessed: 6 February 2021).

Davis, K.E., Kingsbury, B. and Merry, S.E. (2010) 'Indicators as a Technology of Global Governance'. Available at: https://ssrn.com/abstract=1583431 or http://dx.doi.org/10.2139/ssrn.1583431.

Dejusticia (2018) *Acción de tutela*. Available at: https://www.dejusticia.org/wp-content/uploads/2018/01/TutelaCambioClim%C3%A1tico.pdf?x54537&x54537&x54537 (Accessed: 5 December 2021).

Dermendzhiyska, E. (2021) 'Feeling, In Situ', *aeon.co*, 8 October. Available at: https://aeon.co/essays/what-if-emotions-arent-universal-but-specific-to-each-culture?utm_source=pocket-newtab-global-en-GB (Accessed: 22 October 2021).

Dukes, R. (2018) 'From the Labour Constitution to an Economic Sociology of Labour Law', *Jurisprudence*, 9(2), pp. 418–423.

Ewick, P. and Silbey, S., (1998) *The Common Place of Law*. Chicago: University of Chicago Press.

Fineman, M.A. (2022) 'What Vulnerability Theory Is and Is Not', *Vulnerability and the Human Condition*, 1 February. Available at: https://scholarblogs.emory.edu/vulnerability/2021/02/01/is-and-is-not/ (Accessed: 26 April 2022).

Foucault, M., Agamben, G. and Benvenuto, S. (2020) 'Coronavirus and Philosophers', *European Journal of Psychoanalysis* [Preprint]. Available at: https://www.journal-psychoanalysis.eu/coronavirus-and-philosophers/ (Accessed: 15 February 2022).

Franceschini, M.M. (2021) 'Legal Personhood: The Case of Chucho the Andean Bear', *Journal of Animal Ethics*, 11(1), pp. 36–46.

Geary, J. (2011) *I is an Other: The Secret Life of Metaphor and How it Shapes the Way We See the World*. New York: Harper Collins ebook.

Giddens, A. (1984) *The Constitution of Society: Outline of the Theory of Structuration*. Oxford: Polity.

Goffman, E. (1959) *The Presentation of Self in Everyday Life*. Garden City: Doubleday.

Goffman, E. (1967) *Interaction Ritual: Essays in Face-to-Face Behavior*. New York: Doubleday.

Hariri, Y.N. (2020) 'Interview on the Today Programme', *BBC Radio 4'*. Available at: https://www.bbc.co.uk/programmes/m000p8c6 (Accessed: 12 November 2020).

Hellman, D. (2021) 'Big Data and Compounding Injustice', *Virginia Public Law and Legal Theory Research Paper* No. 2021-27 [Preprint]. Available at: https://papers.ssrn.com/sol3/papers.cfm?abstract_id=3840175 (Accessed: 2 May 2022).

Hirsch, P., Michaels, S. and Friedman, R. (1990) 'Clean Models vs. Dirty Hands: Why Economics is Different from Sociology', in Sharon Zukin and Paul DiMaggio (eds) *Structures of Capital: The Social Organization of the Economy*. Cambridge: Cambridge University Press, pp. 39–57.

Kramm, M. (2020) 'When a River Becomes a Person', *Journal of Human Development and Capabilities*, 21(4), pp. 307–319. https://doi.org/10.1080/19452829.2020.1801610.

Krippner, G. et al. (2004) 'Polanyi Symposium: A Conversation on Embeddedness', *Socio-Economic Review*, 2, pp. 109–135.

Krippner, G. and Alvarez, A.S. (2007) 'Embeddedness and the Intellectual Projects of Economic Sociology', *Annual Review of Sociology*, 33, pp. 219–240.

Lakoff, G. (2014) *Don't Think of an Elephant: Know Your Values and Frame the Debate*. Kindle. Chelsea Green Publishing.

Lepore, J. (2021) 'The Elephant Who Could Be a Person', *The Atlantic*, 16 November. Available at: https://www.theatlantic.com/ideas/archive/2021/11/happy-elephant-bronx-zoo-nhrp-lawsuit/620672/ (Accessed: 5 December 2021).

Liang, P.P., Morency, L.-P. and Salakhutdinov, R. (2021) 'Towards Understanding and Mitigating Social Biases in Language Models', *Procedings of the 38th International Conference on Machine Learning, PMLR 139*, [Preprint]. Available at: https://arxiv.org/pdf/2106.13219.pdf (Accessed: 13 April 2022).

Matthews, D. (2021) *Earthbound: The Aesthetics of Sovereignty in the Anthropocene*.Edinburgh: Edinburgh University Press.

Mazzucato, M. (2021) *Mission Economy: A Moonshot Guide to Changing Capitalism*. Penguin.

McCloskey, D.N. (1998) *The Rhetoric of Economics*. 2nd ed. Madison: University of Wisconsin Press.

Meyer, J. and Rowan, B. (1991) 'Institutionalized Organizations: Formal Structure as Myth and Ceremony', in W.P. Powell and P.J. DiMaggio (eds) *The New Institutionalism in Organizational Analysis*. Chicago: University of Chicago Press, pp. 41–62.

Mudge, S.L. (2008) 'What is Neo-Liberalism?', *Socio-Economic Review*, 6(4), pp. 703–731. https://doi.org/10.1093/ser/mwn016.

Norman, J. (2022) *Posthuman Legal Subjectivity: Reimagining the Human in the Anthropocene*. Oxon and New York: Routledge.

OPHDI (2021) *Bhutan's Gross National Happiness Index, Oxford Poverty & Human Development Initiative*. Available at: https://ophi.org.uk/policy/gross-national-happiness-index/.

Oslo European Green Capital 2019 (2019) Sustain Europe. Available at: https://www.sustaineurope.com/oslo-european-green-capital-2019-20191023.html.

Peck, J. (2013) 'Disembedding Polanyi: Exploring Polanyian Economic Geographies', *Environment and Planning A*, 45, pp. 1536–1544. https://doi.org/10.1068/a46253.

Perry-Kessaris, A., (2011) 'Reading the Story of Law and Embeddedness Through a Community Lens: A Polanyi-Meets-Cotterrell Economic Sociology of Law?', *Northern Ireland Legal Quarterly* (Special Issue on Socialising Economic Relationships), 62(4), pp. 401–413.

Perry-Kessaris, A. (2021) *Doing Sociolegal Research in Design Mode.*Oxon and New York: Routledge.

Proctor, K. (2020) 'Saving Lives or UK Economy from Covid a 'False Choice', MPs Warn', *The Guardian*, 26 August. Available at: https://www.theguardian.com/world/2020/aug/26/saving-lives-or-uk-economy-from-covid-a-false-choice-mps-warn (Accessed: 5 December 2021).

Raworth, K. (2018) *Doughnut Economics: Seven Ways to Think Like a 21st-Century Economist.* ebook (Kindle). Random House Business.

Russell, J.A. (2003) 'Core Affect and the Psychological Construction of Emotion', *Psychological Review*, 110(1), pp. 145–172.

Sap, M., Gabriel, S., Qin, L., Jurafsky, D., Smith, N.A. and Choi, Y. (2020) 'Social bias frames: Reasoning about social and power implications of language', In *Proceedings of the 58th Annual Meeting of the Association for Computational Linguistics*, pp.5477–5490. Available at: https://aclanthology.org/2020.acl-main.486.pdf.

Searle, J.R. (2006) 'Social Ontology: Some Basic Principles', *Anthropological Theory*, 6(1), pp. 12–29.

Shariatmadari, D. (2019) *Don't Believe a Word: The Surprising Truth about Language.* Kindle. Weidenfeld & Nicolson.

Smith, J.E. (2021) 'Is Nature Becoming a Person?', *Foreign Policy*, 24 November. Available at: https://foreignpolicy.com/2021/11/24/nature-person-rights-environment-climate-philosophy-law/?utm_source=pocket-newtab-global-en-GB (Accessed: 5 December 2021).

Supiot, A. (2021) 'Foucault's Mistake: Biopolitics, Scientism, and the Rule of Law', *New Left Review*, 132, pp. 125–139.

UNDP (2021) *Human Development Index, United Nations Development Programme: Human Development Reports.* Available at: http://hdr.undp.org/en/content/human-development-index-hdi.

Ura, K. (2015) *The Experience of Gross National Happiness as Development Framework.* 42. ADB South Asia. Available at: https://www.adb.org/sites/default/files/publication/177790/gnh-development-framework.pdf (Accessed: 8 June 2021).

Ura, K. et al. (2012) *An Extensive Analysis of GNH Index.* Centre for Bhutan Studies. Available at: https://ophi.org.uk/wp-content/uploads/Ura_et_al_Extensive_analysis_of_GNH_index_2012.pdf (Accessed: 8 June 2021).

Williams, C. (2022a) 'Using Personas, Vignettes, and Diagrams in Legal Education', in Allbon, E. and Perry-Kessaris, A. (eds) *Design and Visualisation in Legal Education: Access to the Law.*Abingdon and Oxon: Routledge.

Williams, C., (2022b) 'Framing the Future: The Foundation Series, Foundation Models, and Framing AI', *Law, Technology & Humans*, 4(2), pp. 1–11.

Epilogue

Notes about the characters

Ann, Polly, and Lillian are fictionalized personas. Nevertheless, they are each composites based on real people, real places, and real interactions that I have had. As such, while they offer narrative explorations of some of the issues here, they serve to empirically ground a conceptual discussion. If you're interested in the three characters, their back stories, and what they've gone on to do since this book went to press, you can follow their stories at https://claresresearch-blog.com/

I had originally intended to carry out the research that Ann is about to undertake, although Ann is not a fictionalized version of me. Her story was anonymized through the book to hopefully make it as generalizable as possible, and relatable to anyone carrying out empirical research, or pondering the interface between law, economy, and society. Nevertheless, Ann's research will see her flying out to Colombo, Sri Lanka. From there, she will be boarding a train to Hambantota in the south of the country, and then taking a taxi to the small village of Beragama. Ann had read reports about protests in Beragama in 2017, and had vowed to go back and carry out more fieldwork into the relationship between law and economic development. Previously, when Ann had carried out research into development policy and practice in southern Sri Lanka, the funding for infrastructure projects had come from major international development banks that had had their own political ambitions, and which had used their lending as leverage to effect legal and political change within the country. China, by contrast, demanded no such obligations from borrowers. Instead, should the borrower default, they would relinquish ownership of the territory or piece of infrastructure. For leaders around the world with ambitions to leave some sort of legacy, this opened up doors for rampant development, along with some vanity projects, all charged to the Chinese credit card. Along the way, other interests were forgotten. And, so, in 2017, fed up at not being listened to and of being evicted from their ancestral lands while vast amounts of Chinese investment flowed into the area, protests erupted.

For those keen to read more about the unrest that was briefly reported in the news and that prompted Ann to go back for follow-up fieldwork, I recommend the journalism of Amantha Perera for the Beragama protests, and Wade

Shepard for the vast infrastructure development projects that, once completed, never fully opened (Shepard, 2016d, 2016a, 2016b, 2016c; Perera, 2017b, 2017a). Both highlight the deep political and ethnic tensions of communities involved but pose vital questions about the importance of the relationships between law, economy, and society that Ann hopes to follow up.

Bibliography

Perera, A. (2017a) 'China's Billion-Dollar Re-Entry in Sri Lanka Met with Public Protests', *Inter Press Service News Agency*, 9 January. Available at: http://www.ipsnews.net/2017/01/chinas-billion-dollar-re-entry-in-sri-lanka-met-with-public-protests/ (Accessed: 8 October 2018).

Perera, A. (2017b) 'Sri Lankan Rice Farmers Vow to Fight Chinese Investors', *Reuters*, 9 February. Available at: https://www.reuters.com/article/sri-lanka-landrights-investment/sri-lankan-rice-farmers-vow-to-fight-chinese-investors-idUSL5N1FF6FG (Accessed: 13 July 2019).

Shepard, W. (2016a) 'China Requests 15,000 Acres of Land in Sri Lanka to Create a Million Jobs', *Forbes*. Available at: https://www.forbes.com/sites/wadeshepard/2016/07/27/china-just-asked-for-15000-acres-of-land-in-sri-lanka-for-a-million-worker-sez/#116d212d8448 (Accessed: 5 July 2018).

Shepard, W. (2016b) 'For Sale: The World's Emptiest International Airport', *Forbes*. Available at: https://www.forbes.com/sites/wadeshepard/2016/07/18/for-sale-the-worlds-emptiest-international-airport-mattala-international-hambantota-sri-lanka/2/#4e796f541730 (Accessed: 5 July 2018).

Shepard, W. (2016c) 'Sri Lanka's Colombo Port City: The Front Line of China and India's Geopolitical Showdown', *Forbes*, 12 August. Available at: https://www.forbes.com/sites/wadeshepard/2016/08/12/a-look-at-colombo-port-city-the-frontline-of-china-and-indias-geopolitical-showdown/#7c59c2e92675 (Accessed: 13 June 2018).

Shepard, W. (2016d) 'The Story Behind The World's Emptiest International Airport', *Forbes*. Available at: https://www.forbes.com/sites/wadeshepard/2016/05/28/the-story-behind-the-worlds-emptiest-international-airport-sri-lankas-mattala-rajapaksa/#7bf0e4867cea (Accessed: 5 July 2018).

Index

Note: page numbers in *italics* denote figures and in **bold** denote tables

For Product Safety Concerns and Information please contact our EU
representative GPSR@taylorandfrancis.com
Taylor & Francis Verlag GmbH, Kaufingerstraße 24, 80331 München, Germany

www.ingramcontent.com/pod-product-compliance
Ingram Content Group UK Ltd.
Pitfield, Milton Keynes, MK11 3LW, UK
UKHW020140200926
475702UK00005B/828
* 9 7 8 0 3 6 7 7 6 1 4 4 8 *